Newspa

THEMES IN BRITISH SOCIAL HISTORY

edited by John Stevenson

This series covers the important aspects of British social history from the Renaissance to the present day. Topics include education, poverty, health, religion, leisure, crime and popular protest, some of which are treated in more than one volume. The books are written for undergraduates, postgraduates and the general reader, and each volume combines a general approach to the subject with the primary research of the author.

Currently available

Newspapers, Politics and English Society, 1695–1855

HANNAH BARKER

 LONGMAN

An imprint of PEARSON EDUCATION

Harlow, England · London · New York · Reading, Massachusetts · San Francisco · Toronto · Don Mills, Ontario
Sydney · Tokyo · Singapore · Hong Kong · Seoul · Taipei · Cape Town · Madrid · Mexico City · Amsterdam
Munich · Paris · Milan

Pearson Education Limited
Edinburgh Gate
Harlow, Essex CM20 2JE
England
and Associated Companies throughout the world

Visit us on the world wide web at:
http://www.awl-he.com

© Pearson Education Limited 2000

First published 2000

ISBN 0 582 31216 7 cased
ISBN 0 582 31217 5 paperback

British Library Cataloguing-in-Publication Data
A catalogue record for this book is
available from the British Library

Library of Congress Cataloging-in-Publication Data
Barker, Hannah.
    Newspapers, politics and English society, 1695–1855 / Hannah
Barker.
        p.   cm. -- (Themes in British social history)
    Includes bibliographical references (p.   ) and index.
    ISBN 0-582-31216-7 (hbk.). -- ISBN 0-582-31217-5 (pbk.)
    1. Press and politics--Great Britain--History--18th century.
    2. Journalism--Social aspects--Great Britain--History--18th century.
    3. Journalism--Social aspects--Great Britain--History--19th century.
    4. Press and politics--Great Britain--History--19th century.
    5. Great Britain--Social conditions--18th century.   6. Great
Britain--Social conditions--19th century.   7. English newspapers-
-History--18th century.   8. English newspapers--History--19th
century.   I. Title.   II. Series.
PN5124.P6B37   1999
072'.09'033--dc21   99-35486
                                                      CIP

Typeset by 43 in 10/12pt Baskerville
Produced by Addison Wesley Longman Singapore (Pte) Ltd.,
Printed in Singapore

To my father and constant supporter

Rodney Barker

Contents

Acknowledgements

I am grateful to Rodney Barker, Tony Claydon, David Eastwood, John Stevenson, Roey Sweet and David Vincent for reading and commenting upon this book in its earlier forms. It is certainly a better work for their advice, which, as ever, was perceptive, intelligent and generously given. I was also greatly assisted by a grant from Keele University, and by the staffs of the Bodleian, British and Keele University libraries. Terry Bolam kindly took the photograph of the *Staffordshire Advertiser*.

Front page of the *Stafforshire Advertiser*, January 16, 1796

Introduction

The lapsing of the Printing Act in 1695 was a watershed in newspaper history. With the removal of several onerous legal restrictions, printers were able to publish newspapers and other forms of printed material with unprecedented freedom. As a result, during the next 160 years millions of newspapers were produced in England. From only a handful of titles at the beginning of the eighteenth century, the newspaper press expanded rapidly until, by the early nineteenth century, newspapers had become part of the everyday life of English men and women. Newspapers were highly prized by a population hungry for news. Their contents were devoured and dissected, and the information and views they imparted provided a basis for public debate. As Jean Louis de Lolme noted in the late eighteenth century, 'every man, down to the labourer, peruses them with a sort of eagerness'.[1] Increasingly, the formation of public opinion – at least outside the narrow ruling elite – was heavily dependent on newspapers. But this relationship was neither one-way nor uncomplicated, since the newspaper press itself relied on the tenor of public sentiment to determine its own politics. This complex interplay between the press and popular politics meant that newspapers became an integral part of the political world, with their influence and power increasing steadily throughout the eighteenth and nineteenth centuries as the importance of public opinion also grew. 1855 was another important moment in English newspaper history. In this year newspaper taxation was abolished, thus removing the most important government restriction on newspaper production. Yet despite the increased freedom and growth of the press after this date, already by 1855 the newspaper press was widely perceived to be the most crucial factor in forming and articulating public opinion. In addition, it was also thought to have a constitutional role: by

1. J.L. de Lolme, *The Constitution of England, or an Account of the English Government* (London, 1784), p. 300.

defending the rights of citizens and warding against government corruption, the newspaper press was deemed to constitute the 'fourth estate' of the constitution.

Throughout the period 1695–1855 newspapers appeared alongside a wide variety of printed political material, including books, pamphlets, broadsides, verses, songs, cartoons, essay-sheets and magazines. The task of differentiating between them is not always easy (or even desirable). Defining what a newspaper was in the eighteenth and nineteenth centuries, and what differentiated it from other forms of print – most notably essay-sheets and magazines – can be complicated. Contemporaries used a number of phrases to describe what we might want to call newspapers, including 'essay-sheets', 'journals', 'papers' and 'public prints', and successive governments repeatedly failed to find a sufficiently good definition for legislative purposes. By the early nineteenth century, the problem was such that the law was changed to encompass those publications which then and now many might call 'journals' or 'magazines' rather than newspapers. According to the 'Six Acts' of 1819, a newspaper was 'any paper which contained public news, intelligence, or occurrences, any comments thereon or on matters of Church and State; and which was printed for sale and published periodically within twenty-six days; and which was no larger than two sheets and sold for less than 6d. exclusive of duty'.[2]

Historians have generally attempted to be less inclusive, but like those in the eighteenth and nineteenth centuries, they have defined the newspaper in a variety of different ways and with varying degrees of rigidity. This lack of consensus has often meant that individual historical studies have used different words to describe the same publications. In this book, 'newspaper' will be used quite broadly, and will encompass those publications which historians and contemporaries have sometimes preferred to call 'journals' or 'essay-sheets', if, on the whole, they appeared at least weekly, and contained a significant amount of 'news'. Of course, what is meant by news is also not unproblematic. In this study, 'news' will be taken to mean information on recent or current events of interest to the public and forming the subject-matter of public debate. Such a definition is also not uncontentious, and may well be more rigid than that imposed by many in the eighteenth

2. Patricia Hollis, *The Pauper Press: A Study of Working-Class Radicalism of the 1830s* (Oxford, 1970), p. 156.

century, when for some, all types of gossip, anecdote and fashionable, moral or religious discussion were deemed worthy of being termed 'news'. However, this trend too was not without its detractors, and in 1785 the *Daily Universal Register* attacked fashionable 'West-End sheets' for just such a practice. 'Newspapers were originally intended for the conveyance of important intelligence, which concerns the public in general,' announced the *Register*, 'what have we to do with the ridiculous disputes of whimsical ladies, or the infamous assurance of bullies and swindlers, at public places and gaming houses?'[3] Instead the paper argued that:

> A News-Paper ... ought to be the Register of the times and faithful recorder of every species of intelligence; it ought not to be engrossed by any particular object; but, like a well covered table, it should contain something suited to every palate; observations on the dispositions of our own and of foreign Courts should be provided for the political reader; debates should be reported for the amusement or information of those who may be particularly fond of them; and a due attention should be paid to the interests of trade...[4]

Despite the *Register*'s complaints, the mixture of 'serious' news, which it argued should form the basis of newspaper contents, was the model adopted by most newspapers at the time, as well as in subsequent years. Not surprisingly, in a book on newspapers and politics these are the newspapers on which this study is based.

The book is divided into two parts. Part One examines the development of the newspaper press between 1695 and 1855. It begins in chapter 1 by exploring the relationship between newspapers and public opinion. It examines contemporary attitudes towards newspapers, including the powerful ideology of press freedom which developed from the 1730s. In addition, chapter 1 discusses the increasing prominence achieved by public opinion during our period, and the extent to which the newspaper press was believed both to inform and to represent it. Chapter 2 charts the growth of the press and explores reasons for the expansion of newspapers, both numerically and geographically. It shows how provincial newspapers were particularly dependent in this respect on patterns of urban growth and methods of distribution, whilst revealing that for all newspapers it was taxation, rather than a lack

3. Jeremy Black, *The English Press in the Eighteenth Century* (Beckenham, 1987), p. 40.
4. *The History of The Times*, vol. I: *'The Thunderer' in the Making, 1785–1841* (London, 1935), p. 26.

of demand or the speed of technological innovation, that kept sales
at a lower level than they might have been. Chapter 3 moves on to
address newspaper readership and suggests that the audience for
newspapers became more numerous and increasingly socially
diverse between 1695 and 1855. It argues that neither the inability
to read nor the high cost of newspapers necessarily prevented the
bulk of the population from discovering their contents over time,
and that evidence about newspaper readers does not support the
contention that the growth in readership was closely linked to
the rise of the middle classes.

Chapter 4 explores the relationship between newspapers and
politicians. It studies the impact of legislative restrictions on the
press, including taxation, the sedition laws, the implementation of
parliamentary privilege and the use of other less legitimate forms
of government harassment. In addition, this chapter examines
political bribery and the limited effect which this had on newspaper
contents. In doing so, it challenges earlier ideas about the corruption of the eighteenth-century press, by arguing that although
political sponsorship was common, newspapers could not succeed
without popular support. More compelling evidence for the success
of newspapers is provided in chapter 5. This chapter studies
the ways in which newspapers were run and demonstrates the
increases in both profits and the scale of production during our
period. It examines the changing role of newspaper personnel and
how new methods of newsgathering provided for better coverage
and increased speed of reporting as time went on. In addition,
chapter 5 explores in more detail the important relationship
between newspaper politics and readers, and concludes that the
importance of sales to newspaper profits forced papers to echo
the political views of their readers in order to thrive. This was true
not just in London, but also in the provinces, where individual
papers appealed to local forms of public opinion.

Part Two examines in detail the interaction between newspapers
and politics between 1695 and 1855. What emerges from the study
of newspaper involvement in a variety of political episodes is the
increasingly powerful role that newspapers played. Over a period of
many years, the newspaper press helped to widen the political arena
and encouraged ordinary English men and women to believe that
as free citizens living in a free state, they had a right to involve
themselves in the nation's political life and to protest when they
disapproved of government action. Indeed, the press itself became
the principal medium in which to articulate and disseminate

protests against the government, and also played a crucial role in the political education and politicisation of the people 'out-of-doors'. As we shall see, newspapers in the eighteenth and early nineteenth centuries did not dictate to individual politicians or governments as a rule, nor could they effect policy changes on a day-to-day basis. However, as the political elite became increasingly sensitive to the tenor of extra-parliamentary politics, on certain occasions, and particularly during periods of political crisis, the press played a decisive role in altering or promoting existing governmental policy. During episodes as diverse as the Excise crisis in the 1730s, the anti-slavery movement of the 1780s and 1790s, and the reform agitation of 1830–2, newspapers were instrumental in influencing the progress of events, and as such in affecting the course of English history. Moreover, as newspapers helped to articulate and legitimate popular opinion, they also changed the ways in which popular politics operated and participants viewed their involvement. Newspapers were thus vital not only in putting 'the people' into English politics, but in politicising and uniting sections within the increasingly powerful body of 'the public'. By so doing, the newspaper press not only altered the manner in which politics was conducted at the centre, but also the way in which it operated at every level of English life.

PART ONE

*The Development
of the Newspaper Press*

CHAPTER ONE

Newspapers and Public Opinion

Historians have long associated the press with changes in the way the political world operated in the eighteenth and nineteenth centuries. For John Brewer, it formed a central component of an 'alternative structure of politics' which emerged in the 1760s and which spawned radical movements such as that headed by John Wilkes. For Whig historians, on the other hand, the press, and newspapers in particular, were part of the inexorable rise of accountable government and democratic society. Yet newspapers were also used by the ruling elite to promote their own political visions and in some ways to reinforce their control over society. Despite the claims of many Whiggish historians, newspapers did not necessarily support the cause of freedom and were indeed often opposed to 'progressive', reforming movements. As we shall see in Part Two of this book, certain sections of the newspaper press could be politically conservative, and even reactionary, in outlook. However, this does not alter the fact that during our period the ruling elite was increasingly forced to recognise popular politics and the press and to accommodate itself to them.

For many amongst the ruling elite, a diversity of newspaper politics was not apparent and there is much evidence of the unease which popular printed matter in general provoked. This was nothing new in our period. Charles II, like his predecessors, had believed that an unfettered press could promote plots against the government.[1] Between 1695 and 1855, however, the level of anxiety which the press could promote amongst the ruling classes appears

---

1. Lois G. Schwoerer, 'Liberty of the press and public opinion: 1660–1695', in J.R. Jones, ed., *Liberty Secured? Britain before and after 1688*, (Stanford, Calif., 1992), p. 200.

to have risen. In part, this can be linked to the growth in newspaper production and spread of newspaper readership, but it was also dependent on the state of national politics, for it was at times of particular political unrest that the newspaper press could appear most influential and potentially threatening. This trend was apparent from the early eighteenth century, when the political writer John Toland claimed that newspapers could 'poyson the minds of the common people against his Majesty ... vilify his Ministers, & disturb the public peace, to the scandal of all good Government'.[2] Five years later, in 1722, Dr Burscough preached a sermon before the House of Commons in which he claimed: 'Seditious papers are the certain forerunners of public confusion; the tendency is natural; nor is it to be wondered at, that when some write upon the confines of treason, others should act within them.'[3]

In the latter part of the eighteenth century, conservative fears were even more marked. In 1774, the political writer Josiah Tucker conjured up the spectres of arbitrary rule and superstition when he complained that 'this country is as much news-mad and news-ridden as ever it was popery-mad and priest-ridden'.[4] During the wars with revolutionary France, the writer and politician Edmund Burke charged newspapers with deliberately subverting the moral and social order in France and threatening to do the same in Britain.[5] John Reeves, founder of the Loyalist Associations in 1792, was so dismayed by the 'circulation of Newspapers filled with *disloyalty and sedition*' that he published a pamphlet which urged 'all good Subjects, whether Masters or Private families, or Keepers of Inns, Taverns, or Coffee-Houses, to discontinue and discourage the use and circulation of all such disloyal and seditious Newspapers'.[6] The MP William Windham echoed his comments in 1799 when he told the House of Commons: 'He never saw a man with a newspaper in his hand, without regarding him with the sensation that he was taking poison.'[7]

2. Cited in C.Y. Ferdinand, *Benjamin Collins and the Provincial Newspaper Trade in the Eighteenth Century* (Oxford, 1997), pp. 174–5.

3. Cited in Jeremy Black, 'Flying a kite: the political impact of the eighteenth-century press', *Journal of Newspaper and Periodical Studies* I, 2 (1985), p. 13.

4. Jonathan Barry, 'The press and the politics of culture in Bristol, 1660–1775', in Jeremy Black and Jeremy Gregory, eds., *Culture, Politics and Society in Britain, 1660–1800* (Manchester, 1991), p. 65.

5. *The Correspondence of Edmund Burke*, ed. T.W. Copeland (10 vols., Cambridge, 1958–78), vi. 242; vii. 216, 229, 260.

6. Stephen Koss, *The Rise and Fall of the Political Press in Britain*, vol. 1: *The Nineteenth Century* (London, 1981), p. 156.

7. Jeremy Black, *The English Press in the Eighteenth Century* (Beckenham, 1987), p. 139.

The end of hostilities with France in 1815 did little to allay such fears, and the early nineteenth century saw increasing anxieties amongst a ruling class faced with growing demands for reform and on occasion believing the country to be on the brink of revolution. In a speech to the House of Lords in 1819, the Foreign Secretary, Viscount Castlereagh spoke of the danger which Britain faced, and argued

> that a conspiracy existed for the subversion of the constitution and of the rights of property; and that it was intended to subvert the fabric of the constitution in church and state. Among the means adopted for the accomplishment of this end, it was with grief he had to state, that the press was one of the principal. It had greatly contributed to produce the danger against which their lordships had to guard.[8]

Robert Southey, erstwhile reformer turned defender of the establishment, agreed and traced popular unrest directly to those 'weekly apostles of sedition' which found their way 'to the pot-house in town, and the ale-house in the country, inflaming the turbulent temper of the manufacturer, and disturbing the quiet attachment of the peasant to those institutions under which he and his fathers have dwelt in peace'.[9] Such sentiments were also expressed outside parliament. A government informer named W. Waddilove wrote to the Home Office from Hexham in November 1831 enclosing an unstamped paper which he had purchased in the open market and which had been bought 'with great avidity'. Waddilove grimly predicted that 'before this reaches you, the poison will have infected our retired valleys'.[10] When the Poor Law Commissioners asked magistrates and overseers the reasons for the agricultural riots of 1830 and 1831, many replied that newspapers had played a part. A respondent from Dorset blamed trouble there on 'the active dissemination, through the press, of seditious and revolutionary principles, seconded by much distress'. In Kent, riots were ascribed to the writings of Richard Carlile and William Cobbett, 'which are taken exclusively, or nearly so, at all the ale and beerhouses, where they are read and commented upon by the lower classes, who frequented these houses, and would allow no publication of a contrary tendency to

8. Kevin Gilmartin, *Print Politics: The Press and Radical Opposition in Early Nineteenth-century England* (Cambridge, 1996), p. 65.

9. Gilmartin, *Print Politics*, p. 74.

10. Patricia Hollis, *The Pauper Press: A Study in Working-class Radicalism of the 1830s* (Oxford, 1970), p. 36.

be brought into the house, so that the baneful poison had its full operation...'[11]

However, despite the alarm shown by members of the ruling elites at radical and 'seditious' publications, it is worth remembering how limited state action against the press was (as is discussed in chapter 4). No doubt many shared the view of the politician Henry Bankes, expressed in 1819, that the press was 'a tremendous engine in the hands of mischievous men',[12] but the country's rulers either felt unwilling or unable to counteract any but the most extreme of publications. One reason for this was the ambivalence with which many politicians viewed the press. It was true that a hostile press was a thorn in any government's side, but it was equally the case that a supportive press could prove a great advantage.· Moreover, and more importantly, despite the loud declamations made about the threat to constitutional stability posed by newspapers, few, if any, politicians would have believed that the press on its own could initiate radical change in the way in which society was governed or dictate the identity of the party in power. It is unlikely that the former Prime Minister, the Duke of Wellington, really did believe that the country was governed by the 'Gentlemen of the Press' as he stated in 1826, even if he did attribute part of the blame for his downfall in 1830 to his neglect of newspapers.[13]

When trying to suppress newspapers, politicians also came up against powerful ideological opposition, which stemmed from a belief in the sanctity of the liberty of the press. For most of our period, many commentators argued that the press was not a threat to the constitution, but its main form of protection. The 'liberty of the press' was to become a powerful rhetorical concept. For much of the eighteenth century, it was seen as a means of defending the country against corrupt government, by publicising the actions of its rulers and thus taking the role of public watchdog. Later in the nineteenth century, the liberty of the press became a more radical tool in campaigns to reform society. From the early eighteenth century onwards the concept had clearly gained political currency, and politicians seemed keen to treat the concept respectfully, even if their actions belied their words. The Lord Chancellor, Lord Hardwicke, for example, argued in 1739 that 'the liberty of the press is what I think ought to be sacred to every Englishman', and

11. Hollis, *The Pauper Press*, p. 40.
12. Arthur Aspinall, *Politics and the Press, c. 1780–1850* (London, 1949), p. 1.
13. Aspinall, *Politics and the Press*, p. 2.

even Sir William Younge, whilst speaking in favour of a resolution to prohibit the publication of parliamentary debates in 1738, was keen to stress that 'attacking the Liberty of the Press is a point I would be as tender of as any gentleman in this House'.[14]

[Outside parliament, too, commentators made much of the benefits which a free press could bestow.] The *Old England Journal* declared that

> the people of *England* without the *Liberty of the Press* to inform them of the *Fitness* and *Unfitness* of measures, approv'd or condemn'd by those whom they have *trusted*, and *whom they may trust again*, would be in as blind a state of subjection, as if they lived under the most arbitrary and inquisitorial Government.[15]

Bob Harris asserts that it was 'near commonplace' in the 1740s to argue that the press 'was vital to the exercise of the people's alleged right to examine "the measures of every administration"'. He cites a pamphlet written by the Earl of Marchmont, which claimed that it remained

> a Privilege of the subject to pass his publick judgement on measures, to point out where he thinks they may have been carried on wrong, to shew mankind the dangerous tendency of them, to exhort them to lawful means of obtaining a Remedy, and to apprise them against any future Inconveniences they may be brought under; all this the Freedom of the Press allows us...[16]

[The political writer William Arnall thought that the liberty of the press was not only 'a valuable Inheritance to every *Briton*', but also *'ESSENTIAL TO A FREE PEOPLE'*.] His fellow writer, Ralph Courteville, argued that the liberty of the press 'is in the highest Sense the Palladium of all other Liberty'.[17]

By the middle of the eighteenth century, such ideas were firmly embedded in popular rhetoric. In 1757, Robert Raikes of the *Glocester Journal* asserted that the recent increase in stamp duty was part of a design 'to subvert the LIBERTY of the PRESS, on which every other Liberty of an Englishman in some Measure depends; or to suppress that Kind of Intelligence which all my Countrymen have

14. Simon Targett, 'Sir Robert Walpole's newspapers 1722–42: propaganda and politics in the age of Whig supremacy' (Cambridge University PhD thesis, 1991), p. 85.
15. Bob Harris, *A Patriot Press: National Politics and the London Press in the 1740s* (Oxford, 1993), p. 32.
16. Harris, *Patriot Press*, p. 31.
17. Targett, 'Sir Robert Walpole's newspapers', pp. 85–6.

a Right, and an Interest to know'.[18] Indeed, it was common to view any unpopular government measure, especially one concerning taxation, as an infringement of liberty and freedom. But press freedom was increasingly depicted as a unique form of liberty as it offered particular protection to the rest of English men and women's much vaunted 'rights'. As the century progressed, these arguments became bound up with radical ideas about the historic rights and freedoms of the English. In 1762, the radical politician John Wilkes proclaimed that 'the liberty of the press is the birthright of a Briton, and is justly esteemed the firmest bulwark of the liberties of this country'.[19] A 1764 pamphlet argued that 'The liberty of exposing and opposing a bad Administration by the pen is among the necessary privileges of a free people, and is perhaps the greatest benefit that can be derived from the liberty of the press.'[20] Even the conservative lawyer William Blackstone defended a free press: 'The liberty of the press is indeed essential to the nature of a free state. ... Every man has an undoubted right to lay what sentiment he pleases before the public; to forbid this, is to destroy the freedom of the press.' However, he also warned that 'if he publishes what is improper, mischievious or illegal, he must take the consequences of his own temerity...'[21] The philosopher Jeremy Bentham agreed, and in 1776 argued that a free government depended in part on the liberty of the press 'or the security with which every man, be he of one class or other, may make known his complaints and remonstrances to the whole community'.[22]

By the late eighteenth century it was commonly believed that the freedom of the press was a Revolution principle: established in theory in 1688 and put into practice with the lapsing of the Licensing Act in 1695 which ended the printing monopoly of those with government licences. But as G.C. Gibbs has pointed out, the legislative changes of 1695 did not secure any rights for the press,

18. R.M. Wiles, *Freshest Advices: Early Provincial Newspapers in England* (Columbus, Oh., 1965), p. 21.

19. Robert R. Rea, '"The liberty of the press" as an issue in English politics, 1792–1793', *The Historian*, **xxiv**, 1 (1961), p. 26.

20. Eckhart Hellmuth, 'The palladium of all other English liberties: reflections on the liberty of the press in England during the 1760s and 1770s', in E. Hellmuth, ed., *The Transformation of Political Culture: England and Germany in the Late Eighteenth Century* (Oxford, 1990), p. 493.

21. H.T. Dickinson, *The Politics of the People in Eighteenth-century Britain* (Basingstoke, 1995), p. 169.

22. Jeremy Bentham, 'A Fragment on Government' [1776], published in *The Collected Works of Jeremy Bentham*, gen. ed. J.H. Burns, *Principles of Legislation*, ed. J.H. Burns and H.L.A. Hart (London, 1977), p. 485.

but merely removed restrictions, whilst the climate of opinion amongst MPs, ministers and peers in the years immediately following 1695 was not one which favoured the establishment of any such rights, but rather the imposition of regulations and even some form of pre-publication censorship.[23] [According to Eckhart Hellmuth, debates about the freedom of the press were revitalised in the 1760s and 1770s as extra-parliamentary activity increasingly challenged the old parliamentary elites.] Hellmuth argues that the idea of a free press as an instrument to control parliament was derived from a principle of popular sovereignty. Such reflections were not new, but by the 1760s 'the people' were conceived of more broadly than before and reflections on the press began to take on more populist connotations. It was more persistently argued that the press should constitute a tribunal for authority, and thus without explicitly calling the press a fourth estate, radicals emphasised ideas that pointed in the direction of this theoretical concept.[24]

Although the press was not depicted as a 'fourth estate' until the 1820s, the Swiss writer and former lawyer Jean de Lolme described censorial power in England as resting with the people, supported by a free press, as early as 1771.[25] In his view, the liberty of the press provided the 'extreme security' of the English constitution:

> ...it is the public notoriety of all things, that constitutes the supplemental power, or check, which ... is so useful to remedy the unavoidable insufficiency of the laws, and keep within their respective bounds all those persons who enjoy any share of public authority. As they are thereby sensible that all their actions are exposed to public view, they dare not venture upon those acts of partiality, those secret connivances at the iniquities of particular persons, or those vexatious practices, which the Man in office is but too apt to be guilty of, when, exercising his office at a distance from the public eye, and as it were in a corner, he is satisfied that provided he be cautious, he may dispense with being just.[26]

Another foreign observer, the German writer Christian Goede, expressed similar views in the early nineteenth century. He described the liberty of the press as 'an invaluable palladium' which the English people held 'by the right of prescription', and

23. Targett, 'Sir Robert Walpole's newspapers', pp. 85–6.
24. Hellmuth, 'The palladium of all other English liberties', pp. 498–501.
25. J.A.W. Gunn, *Beyond Liberty and Property: The Process of Self-Recognition in Eighteenth-century Political Thought* (Kingston, Ont., 1983), p. 90.
26. Jean Louis de Lolme, *The Constitution of England, or an Account of the English Government* (London, 1784), pp. 299–300.

in which 'public characters, public bodies, or objects comprehending the national welfare, are all liable to be called before the tribunal of the public'.[27] In just such a move, the *Craftsman* was one of the first newspapers to threaten to publish the names of MPs who did not attend the Commons.[28] As a result of such action, Lord Egremont recorded in his diary in 1742 that the Tory MP for Devon, Sir William Courtenay, had been mobbed at Exeter for 'not being up at parliament to attend his duty'.[29] In 1756, one London paper remarked that the Ministry should remember 'that the MONITOR will not fail to tell them [the people] of their doings'.[30] Dr Johnson noted wryly that 'the liberty of the press is a blessing when we are inclined to write against others, and a calamity when we find ourselved overborne by a multitude of our assailants'.[31]

For some, then, the liberty of the press became a central pillar of the constitution. 'Against venal Lords, Commons, or juries', claimed the Whig politician, Richard Brinsley Sheridan, 'against despotism of any kind or in any shape – let me but array a free Press, and the liberties of England will stand unshaken'.[32] As we shall see, such arguments were increasingly used, not just to ensure the proper functioning of the existing constitution, but also to campaign for a greater say amongst the population at large about how the country was run. Crucial to this development was the use of the press as a source of information and a form of political education. For men such as Thomas Turner, a resident of East Hoathly in Sussex, newspapers were a vital link to the wider world. His diary from the mid-eighteenth century records that he read both the local Lewes paper and the London *Gazette* on a regular basis, and it was from these sources that many of his political opinions stemmed.[33] As Nathaniel Cole, a London lawyer, wrote to a rural correspondent, James Brockman, in 1746:

To be acquainted with the occurrences here is I am sensible what Gentlemen who reside at a distance are generally desirous of. But the

27. Christian August Gottlieb Goede, *The Stranger in England: or, Travels in Great Britain* (3 vols., London, 1807), i. 216.

28. Michael Harris, 'Print and politics in the age of Walpole', in Jeremy Black, ed., *Britain in the Age of Walpole* (London, 1984), p. 208.

29. Harris, *Patriot Press*, p. 28.

30. Marie Peters, *Pitt and Popularity: The Patriot Minister and London Opinion during the Seven Years' War* (Oxford, 1980), p. 64.

31. Rea, '"The liberty of the press" as an issue in English politics', p. 6.

32. Aspinall, *Politics and the Press*, p. 33.

33. *The Diary of Thomas Turner*, ed. David Vaisey (Oxford, 1985), pp. 6, 43, 62, 80–1, 99, 124, 153–4, 191.

papers which are daily exhibited furnish every advice both foreign and domestic within 12 hours after it is known so as to leave nothing of that kind for the subject of a private letter to a particular friend.[34]

Thus a writer in *Lloyd's Evening Post* noted in 1780: 'Without newspapers ... our Country Villager, the Curate, and the Blacksmith, would lose the self-satisfaction of being as wise [as] our First Minister of State.'[35]

The degree of political knowledge and opinion that the wider public was privy to was the cause of some complaint. One commentator noted sarcastically in 1766:

> at this fortunate period, there is not a citizen, within the bills of mortality, but what [*sic*] is capable of filling the first offices of government, – the veriest drudge, who now wears a leathern apron, can tell how far a secretary of state's power ought to extend; and expatiate on the illegality of General Warrants with the perspicuity of a *Camden*.[36]

In 1823 the *London Gazette* also noted, rather sneeringly, that everywhere in Birmingham there was a 'voluntary disposition among the inhabitants to the investigations of the maxims of Government and the conduct of their rulers; and many a *lean unwashed artisan* will discourse upon these topics quite as rationally as some of the theorists in higher places'.[37]

[Amongst less hostile commentators, knowledge was seen as a crucial weapon for the common man in the fight against unfair government. The Manchester radical Thomas Cooper informed Edmund Burke in 1792 that 'ignorance was the ally of the courts, and information was the ally of the people'.[38] The radical writer William Godwin was cited in a 1793 edition of the *Sheffield Register* as saying: 'In the invention of printing is contained the embryo, which in its maturity and vigour is destined to annihilate the Slavery of the Human Race.'[39] Hollis has shown that many nineteenth-century

34. Karl Schweizer and Jeremy Black, eds., *Politics and the Press in Hanoverian Britain* (Lewiston, NY, 1989), p. vii.

35. Solomon Lutnick, *The American Revolution and the British Press 1775–1783* (Columbia, Mo., 1967), p. 1.

36. *An Apology for the Ministerial Life and Actions of a Celebrated Favourite* (1766), cited in John Brewer, *Party Ideology and Popular Politics at the Accession of George III* (Cambridge, 1976), p. 140.

37. Asa Briggs, 'Press and public in early nineteenth-century Birmingham', *Dugdale Society Occasional Papers*, 8 (1949), p. 18.

38. Martin John Smith, 'English radical newspapers in the French Revolutionary era' (London University PhD thesis, 1979), (p. 151.

39. M.E. Happs, 'The Sheffield newspaper press and parliamentary reform, 1787–1832', (Oxford University BLitt thesis, 1973), p. 6.

radicals, in common with Godwin, believed that a free press was 'the portal through which working men could pass into political society'.[40] Through the press, it was believed, working people could be enlightened. John Wade's introductory essay in the *Gorgon* in 1818 argued that 'Before the commencement of these weekly papers, the labouring classes were, in a great measure, precluded from political information. ... But how wonderfully is the scene changed during the last eighteen months! What a glare of light has been cast into every cottage and workshop of the kingdom!'[41] The belief that information and enlightenment went hand in hand was reiterated by the Manchester reformer Richard Cobden, in 1844: 'Knowledge is the power – knowledge alone – by which we shall bring this foul system to the dust.'[42] Newspapers themselves increasingly encouraged such interpretations of their role. Many used symbols such as Hermes, messenger of the gods, and the all-seeing eye with the motto 'nunquam dormio' [I never sleep]. Titles such as the 'Sun', the 'Star', the 'Comet' and the 'Lantern' suggested the enlightening effects which the newspaper press bestowed on society, whilst the guiding and protecting proper-ties of newspapers were apparent in titles such as 'Champion', 'Moderator', 'Vindicator' and 'Sentinel'.[43]

The printing press as the defender of English liberty was also an enduring motif. It could be seen, for example, in the caricatures of George Cruikshank after the Napoleonic Wars, and found its way into more popular cultural forms. The reform celebrations which took place in Sheffield in June 1832 included a procession where a Mr Gordon, the oldest printer in Sheffield, appeared on horseback in the guise of William Caxton, the inventor of the printing press. He was followed by a 'printing press at work' supported on planks and decorated with the motto 'Dispeller of darkness'. A group of typefounders marched behind carrying a banner which proclaimed 'Types are the seeds of knowledge, and knowledge the source of Reform'. At the public banquet given at the end of the day, toasts were drunk 'to the perfect liberty of the press'.[44]

40. Hollis, *Pauper Press*, pp. 18–23.
41. Gilmartin, *Print Politics*, p. 99.
42. Brian Harrison, 'Press and pressure group in modern Britain', in Joanne Shattock and Michael Wolff, eds., *The Victorian Periodical Press: Samplings and Soundings* (Leicester, 1982), p. 264.
43. Aled Jones, *Powers of the Press: Newspapers, Power and the Public in Nineteeth-Century England* (Aldershot, 1996), pp. 31–3.
44. Happs, 'The Sheffield newspaper press and parliamentary reform, 1787–1832', p. 153.

Yet despite the general enthusiasm shown for the enlightening effects of print, throughout our period some commentators who supported a free press still warned of its propensity to delude the public if used corruptly. The *London Journal* asked in 1732 whether the liberty of the press was 'a Liberty of Writing without being *confined to Truth*, a *Liberty* of Lying, without being liable to Restraint or Punishment, and a *Liberty* of *Defamation*, without being obliged to make Reparations for Wrongs, or Satisfaction for Injuries?'[45] The Whig writer Vicesimus Knox was convinced of the potential for harm. In 1795 he wrote:

> Perhaps there is nothing which contributes so much to diffuse the spirit of despotism as venal newspapers, hired by the possessors of power, for the purpose of defending and prolonging their possession. The more ignorant classes have a wonderful propensity to be credulous in all that they see in print, and will obstinately continue to believe a newspaper, to which they have been accustomed, even when notorious facts give it the lie.[46]

William Cobbett, later a radical writer, argued whilst still a conservative in 1807 that the press was leading the people into serfdom, rather than political emancipation:

> If ever there was in the world a thing completely perverted from its original design and tendency, it is the press of England: which instead of enlightening does, as far as it has any power, keep the people in ignorance; which, instead of cherishing notions of liberty, tends to making the people slaves; and which instead of being their guardian, is the most efficient instrument in the hands of all those who oppress, or who wish to oppress them.[47]

Cobbett was equally critical of some sections of the press over twenty years later, after his politics had assumed a more radical bent. He claimed in 1829 that George IV 'lived in almost total seclusion from the eyes of the people' and yet he was not hidden from them nor alienated from them (as he should have been), since they were 'daily informed, by the newspapers, of his dinner parties at his cottage; of his rides about Windsor-Park'.[48]

Not only could the proper role of the press be perverted, but some conservative commentators denied that the public had any right to know about, or comment on, politics at all. In particular,

45. Targett, 'Sir Robert Walpole's newspapers', p. 88.
46. Vicesimus Knox, *The Works of Vicesimus Knox* (7 vols., London, 1824), v. 174.
47. Jones, *Powers of the Press*, p. 17.
48. Lucy Brown, *Victorian News and Newspapers* (Oxford, 1985), p. 147.

they attacked the legitimacy of popular sovereignty implied by the concept of the liberty of the press. William Pulteney, who had championed the freedom of the press in *The Craftsman*, gave his support in 1738 to a unanimous vote in the Commons to extend the privilege over the publication of proceedings:

> I think that no appeals should be made to the public with regard to what is said in this assembly, and to print or publish the speeches of gentlemen in this House, even though they were not misrepresented, looks very much like making them accountable without doors for what they say within.[49]

Sixty years later, William Windham MP blamed parliamentary reporting for the naval riots of 1797. He argued that the press was changing the relationship between the people and the House of Commons, since it gave

> the People an opportunity of sitting in judgement every day on the measures under discussion in that House, tumultuously to express its disapprobation or approbation – and favoured the propensity of all vulgar minds, perhaps also of minds of no mean endowments, to form premature or intemperate decisions upon the whole matter, long before the details of its parts and the character of its principles could be discussed and unfolded by the Legislature.[50]

But protests such as this were increasingly swimming against the tide, as newspapers became yet more entrenched in English politics at all levels and championing the liberty of the press ceased to be the preserve of radicals and reformers. The potency of ideas about press freedom and the degree to which print had become an accepted part of everyday life was such that many nineteenth-century conservative commentators began to argue for the positive effects of the press. For them, newspapers and other printed material were not a threat to the status quo at all, but a possible means of its defence. In 1808, James Graham argued in an address to the Literary and Philosophical Society of Newcastle upon Tyne that popular insurrections were not the result of food shortages, price rises or unemployment, but rather the inability of those in power to explain to the lower orders why such things occurred. Social conflict was thus the result of poor communication between government and the people: a situation which could be easily

49. Targett, 'Sir Robert Walpole's newspapers', p. 39.

50. Jeremy Black, 'Politicisation and the press in Hanoverian England', in Robin Myers and Michael Harris, *Serials and Their Readers, 1620–1914* (Winchester, 1993), p. 75.

rectified. By the 1820s such ideas were gaining increasing currency. Social reformers, such as Joseph Livesay and Charles Knight, blamed Britain's difficulties not upon poverty, but on 'the want of mental culture and material worth' amongst the British people, thereby expressing a belief in both the corrupting and the redeeming qualities of popular journalism. In 1832 Knight began the *Penny Magazine* in an attempt to supply the lower orders with more wholesome material than they were used to reading in newspapers, and in 1838 Livesay launched the *Moral Reformer* with the same intention.[51] Whilst middle-class radicals argued that the repeal of the Stamp Act would lead to social peace and popular education,[52] the philosopher James Mill adopted a rather different approach. Instead of seeking to re-educate the people, he argued that the press could act as a 'safety valve' for popular protest by allowing the lower classes to abuse the government.[53] Far from encouraging unrest, Mill believed that the press diverted revolutionary impulses amongst the population. The argument was not new; it had been used to defend satire aimed at Sir Robert Walpole in the early eighteenth century.

It was a belief in the potentially positive effects of a 'respectable' press, coupled with an acknowledgement that the 'harmful' and seditious unstamped press was beyond legislative control, which led the government to reduce Stamp Duty in 1836 and remove it altogether in 1855.[54] By freeing the more respectable sections of the newspaper press from the payment of duties which had placed them at an unfair disadvantage to their unstamped – and non-tax paying – counterparts, it was hoped that more conservative – or at least less seditious – sections of the press would thrive. To a great extent the ploy succeeded, since the Sunday papers, which became the staple reading matter of the working classes from the 1840s onwards, were clear beneficiaries of the government's action. Although often radical, they were radical within the framework of a liberal consensus, and did not challenge the very basis of government as many unstamped newspapers had done. With newspapers sold so much more cheaply, the government also managed to reduce another source of unease: the collective reading of newspapers. As we shall see, this type of group activity was linked

---

51. Jones, *Powers of the Press*, pp. 99–107.
52. Hollis, *Pauper Press*, pp. 18–23
53. Hollis, *Pauper Press*, p. 14.
54. Alan J. Lee, *The Origins of the Popular Press in England, 1855–1914* (London, 1976), ch. 3.

to radical, subversive political activity and anti-social behaviour in a way which solitary reading was not. As the Chancellor of the Exchequer argued in a debate on the removal of Stamp Tax in 1836, 'he would rather that the poor man should have the newspaper in his cottage than that he should be sent to a public house to read it', where he would listen to and discuss the news in the company of those who were not respectable, sober or loyal.[55]

As this discussion of the freedom of the press has made clear, throughout our period an increasingly politicised public, both informed and represented by newspapers and other forms of print, was having a growing impact on the nation's political life. This phenomenon became known as 'public opinion'. According to Gunn, the concept of public opinion had a political application before the mid-eighteenth century. As early as the 1730s there had been references made to the 'opinion of the people', but it was in the second half of the century that 'public opinion' was spoken of more commonly.[56] Contemporaries were vague and divided about what public opinion meant, and it is equally difficult to pin down definitions within existing historiography. However, despite such ambiguities, it seems evident that eighteenth-century Britain witnessed the emergence of a dynamic extra-parliamentary political culture, and that many contemporaries believed that beyond the world of the political elite, opinion was being formed and expressed which was at once powerful, coherent and legitimate.[57]

In this context, public opinion can perhaps best be described as a body of argument or discussion about politics, which took place largely outside the governing elite. Its existence depended on the belief that those who participated in and constituted it – 'the people' or 'the public' – were more than simply subjects; they were in some sense citizens. These individuals were thought to have a legitimate interest in the public affairs of their nation, which they could pursue and express without challenging the broad constitutional structures within which they lived. For although

55. David Vincent, *Literacy and Popular Culture: England 1750–1914* (Cambridge, 1989), pp. 234–6.

56. Gunn, *Beyond Liberty and Property*, p. 263.

57. In particular, see Brewer, *Party Ideology and Popular Politics*; E.P. Thompson, 'Eighteenth-century English society: class struggle without class?', *Social History*, **3** (1978), 123–65; Nicholas Rogers, *Whigs and Cities: Popular Politics in the Age of Walpole and Pitt* (Oxford, 1989); Frank O'Gorman, *Voters, Patrons, and Parties: The Unreformed Electorate of Hanoverian England, 1734–1832* (Oxford, 1989); Linda Colley, *Britons: Forging the Nation 1707–1837* (New Haven, Conn., 1992); Kathleen Wilson, *The Sense of the People: Politics, Culture and Imperialism in England, 1715–1785* (Cambridge, 1995).

'the public', and 'the people' in particular, were often conceived of as having interests in opposition to those in power, 'public opinion' in England was seldom or never revolutionary. It was instead a tribunal based outside the political structures of the state where state power could be judged and criticised by those who deemed themselves fit to be included within the boundaries of the political nation. Within this context, the press not only allowed the exchange of information and ideas, but also what Jürgen Habermas describes as an 'institutional context' where debate could happen.[58] Newspapers thus became, to all intents and purposes, a major forum for the formation of public opinion and one of the main channels through which public opinion could be expressed.

Quite who produced public opinion though was hotly debated throughout our period, and contemporaries could not agree on the identity of 'the public'. Edmund Burke's estimate of the political nation in the 1790s was 400,000. 'This,' he claimed, 'is the British publick.'[59] The radical politician John Jebb's interpretation from the same period, on the other hand, encompassed all adult males.[60] For many in the eighteenth and nineteenth centuries, 'the people' described those whose constitutional standing, education or wealth gave them a legitimate say in the nation's affairs; for others, the term was synonymous with the mob. Such varieties of meaning often arose from political expediency. Few political activists, in or out of power, would not have claimed to represent, or to aim to protect, the public interest, although many might have wished to limit the numbers, or more importantly, the social status, of those whom they supposedly served. Yet for most politicians in the early eighteenth century, 'the people' excluded most of the population. In 1702, the political writer Daniel Defoe asserted that the 'people' should not be confounded with the 'inhabitants', but constituted freeholders, 'the proper owners of the country'.[61] According to Targett, Walpole's attempts to influence the political nation were firmly focused on the parliamentary classes.[62] For the Prime

---

58. Jürgen Habermas, *The Structural Transformation of the Public Sphere*, trans. Thomas Burger (Cambridge, Mass., 1989). See also Geoff Eley, 'Re-thinking the political: social history and political culture in 18th and 19th century Britain', *Archiv für Sozial Geschichte*, **XXI** (1981), 427–57.

59. Edmund Burke, 'First letter on a regicide peace' [1796], in *The Works of the Right Honourable Edmund Burke* (8 vols., London, 1854–71), viii. 140.

60. *The Works Theological, Medical, Political, and Miscellaneous of John Jebb ... With Memoirs of the Life of the Author*, ed. John Disney (3 vols., London, 1787), i. 147.

61. Gunn, *Beyond Liberty and Property*, p. 75.

62. Targett, 'Sir Robert Walpole's newspapers', p. 108.

Minister Henry Pelham, the opinions of the people referred to his own opinions and those of a small circle of his acquaintances. 'The people' in its wider sense was merely 'a sort of ghost or hobgoblin', used to frighten those in power.[63]

Yet for others, the public was increasingly drawn from a much broader section of society. Indeed for many, it was access to print which secured membership. John Brewer has argued that the 1760s witnessed the development of a 'political nation' that was increasingly socially diverse, and certainly much larger than the parliamentary classes alone. Brewer describes the middle and lower orders of this period as politically conscious and part of the 'alternative structure of politics' of Hanoverian England. 'One is left with the impression', he concludes, 'that those who scorned the humble politician were satirising a phenomenon which, for all their disapproval, they were powerless to change.'[64] Since politicisation and access to print culture are seen to go hand-in-hand, Brewer, like many in the eighteenth century, implicitly equates the wider political nation with the readers of political material, most importantly newspapers, journals, pamphlets and handbills. Thus the increasing availability of such matter and rising readership suggest a growth in the numbers of politically aware and interested citizens who found a focus for their political activity in issues such as Wilkes and America.[65]

Yet some would date such developments even earlier. According to Michael Harris, by the time Walpole became Prime Minister, 'the London press had long been accepted as an important and legitimate component of the political system', since 'no other medium offered such ease of dispersal and range of regular access to the nation at large . . . '[66] Joseph Danvers, the independent Member of Parliament for Totnes, observed in the Commons in 1738:

> I believe the people of Great Britain are governed by a power that never was heard of as a supreme authority in any age or country before . . . it is the government of the press. The stuff which our weekly newspapers are filled with, is received with greater reverence than acts of parliament; and the sentiments of one of these scribblers have more weight with the multitude than the opinions of the best politicians in the kingdom.[67]

63. Gunn, *Beyond Liberty and Property*, p. 80.
64. Brewer, *Party Ideology*, p. 141.
65. Brewer, *Party Ideology*, ch. 8.
66. Michael Harris, *London Newspapers in the Age of Walpole: A Study in the Origins of the Modern English Press* (London, 1987), p. 113.
67. Targett, 'Sir Robert Walpole's newspapers', p. 6.

Indeed, the opposition press under Walpole encouraged its readers to see the publication of constituency instructions to MPs as expressing the 'sense of the people' on certain issues. This provoked a vigorous debate on the legitimacy of such instructions and of the proper role of the 'people' in the political process.[68]

The newspapers themselves encouraged readers to believe that they had a close relationship with each other, and most newspapers claimed to represent public opinion in some way, particularly by the nineteenth century. The *Leicester Chronicle* of 1843 announced that 'obliged as its conductors often are to mirror the world as it is than to picture it as it should be – compelled to accompany the main body in the march of improvement instead of going a step in advance, as they frequently would, it may be assumed that they represent with general fidelity the views of their supporters'.[69] Feargus O'Connor, editor of the *Northern Star*, insisted that the paper was a 'mirror' of the people's mind. According to Epstein, this was central to the very concept of a 'people's paper'. Thus one of the *Star*'s writers, the Rev. William Hill, wrote in 1842: 'I have ever sought to make it rather a reflex of your minds than a medium through which to exhibit any supposed talent or intelligence of my own. This is precisely my conception of what a people's organ should be ...'[70]

In addition to proclaiming their allegiance to public opinion, newspapers also used more subtle methods to encourage their readers to believe that they spoke with 'the voice of the people'. Using terms such as 'the people', 'Englishmen' and 'the public', from the mid-eighteenth century onwards, newspapers increasingly addressed much wider (and less easily definable) sections of the population, rather than presuming to speak only to freeholders, voters or the rich. In addition, letter-writers used pseudonyms to suggest that an individual was speaking not for himself or herself, but as the representative of a wider social group, or even of the public as a whole. Thus signatures, such as 'one of the people' and 'an Englishman', were common throughout our period, as were occupational descriptions such as 'a farmer', 'a weaver' or 'a tailor'.

68. Rogers, *Whigs and Cities*, pp. 246–50; and Kathleen Wilson, 'Inventing revolution: 1688 and eighteenth-century popular politics', *Journal of British Studies* **28** (1989).

69. Derek Fraser, 'The press in Leicester c. 1790–1850s', *Transactions of the Leicestershire Archaeological and Historical Society* **xlii** (1966–7), p. 53.

70. James Epstein, 'Feargus O'Connor and the *Northern Star*', *International Review of Social History* **xxi** (1976), p. 85.

Rather than alienating readers, the anonymity of many newspaper contributions served to promote newspapers, and the political world that they described, as inclusive and accessible.

For conservatives, one of the problems inherent in allowing the public – as defined by readers – a voice in politics was that it was largely made up of the sort of people who could not be entrusted to govern competently, or even to advise a government wisely. Lord Perceval's 1743 pamphlet, *Faction Detected by the Evidence of Facts*, reveals his alarm at the way in which newspapers appeared to challenge the relationship between property and government by opening up both political debate and influence to those amongst the middling and lower orders. 'Shall every Cobbler in his stall pretend a knowledge of political Affairs, superior to that of the best ... the greatest men of this and all former Ages, who in their whole Turn of Life have adapted and dedicated wholly to the study of Politicks and Government?' he asked. It was, Perceval argued, 'ridiculous vanity' to suppose that 'men who have not interest in the state, but the profits of their Daily labour' should have a greater concern for their country than 'those who have vast properties to take care of'.[71]

Similar concerns were expressed in the nineteenth century. In 1834, Sir Archibald Alison, the Tory High Sheriff of Lanarkshire, wrote against the 'democratic' nature of the press, which its immense growth had brought about. Since 'nine-tenths of mankind adopt their opinions' from newspapers, most readers were decidedly humble, meaning that 'the superior number of the lower orders' gave them 'a decided preponderance over all the better classes of society'. According to Alison, this was very dangerous, since the press's 'democratic character shakes the foundations of government: its licentious tendency saps the bulwarks of morals; its ascendancy over property gives the victory over all the institutions of society'.[72] As the conservative politician Lord Ellenborough reported ruefully of Wellington in 1830, 'The duke relies upon the support of the "respectable people" and despises the rabble, but the rabble read newspapers.'[73]

As our period progressed, public opinion was not just talked about more often, but it also became a more important part of political life. Yet for much of the eighteenth century, Gunn argues,

71. Harris, *Patriot Press*, p. 20.
72. Jones, *Powers of the Press*, pp. 157–9.
73. Aspinall, *Politics and the Press*, p. 372.

'the idea of the public as a constant actor in the political process did not materialise'. Instead, when it suited them, politicians appealed to opinion in the country, but they accorded it no permanent say in public affairs.[74] Gunn claims that after 1784 this began to change, once 'the press had absorbed the political functions of the pulpit and, as the necessary stimulant to public opinion and vehicle of it, increasingly dominated the political system'.[75] John Brewer broadly concurs. He argues that despite the interest that politicians such as Bute, Burke, Rockingham and Grenville showed in the press in the 1760s, this should not be mistaken for a belief on their part that the press was somehow a 'fourth estate', and in some way representative of public opinion, nor that they saw the public as playing an enduring role in national politics. However, this ideology of political distance was increasingly undercut by the press as it demystified politics and suggested radical alternatives for rule.[76]

Despite such shifts, nineteenth-century politicians were still divided in their attitude towards public opinion. Ivon Asquith argues that in the early nineteenth century, the Whigs were split. The more conservative of their number regarded extra-parliamentary opinion as a useful check upon the encroachments of government and particularly the influence of the Crown, but defined public opinion as emanating from the propertied and educated classes, since 'they distrusted it as a volatile force that needed to be led and tempered by the aristocracy'. The more forward-looking Whigs viewed public opinion as a dynamic force which could take the initiative in politics and were less afraid that it would get out of control. As a result, they were more willing to mobilise radical and lower-class opinion in order to put pressure on the government.[77] Conservative politicians were, not surprisingly, less keen. Robert Peel wrote to his colleague, John Croker, in 1820 of 'that great compound of folly, weakness, prejudice, wrong feeling, right feeling, obstinacy and newspaper paragraphs which is called public opinion...'[78] Yet despite the general hostility and mixture of opinions amongst politicians, it does seem that they

74. Gunn, *Beyond Liberty and Property*, p. 273.
75. Gunn, *Beyond Liberty and Property*, pp. 286–7.
76. Brewer, *Party Ideology*, pp. 235–8.
77. Ivon Asquith, 'The Whig Party and the press in the early nineteenth century', *Bulletin of the Institute of Historical Research* (1976), pp. 222–3.
78. *History of The Times*, vol. I: *'The Thunderer' in the Making, 1785–1841* (London, 1935), p. 242.

took public opinion increasingly seriously, and that its links with the press in the nineteenth century at least were clearly acknowledged. Hence, in 1831, John Hobhouse, in an address to the House of Commons stated that the press was the only organ of public opinion capable of dictating to the government, since nothing else could speak the sense of the people.[79] Still, the degree to which the press did influence politics – both inside parliament and in the country as a whole – is far from clear. It is this issue which will be explored in Part Two.

Conclusion

Throughout our period, the potentially seditious influence of the press caused politicians great alarm. Yet only limited action was taken against newspapers. One reason for this was a powerful ideology of press freedom which developed from the 1730s. Increasingly, the liberty of the press was seen as part of the traditional rights and liberties of the English, and the main form of defence against corrupt government. The press was a vital source of information for the population at large, and thus crucial for radicals, who believed that knowledge was the key to reform. Some conservative thinkers also argued that the press could dampen popular unrest, but others held that the people had no right to know how government operated. Despite such hostility, public opinion – which was both informed and represented by the press – became an increasingly powerful force. Even if its meaning, and those who produced it, were not easy to define, it is clear that public opinion was increasingly associated with those who read newspapers and other forms of printed matter, and that this was a trend encouraged by the newspapers themselves.

79. Aspinall, *Politics and the Press*, p. 3.

CHAPTER TWO

The Growth of Newspapers

There was a dramatic increase in the number of newspapers produced in England during the eighteenth and nineteenth centuries. This was most noticeable outside the capital. Prior to the lapse of the Printing Act in 1695, there had been no provincial newspapers in England. During the opening decade of the eighteenth century, however, a handful of papers emerged in Norwich, Bristol and Exeter. By the early 1720s over twenty provincial newspapers were in production, and by the mid-century this figure had risen to over forty. A surge in the last two decades of the eighteenth century meant that by 1800 more than seventy provincial newspapers were published each week, while an even greater rate of increase in the early nineteenth century saw numbers reach 130 in 1832 and over 200 a decade later.[1] In London, the pace of change was less striking, primarily because numbers were high from the opening decades of the eighteenth century. As early as 1719, one paper complained that 'at present both city, town and country, are over-flowed every day with an inundation of newspapers', whilst in 1733, the *British Observator* claimed that 'it is grown a general complaint that there are already such a glut of newspapers and weekly pamphlets'.[2] The capital's printers had been even quicker than those in the provinces to take advantage of the lapse of the Printing Act, so that in 1712 there were probably twelve papers produced in the capital. By the middle of the century London had eighteen newspapers: six weeklies, six tri-weekies and six dailies,

---

1. Hannah Barker, *Newspapers, Politics, and Public Opinion in Late Eighteenth-Century England* (Oxford, 1998), p. 111; A.P. Watson, 'Newpaper circulations, 1800–1954', *Transactions of the Manchester Statistical Society* (1955), p. 16.
2. Jeremy Black, *The English Press in the Eighteenth Century* (Beckenham, 1987), pp. 12–13.

and in 1783, nine dailies and ten bi- or tri-weeklies were published each week. This number had risen to fourteen dailies, seven tri-weeklies and two weeklies by 1790, and in 1811, swelled by the emergence of the Sunday press, the total figure had reached fifty-two.[3] However, as we shall see, not all papers were equal in stature. This was particularly true in the early nineteenth century, when sales could vary dramatically between newspapers. Moreover, in this latter period, the increasing domination of the market by *The Times* was such that the number of London dailies actually fell from fourteen to ten between 1790 and 1855, even though total sales of daily papers in the capital had risen.[4]

The increase in titles, then, does not tell the whole story of newspaper growth. To assess this more fully, we need to look at the striking increase in newspaper circulation between 1695 and 1855. Since newspapers were taxed for much of this period (as is discussed in detail in chapter 4), some Treasury records are useful here, but unfortunately much of the relevant material has not survived and other sources are notoriously unreliable. This makes it difficult to give newspaper circulation figures, at least before the 1830s, with any degree of certainty. Informed estimates, however, can still be made. Sutherland has calculated an annual newspaper circulation of around 2.3 million in 1704. According to Snyder this had risen marginally to 2.4 million by 1712–13. Some Treasury records for the mid-century have survived, which show that 7.3 million newspaper stamps (a stamp appearing on each legitimately produced paper as a record of the tax paid) were issued in 1750, 9.4 million in 1760 and 12.6 million in 1775. In 1801, a total of 16.4 million stamps were issued – 7 million for London papers and 9.4 million for those produced in the provinces. By 1816, the total sale of stamps had reached over 22 million and in 1837 this figure had risen again to more than 39 million.[5] The increase in newspaper sales between the early eighteenth and mid-nineteenth centuries that such,

3. Black, *English Press*, p. 14; Michael Harris, *London Newspapers in the Age of Walpole: A Study in the Origins of the Modern English Press* (London, 1987), p. 31.

4. Ivon Asquith, 'The structure, ownership and control of the press, 1780–1855', in George Boyce, James Curran and Pauline Wingate, eds., *Newspaper History from the Seventeenth Century to the Present Day* (London, 1978), p. 99.

5. James R. Sutherland, 'The circulation of newspapers and literary periodicals, 1700–30', *Library*, 4th ser., **15** (1934); Black, *English Press*, pp. 104–5; Henry L. Snyder, 'The circulation of newspapers in the reign of Queen Anne', *Library*, 5th ser., **xxiii** (1969); I.R. Christie, 'British newpapers in the later Georgian age', in I.R. Christie, *Myth and Reality in Late-Eighteenth-Century British Politics and Other Papers* (London, 1970), p. 313.

admittedly patchy, evidence reveals is clearly impressive, with circulation increasing twenty-fold between 1695 and 1855. But as we shall see below and in chapter 4, the true picture of growth is likely to be greater still, since some papers managed to avoid paying tax and thus are excluded from official statistics.

Even in the case of the legitimate press, the figures given are not easy to break down, particularly between London and provincial sales, except when Stamp Office records are explicitly organised to show this. It does seem likely that despite the increasing prominence of the provincial press, London remained at the centre of the newspaper industry throughout our period. At the start of the eighteenth century, newspaper sales in the capital have been estimated at around 44,000 per week,[6] with papers such as the *Daily Courant* selling about 1,000 copies a day.[7] After the introduction of Stamp Tax in 1712, it has been calculated that there was a temporary decline in total weekly sales, from a high of 67,000 just before the Act to only 44,000 after it. Although this setback did not last long, the sale of individual papers increased only slowly during the eighteenth century. Michael Harris has estimated that individual circulations of London weekly papers in the 1720s and 1740s were between 1,000 and 2,000. However, during periods of particular political controversy, and with access to a national market, very popular journals such as the *London Journal, Mist's Weekly Journal* and *The Craftsman* each achieved sales of over 10,000.[8] During the 1730s and 1740s there was also a dramatic expansion of the cheap unstamped press, which was produced illegally without the payment of stamp duty and which contemporary estimates put at 50–60,000 copies a week. Although such publications were almost completely suppressed by new legislation in 1743, overall newspaper production may not have fallen much, since this was a move which benefited legitimate publications. Indeed, Harris states that, by 1746, some London dailies were selling as many as 5,000 copies per issue. He estimates that the total weekly sale of London papers in this period was 100,000 – a figure supported by the taxation records for 1750.[9]

By the latter part of the eighteenth century, sales of newspapers in the capital had probably trebled. The political agent Dennis

6. Sutherland, 'Circulation of newspapers', p. 113.

7. Snyder, 'Circulation of newspapers', p. 210.

8. Harris, *London Newspapers in the Age of Walpole*, pp. 55–7; K.L. Joshi, 'The London Journal, 1719–1738', *Journal of the University of Bombay*, **9** (1940), p. 54.

9. Harris, *London Newspapers in the Age of Walpole*, p. 190.

⌈O'Bryen wrote to Edmund Burke, in 1782, that '... there are 25 thousand papers published every day in London'[10] (or about 300,000 a week).⌉The same figure was calculated by the historian Jeremy Black in his work on the eighteenth-century newspaper press.[11] The account book of one paper dating from this period shows that sales of at least 1,500 copies a day were needed in order for a paper to stay solvent.[12] But most daily newspapers would have fared much better than this. Henry Bate, editor of the *Morning Post*, claimed to have achieved sales of 5,000 copies a day in 1778.[13] In the following year, Johann Wilhelm von Archenholz, a Prussian traveller and writer, estimated that the *Public Advertiser* sold between 3,000 and 4,500 papers a day, and that the *Daily Advertiser* achieved sales of 5,000 copies.[14] It is likely that most of the nine London daily newspapers in 1780 had circulations of between 2,000 and 5,000, with the eight tri-weekly papers and nine weekly papers also selling somewhere in this region.

Despite the rise in overall circulation, the sales in individual papers did not increase dramatically in the early years of the nineteenth century. According to government estimates in 1811, seven London papers had circulations of around 3,000, with the *Courier*, *The Times* and the *Evening Mail* enjoying sales of over 5,000.[15] By the 1840s, however, the situation had changed a good deal. Now one paper, *The Times*, dominated the field, with daily sales of 40,000. Other papers had sales approaching 10,000, but many did not reach half that.[16] Occasionally, newspapers did achieve equally impressive sales in the early nineteenth century, but these were not dailies. In November 1816, sales of the *Political Register* rose to between 40,000 and 50,000 a week, but fell sharply after the 1820 Duties Act increased the price from 2d to 6d,[17] and

10. Dennis O'Bryen to Edmund Burke, March 1782, Wentworth Woodhouse Muniments, Sheffield City Archives, BK 1/1557.

11. Black, *English Press*, p. 104; Joseph Addison, 'Essay No. 10', *The Spectator*, ed. Donald F. Bond (5 vols., Oxford, 1965), i. 44.

12. Papers of the *Gazetteer*, Public Records Office, C104/67.

13. Cited in Solomon Lutnick, *The American Revolution and the British Press: 1775–1783* (Colombia, Mo., 1967), p. 28.

14. Johann Wilhelm von Archenholz, *A Picture of England* (Dublin, 1791), p. 42.

15. Christie, 'British newspapers', p. 323.

16. A.P. Wadsworth, 'Newspaper circulations, 1800–1954', *Transactions of the Manchester Statistical Society* (1955), pp. 7–9; Asquith, 'The structure, ownership and control of the press', p. 100.

17. A. Aspinall, 'The circulation of newspapers in the early nineteenth century', *Review of English Studies*, **xxii**, 85 (1946), pp. 39–41.

the *Penny Magazine* soon achieved sales of 200,000 after its launch in 1832.[18] In the 1840s, the newly launched *Illustrated London News* also appeared to achieve spectacularly high sales and claimed a circulation of 100,000 at the end of 1842.[19] Overall in London, however, the circulations of individual newspapers were relatively slow to rise during the eighteenth and early nineteenth centuries, although steady and significant progress was made. Apart from the unique success of *The Times*, it was the newer forms of newspapers – such as the Sunday and 'radical' presses – which made the most impressive gains. The most successful unstamped radical paper, the *Poor Man's Guardian*, sold between 12,000 and 15,000 copies for most of 1832 and 1833, but it was still outsold by two other radical publications of the early nineteenth century, Cobbett's *Register* and the *Northern Star*, both of which were produced legally and paid tax.[20] First published in Leeds, the *Star* was soon selling over 10,000 copies a week and probably reached sales of over 50,000 during part of 1839.[21] Yet Hollis has estimated that, on average, sales of the unstamped press as a whole in 1836 still probably outstripped those of stamped papers.[22] As far as the Sunday press was concerned, it was technically illegal to sell newspapers on the Sabbath throughout our period (in fact, only milk and mackerel could be sold legally). However, the law was not rigorously enforced, and Sunday newspapers appeared from 1779. By 1812, at least eighteen Sunday papers were published in London. Although they were the subject of much criticism, they were to prove highly successful and by the end of our period had begun to outsell most other forms of newspapers. The *Weekly Dispatch*, for example, had a circulation of over 50,000 per week in the 1840s, whilst most other Sunday papers sold between 10,000 and 30,000.[23] Williams estimates the total sales of Sunday newspapers at the end of the 1840s as 270,000.[24] By the 1850s and 1860s, Sunday papers such as *Lloyd's Weekly* and *Reynold's Newspaper* had

18. Aled Jones, *Powers of the Press: Newspapers, Power and the Public in Nineteenth-Century England* (Aldershot, 1996), p. 105.

19. G.A. Cranfield, *The Development of the Provincial Newspaper* (Oxford, 1962), p. 171.

20. Patricia Hollis, *The Pauper Press: A Study of Working-Class Radicalism of the 1830s* (Oxford, 1970), p. 118.

21. Donald Read, *Press and People 1790–1850: Opinion in Three English Cities* (Aldershot, 1993), pp. 99–101.

22. Hollis, *The Pauper Press*, p. 105.

23. Wadsworth, 'Newspaper circulations, 1800–1954', p. 13.

24. R. Williams, *The Long Revolution* (London, 1961), p. 54.

established themselves as the most popular newspapers for the mass working-class readership. The politics of such papers was certainly populist and even 'radical' in tone (in a liberal, consensual sense), yet unlike the radical press of the earlier nineteenth century, their sales were far less volatile.

Outside London, despite the boom in the number of titles, sales of individual papers were generally less impressive. In her study of the *Salisbury Journal*, Christine Ferdinand has suggested that the paper may have sold only 200 copies a week when it started in the 1730s, although this soon rose to 2,000 by the 1740s, and reached 4,000 by 1780.[25] In a more wide-ranging study covering provincial newspapers throughout England, Cranfield has also estimated that circulations were typically only 100–200 in the first decades of the eighteenth century, but that this quickly rose to 1,000–2,000 by the mid-century.[26] It is clear that by the second half of the eighteenth century most papers would have struggled financially with sales of only 1,000.[27] The records of the *Chelmsford Chronicle* – an only moderately successful paper – show that its figures were over twice this, whilst other papers claimed even higher circulations.[28] Christopher Etherington's *York Chronicle*, for example, appears to have reached a circulation of up to 2,500 between 1772 and 1777.[29] The *Salisbury Journal* claimed to have a circulation of 4,000 in 1780,[30] and James Bowling, editor of the *Leeds Mercury* and 'a gentleman of considerable talent', was attributed with increasing the circulation of his paper to 3,000 copies in the 1790s.[31]

The trend of slow growth continued into the nineteenth century. Based partly on Stamp Office records, Wadsworth estimates that a majority of provincial newspapers produced fewer than 2,000 copies a week before 1850. Papers such as the *Leeds Mercury*, *Stamford Mercury* and the *Liverpool Mercury*, which achieved sales of around 4,000 in the 1830s and over 6,000 in the 1840s, were important exceptions to this general trend. So too was the *Manchester Guardian*. Founded in 1821, it sold about 3,000 copies a week

25. C.Y. Ferdinand, *Benjamin Collins and the Provincial Newspaper Trade in the Eighteenth Century* (Oxford, 1997), pp. 125–8.
26. Cranfield, *Development of the Provincial Newspaper*, p. 176.
27. Barker, *Newspapers, Politics, and Public Opinon*, p. 114.
28. Essex Record Office, Acc. 5197, D/F, 66/1. See also 'The Leeds Mercury', *Effective Advertiser* (March 1886), p. 27; W.J. Clarke, *Early Nottingham Printers and Printing* (2nd edn, Nottingham, 1953), p. 20.
29. R. Davies, *A Memoir of the York Press* (London, 1868), pp. 331–4.
30. Ferdinand, *Benjamin Collins*, p. 128.
31. 'The Leeds Mercury', p. 27.

in 1830, but this had risen to over 11,000 by 1840 (with the paper appearing twice a week), and had increased to almost 20,000 by mid-century.[32] During the same period, the sales of other Manchester papers ranged from 1,400 to 6,500 for the *Manchester Times*, and 2,000 to 6,000 for the *Manchester Chronicle*.[33] It has been claimed that the most successful paper in Sunderland in the 1840s was the *Sunderland Herald*, which sold only 1,200 copies a week.[34] This appears particularly unimpressive compared with the presses of other towns. In Exeter during the same period the popular *Western Gazette*, one of five papers produced in the town, sold between 2,000 and 3,500 papers a week,[35] whilst Michael Murphy claims that the three Cambridge newspapers sold around 5,000 copies a week in the 1840s.[36] The total newspaper production of provincial towns which such figures reveal is impressive when compared with the early eighteenth century, but is still nothing like the huge increase witnessed in the later nineteenth and twentieth centuries.

Such growth also needs to be considered in relation to demographic trends, since the population of England grew rapidly between 1695 and 1855. However, the increase in newspaper production was more than simply a reflection of this. Throughout the period, the growth rate of the newspapers was greater than that of the country's population and particularly its adult population (those over 14 years old). Indeed, between the opening decades of the eighteenth century and of the nineteenth, newspaper production more than quadrupled in proportion to the number of adults in England.[37] The proliferation of newspapers can be seen as part of a more general surge in the production of all kinds of printed matter in the eighteenth and nineteenth centuries. Of course, the period of English history from around 1780 onwards has traditionally been associated with great advances in manufacturing output, but many historians now argue that the earlier eighteenth century

32. Wadsworth, 'Newspaper circulations, 1800–1954', pp. 16–17.

33. Read, *Press and People*, pp. 213–17.

34. Maurice Milne, 'Survival of the fittest? Sunderland newspapers in the nineteenth century', in Joanne Shattock and Michael Wolff, eds., *The Victorian Periodical Press: Samplings and Soundings* (Leicester, 1982), p. 197.

35. Richard S. Lambert, *The Cobbett of the West: A Study of Thomas Latimer and the Struggle Between Pulpit and Press at Exeter* (London, 1939), p. 148.

36. Michael J. Murphy, *Cambridge Newspapers and Opinion 1780–1850* (Cambridge, 1977), p. 111.

37. Population figures taken from E.A. Wrigley and R.S. Schofield, *The Population History of England 1541–1871: A Reconstruction* (Cambridge, 1989), pp. 207 and 216.

was also a time of important development. It is claimed that a 'consumer revolution' – in which production and consumption of all types of material possessions rose at an unprecedented rate – was in evidence throughout most of the eighteenth century.[38] Spurred on by social emulation and supported by the nation's increasing prosperity, English men and women are thought to have both produced and consumed at unprecedented levels. This model of growth is certainly borne out by the rate of newspaper increase, which was broadly consistent throughout the eighteenth century (although it is also noticeable how steeply it rose after around 1800).

The period 1695–1855 also witnessed unprecedented levels of urban growth. Towns across England expanded rapidly, so that by the end of our period the proportion of the population living in urban centres had overtaken that of rural areas. This development was, of course, allied to the 'consumer revolution' and had great implications for the expansion of the newspaper press. It was in towns where newspapers were not only produced, but also largely consumed. Here the newspaper press could thrive, surrounded by a large and accessible market and other features of urban development which encouraged the popularity and circulation of newspapers. These included inns, shops, book clubs, coffee-houses and, most importantly, a vigorous and active local political culture whose participants demanded a steady source of news, information and debate.[39] Not only does the pattern of eighteenth-century newspaper growth appear at odds with more traditional accounts of an economic watershed occurring around 1780, but it also seems to counter the claim made by some press historians that the proliferation of papers can be linked to periods of particularly vigorous activity in the country's domestic or foreign affairs.[40] Although

38. Neil McKendrick, John Brewer and J.H. Plumb, *The Birth of a Consumer Society: The Commercialization of Eighteenth-Century England* (London, 1983).

39. On urban growth and the culture of provincial towns, see Penelope Corfield, *The Impact of English Towns, 1700–1800* (Oxford, 1982); Peter Clark, ed., *The Transformation of English Provincial Towns 1660–1800* (London, 1984); Nicholas Rogers, *Whigs and Cities: Popular Politics in the Age of Walpole and Pitt* (Oxford, 1989); Frank O'Gorman, *Voters, Patrons, and Parties: The Unreformed Electorate of Hanoverian England, 1734–1832* (Oxford, 1989); Peter Borsay, ed., *The Eighteenth-century Town* (Harlow, 1990); Kathleen Wilson, *The Sense of the People: Politics, Culture and Imperialism in England, 1715–1785* (Cambridge, 1995); H.T. Dickinson, *The Politics of the People in Eighteenth-Century Britain* (Basingstoke, 1995); Rosemary Sweet, *The English Town, 1680–1840: Government, Society and Culture* (Harlow, 1999).

40. Cranfield, *The Development of the Provincial Newspaper*, pp. 20–1; Bob Harris, *Politics and the Rise of the Press: Britain and France, 1620–1800* (London, 1996), p. 11.

there were periods when a rapid increase in titles coincided with important political events (in the early 1740s when the Jacobite threat loomed large and during the period of the French Revolution, for example), there was no rise in newspaper numbers as a result of political instability in the 1760s or during the American Revolution, and yet the production of papers rose steeply in the less fraught early 1770s and the late 1780s.[41] The sharp rise in newspaper production after 1800 is similarly unlikely to be solely the result of political foment. This is not to deny that radical movements in particular promoted the new titles in the 1810s, 1830s and 1840s, but, as in the eighteenth century, a generally even pattern of growth denies the use of narrowly political explanations.

Brian Harrison has argued that the cheapness of presses and letterpress in the early nineteenth century made it easy to set up new ventures and that this was one of the reasons why the production of officially stamped paper more than trebled between 1801 and 1831.[42] It is undoubtedly true that improvements in printing technology, which resulted not only in more efficient production methods, but also lowered the price of some printing materials and machinery, played a part in increasing newspaper production. However, the impact of such developments was limited in the eighteenth and early nineteenth centuries in comparison to later periods. For much of the period under discussion, newspaper printing was done using an unmechanised hand-press. By this method, printers could produce 250 impressions an hour (or about one whole newspaper every 30 seconds). By modern printing standards, this was an incredibly slow and laborious process. In order for publishers to meet demand, they often had to replicate printing work on more than one press: a particularly expensive option which entailed duplicate composition. In the provinces, although additional composition charges were largely avoided because weekly publication allowed printers several days to produce each paper, pressures of time and the slowness of printing meant that much of what appeared in print could be days old, and newer intelligence had to be rushed into print in order to beat the arrival of London papers by coach.

Yet despite the inconveniences associated with traditional methods of production, technological innovation was slow to

41. Barker, *Newspapers, Politics, and Public Opinion*, pp. 110–11.
42. Brian Harrison, 'Press and pressure group in modern Britain', in Shattock and Wolff, eds., *Victorian Periodical Press*, p. 277.

emerge. The introduction of the Stanhope press in 1800, which had an iron rather than a wooden frame, allowed for the production of clearer impressions, but did not increase the rate of printing.[43] In 1814, John Walter II of *The Times* bought two of Koenig's new steam-driven printing machines. These could produce 1,000 impressions an hour compared to the 250 which older presses were capable of, did away with the need for duplicate composition (where the same text had to be typeset more than once) and also allowed for later printing (and thus the inclusion of more up-to-date news). However, the machines were comparatively expensive and other papers were slow to follow Walter's lead. The *Morning Herald* waited until 1822, and other London papers did not follow suit until the following decade. Some provincial newspapers moved more quickly: the *Manchester Courier* bought a steam press in 1825, followed by the *Manchester Guardian* three years later, with papers such as the Exeter *Western Times* buying in steam presses in the mid-1830s.[44] In fact, by the 1830s, steam presses were becoming commonplace, and even the unstamped *Poor Man's Guardian* and the *Northern Star* were produced using the new technology.[45]

By 1827, *The Times*'s circulation of over 10,000 was beyond the capabilities of the old plant, and Walter introduced Cowper and Applegarth's Four-Feeder machine in order to print 4,000 impressions an hour. The method of feeding was again improved in 1847, when Applegarth invented a vertical feeder for the paper. But *The Times* was the only newspaper with sales great enough to warrant such innovations prior to the mid-nineteenth century.[46] For the period under discussion here, it was demand, kept down by high prices, rather than problems of supply, which kept the rise in newspaper circulation steady. In the second half of the nineteenth century, by comparison, the reduction and eventual abolition of newspaper taxes and the resultant and dramatic drop in prices meant that the situation was very different. After 1855, the market for newspapers increased at such a rate that advances in printing technology became essential in order for publishers to meet demand. However, some aspects of newspaper production

43. Asquith, 'The structure, ownership and control of the press', p. 101; A.E. Musson, 'Newspaper printing in the industrial revolution', *Economic History Review*, 2nd ser., **x**, 3 (1958).

44. Lambert, *The Cobbett of the West*, p. 97.

45. Asquith, 'The structure, ownership and control of the press', p. 101.

46. Ellic Howe, *Newspaper Printing in the Nineteenth Century* (London, 1943), pp. 1–16.

developed slowly, and there was little change in the composing room, for example, until the late nineteenth century.[47]

Because of their impact on the price of a newspaper, taxes acted as a significant brake on the growth of the newspaper press prior to 1855. A Stamp Tax payable on every paper was introduced in 1712, and was quickly followed by taxes on advertisements. Taxation was increased eight times before 1836, after which both sales and advertising duty were reduced prior to their complete removal in 1855. Before 1712, most papers cost 1d. The 1725 Act caused a rise from $1\frac{1}{2}$d to 2d, and in 1757 prices increased to $2\frac{1}{2}$d. In 1776 the price went up again to 3d; by end of 1780s it was 4d, rising in 1790s to 6d, before reaching a high point of 7d at the end of the Napoleonic Wars, and thereafter dropping to 5d in 1836 and 4d in 1855.[48] After 1855, the sale of newspapers rose almost exponentially, but before the mid-nineteenth century, the nature of government legislation greatly influenced the speed at which the press developed. Despite the relative freedom of the British press in comparison with its European counterparts, the taxes to which it was subject ensured that the price of legally produced papers was never low. The 1757 price of $2\frac{1}{2}$d, for example, constituted about 5 per cent of a London labourer's weekly wage, and almost 10 per cent of an agricultural labourer's, whilst for craftsmen, the figure was approximately 4 per cent. The highest price of 7d, reached in 1815, appears to have constituted a lower percentage of some workers' pay. For London artisans, the cost of a newspaper was about 2 per cent of their weekly wage, but it was still between 6 and 12 per cent of the wage received by labourers outside the capital, such as pitmen on the Tyne and Wear and lead miners in the Pennines.[49] It was the constant complaint of newspaper publishers that advertising and sales taxes threatened to ruin their businesses, and the success of unstamped newspapers at various points between 1695 and 1855 suggests that a cheap press could ensure a larger market than could more expensive, stamped papers.

Whilst high prices kept sales down overall, other factors influenced further aspects of the pattern of newspaper development, particularly in the provinces. In the first half of the eighteenth

47. Musson, 'Newspaper printing in the industrial revolution', p. 421.

48. Black, *English Press*, pp. 104–5; Wadsworth, 'Newspaper circulations, 1800–1954', p. 3.

49. John Rule, *Albion's People: English Society, 1714–1815* (Harlow, 1992), pp. 168 and 182–4.

century, the importance of receiving news from London meant that proximity to a post road could be a deciding factor in the establishment of a paper. Cranfield notes that when daily posts were extended to Middlewich, Warrington and Liverpool in 1755, all three towns began newspapers in less than a year.[50] By the mid-eighteenth century, and with the continuing growth of the turnpike road system and the relative speed of communication which this afforded, most towns of standing had their own newspaper. However, access to a good road, a large population or the town's position as an administrative, economic, judicial or social centre did not guarantee the appearance of a paper. Although urbanisation naturally encouraged the development of the provincial press in the long term, the pattern of industrial growth in England, and the way in which provincial newspapers were established, did not necessarily coincide. Birmingham did not have a paper until 1732, Coventry waited until 1741 and Leicester until 1753, whilst much smaller towns such as St Ives, Whitehaven and Lewes had papers far earlier. Indeed even in the late eighteenth century, towns such as Lincoln, Colchester and Carlisle were not producing their own newspapers.

Even if conditions were favourable, they could not be exploited successfully by everyone. What mattered most was the existence of a printer who was willing and competent enough to set up a newspaper. Thus in the early eighteenth century, an exodus of printers from the capital meant that southern England produced most papers, but after 1725, the North and Midlands soon started to catch up as printers travelled further afield to exploit new markets.[51] In the later part of the eighteenth century, the establishment of increasing numbers of newspapers in the provinces meant that competition between them was potentially fierce. In areas such as the English Midlands, it appears that saturation point had been reached between the 1760s and 1770s. Such was the number of newspapers published there, and the blanket coverage of the region which resulted, that when new papers were started in Hereford and Shrewsbury in the 1770s, their publishers were forced to be more imaginative than their neighbours in seeking out readers and looked to the previously under-exploited area of Wales to the west, rather than concentrating their efforts on securing an English readership to the east.[52] Despite the somewhat random

50. Cranfield, *Development of the Provincial Newspaper*, p. 23.
51. Cranfield, *Development of the Provincial Newspaper*, pp. 25–6.
52. Barker, *Newspapers, Politics, and Public Opinion*, pp. 122–4.

pattern in which they emerged though, by the early nineteenth century provincial newspapers were firmly established in most towns across the country.

Provincial newspapers were heavily dependent on sales made outside the town in which they were published. A good distribution system for the surrounding area was therefore vital to the survival of individual papers.[53] This usually comprised a system of agents and newsmen, the latter delivering papers largely on foot and often travelling long distances. The use of newsmen to deliver papers around the countryside has been well documented by Cranfield and Wiles for the earlier part of the century,[54] and more recently by Christine Ferdinand in the case of the *Salisbury Journal*.[55] Ferdinand has demonstrated how newspaper distribution operated on several levels: from the paper's own shop, to a series of agents in local towns and finally to the carriers and newsmen who delivered to villages and rural areas.[56] The *Salisbury Journal* was a particularly well-run provincial newspaper and its model of distribution was repeated by other successful papers across the country. Thus, when the *Salopian Journal* was established in 1790, the proprietors were acutely aware of the importance of circulating the paper widely and efficiently. They spent a good deal of time and effort advertising the paper in the locality and employed five newsmen to deliver the paper to towns up to 50 miles away.[57]

Although they usually travelled on foot rather than on horseback, and thus would have served only relatively nearby areas of the surrounding countryside (up to about 50 miles), newsmen probably delivered the bulk of provincial papers not sold in town during our period. Such arrangements could prove very efficient. Andrew has noted that the *Derby Mercury*'s local distribution network in the 1770s ensured that the paper, which was printed on a Thursday morning, would reach most of its readers in nearby villages by the

53. Looney has suggested that over half of the copies of provincial newspapers produced were sold outside their town of publication: J.J. Looney, 'Advertising and society in England, 1720–1820: A statistical analysis of Yorkshire newspaper advertisements' (Princeton University PhD thesis, 1983), p. 41. However, there is no way to be sure of the proportions.

54. Cranfield, *Development of the Provincial Newspaper*, pp. 190ff; R.M. Wiles, *Freshest Advices: Early Provincial Newspapers in England* (Columbus, Oh., 1965), pp. 95ff.

55. Ferdinand, *Benjamin Collins*, and 'Local distribution networks in eighteenth-century England', in R. Myers and M. Harris, eds., *Spreading the Word: The Distribution Networks of Print 1550–1850* (Winchester, 1990).

56. Ferdinand, *Benjamin Collins*, ch. 2.

57. Minutes book and account book of the *Salopian Journal*, Shropshire Records and Research Unit, MS 1923.

same evening, and the rest by the Friday morning.[58] Sometimes quite complicated local arrangements were involved. A Norfolk clergyman, James Woodforde, recorded in 1799 that he received newspapers at his village of Weston Longville from 'Sarah Grant from the Poor House on Hungate Common', after they had been left there for him by his butcher the night before.[59] As late as 1830, newspapers in Devonshire were still being delivered in similarly indirect ways. William Hunt, who grew up in Honiton, recalled that 'People who lived out of the way used to await, at a certain village on the roadside, the passing of the messenger, and thus obtain their paper'.[60] However, despite the continuities apparent in distribution methods, shifts towards more modern forms – less dependent on newsmen and the sort of makeshift arrangements described by Woodforde and Hunt – are apparent. A case in point is provided by David Ayerst's description of the distribution of the *Manchester Guardian* in the 1830s and 1840s, where he notes a decline in the distribution of newspapers by the firm's newsmen or through its shop between 1830 and 1845, with newspapers increasingly sold by agents in neighbouring towns, or distributed by post instead.[61]

From the late seventeenth century onwards, provincial distribution was also crucial to a large section of the London press. Michael Harris has described how the principal London papers of the 1690s picked up and extended the distribution of the more established manuscript newsletters, whilst in the early eighteenth century, tri-weekly newspapers began which were specifically aimed at a provincial market. These were invariably published on Tuesdays, Thursdays and Saturdays, to coincide with the dispatch of mails from the capital. From 1712, they were joined by weekly journal-form papers, which also sold widely outside London. The dependence of certain London newspapers on provincial sales was a constant feature of the newspaper trade throughout the eighteenth and nineteenth centuries. The capital's daily papers, however, were unable to compete on an equal footing with tri-weekly and weekly papers during much of the eighteenth century. Instead,

58. J.D. Andrew, 'The Derbyshire newspaper press, 1720–1855' (University of Reading MA thesis, 1954), p. 170.

59. Diary entry dated 17 February 1799. Woodforde also noted that severe weather had prevented the distribution of the Ipswich paper to some areas two weeks earlier: James Woodforde, *The Diary of a Country Parson, 1758–1802* (Oxford, 1978), pp. 579 and 576.

60. William Hunt, *Then and Now; Or, Fifty Years of Newspaper Work* (Hull, 1887), pp. 1–2.

61. David Ayerst, *Guardian: Biography of a Newspaper* (London, 1971), p. 83.

they secured the bulk of their sales within the capital: selling mostly from small pamphlet shops, through hawkers who roamed the streets, or using newsmen who delivered to more outlying areas.[62]

For those London papers that were distributed in the provinces, the postal system was one of the main methods used. Post Office employees – the Clerks of the Road – had used their franking privilege (by which they could send items by post free of charge) to send newspapers around the country from the seventeenth century. Greenwood describes how, by the middle of the eighteenth century, this practice had grown to such an extent that the Clerks were dependent upon the money they received from publishers for distributing their newspapers, and employed fifty people to carry newspapers from presses and prepare them for posting. Members of Parliament, who also had franking privileges, increasingly made use of them to send newspapers to their families, friends and constituents, and by 1789, over 65,000 newspapers a week were sent in this way. Such was the extent to which the system was abused that in the 1790s the franking system for newspapers was abolished and anyone could send newspapers by post free of charge. Even dealers could send papers in bulk, as long as they were delivered to the Post Office by 6 pm, two hours before the posts left for the provinces. The Clerks continued to operate as newspaper distributors, but, not surprisingly, with their privileges gone their share of the market dropped steadily. Still, the postal service continued to act as the main distributor of London newspapers throughout the country. By 1829, almost 12 million newspapers were circulated in this way every year.[63] As the post itself improved, and communications throughout the country became faster with the spread of turnpike roads in the eighteenth century and the development of the railway in the nineteenth, the capital's newspapers became increasingly attractive to provincial newspaper readers as a means of discovering the latest national and international news. Yet even with such improvements, provincial newspapers remained popular: a phenomenon which will be explained in chapter 5.

One final aspect of the development of newspapers in the eighteenth and nineteenth centuries concerns their appearance. This changed relatively little for much of the period. At the beginning of the eighteenth century, newspapers were rather brief

62. Harris, *London Newspapers in the Age of Walpole*, pp. 33–9.
63. Jeremy Greenwood, *Newspapers and the Post Office, 1635–1834* (Reigate, 1971), unpaginated.

productions, often consisting of a single leaf printed with two columns per page. The 1712 Stamp Act contained a loophole which meant that papers of over six pages could escape taxation, and until this practice was made illegal by a subsequent Act in 1725, most newspapers adopted the multi-page format on the grounds of economic expediency (even though, as Morison notes, publishers often had problems filling six pages).[64] After 1725, newspapers were printed on four pages (achieved by folding a single piece of paper in half). This basic format survived for the rest of the century, although the use of greater numbers of columns and smaller print, coupled with larger paper size, was to increase the amount of text each newspaper carried. From the 1760s, more and more papers were produced with four columns on each page. This basic format continued into the nineteenth century, until in 1819, *The Times* began to publish five-column pages, and by the 1830s, as a result of technological improvements, eight-page, six-column papers predominated in the capital.[65]

Eighteenth-century newspapers in particular can appear jumbled and confusing to the modern reader. There was little improvement in the organisation of the news printed until the end of the century when some papers began to introduce sub-headings more systematically. Even with this development, it can still be difficult to find individual stories from amongst a mass of largely undifferentiated and tightly spaced text. In the provinces, the layout of provincial papers continued to be governed by the arrival of the London posts until the introduction of steam-powered printing in the 1830s. Prior to this date, most papers printed their outer pages first, and included news from the most recent post on the inner pages. Although this method meant that provincial newspapers were published soon after the last post had arrived, it had the unfortunate consequence of allowing old and new news to appear in the same issue, with one often contradicting the other. Production problems such as this contributed to the failure of provincial newspapers to appear on anything but a weekly basis before the mid-nineteenth century, the only exceptions being the publication of a few bi-weekly papers in places such as Canterbury and Manchester.[66] For the most

64. Stanley Morison, *The English Newspaper: Some Account of the Physical Development of Journals Printed in London Between 1622 and the Present Day* (Cambridge, 1932), p. 86.
65. Black, *English Press*, pp. 278–9; Morison, *The English Newspaper*, pp. 84–6 and 205–16.
66. Wadsworth, 'Newspaper circulations, 1800–1954', p. 6.

part though, the capital's press appeared conspicuously more modern than its provincial counterpart.

Conclusion

Despite the difficulties inherent in trying to estimate the number of newspapers published in England between 1695 and 1855, it is clear that the press grew significantly and that this trend was most striking in the provinces. This picture of newspaper growth remains valid even when one takes into account the population boom with which it coincided. The sales of individual papers increased from just a few hundred in the early eighteenth century, to many thousand at the end of our period. In addition, the number of titles rose dramatically. When viewed across the period as a whole, newspapers proliferated in a fairly steady manner, and it does not appear that sudden economic growth or short-term political developments were significant causes, although political events did initiate the production of particular papers at certain times. In the provinces, the spread of newspapers in the eighteenth century was affected by urban growth and improvements in communications, but also vital was the existence of skilled entrepreneurial printers.

Efficient methods of distribution were also essential for provincial papers throughout the eighteenth and nineteenth centuries (since a significant proportion of sales was made outside of the town of production) as well as to those London papers which relied on a provincial readership. Various methods of circulating newspapers were used, including the newsmen who delivered to wide areas on foot, but the postal service played an increasingly prominent role. For much of the period under discussion, the methods by which newspapers were printed did not change. For most papers, new technology only began to affect the rate of production from the 1830s. It was taxation, and the high prices which it necessitated, rather than a lack of technological innovation, which kept sales at a lower level than might have been. This lack of innovation was also apparent in the ways in which the content of newspapers was organised and presented. During the bulk of the eighteenth century this seemed random and incoherent, although in the last decades of the century greater use was made of sub-headings and other techniques to help readers negotiate their way around ever larger amounts of dense text. It is to these readers, and the manner in which they read newspapers, that we now turn.

CHAPTER THREE

Newspaper Readers

If it is difficult to establish how many newspapers were published in the eighteenth and nineteenth centuries, it is even harder to discover how many people read them and who those people were. The gender composition of newspaper readers is particularly opaque. Although it is evident that women read newspapers, the size of the female readership remains extremely unclear, even in comparison with the vexed issue of readers' social status. The figures given in chapter 2 for the payment of newspaper stamps suggest that the sales of stamped newspapers more than quadrupled in proportion to the adult population between the early eighteenth and early nineteenth centuries. However, this increase was not as dramatic as might first appear, since the proportion of newspapers to population remained extremely low for most of the period under discussion, even if we take into account the unstamped press. In 1712, just over one stamped newspaper was produced each year for every two adults in England. By 1760, the ratio was closer to 3:2, and at the turn of the century it had jumped to almost to 3:1. By the 1830s, more than three taxed newspapers were produced annually per adult head of population, with perhaps as many unstamped papers being published at the same time. Although the growth in production was significant, these calculations suggest that newspaper readers comprised a tiny percentage of the total population. But newspaper readership was likely to have been much higher than these figures suggest. Relatively few papers would have been read by just one person. In the early eighteenth century, Joseph Addison estimated that at least twenty people read each copy of the *Spectator*.[1]

1. Jeremy Black, *The English Press in the Eighteenth Century* (Beckenham, 1987), p. 104; Joseph Addison, 'Essay No. 10', *The Spectator*, ed. Donald F. Bond (5 vols., Oxford, 1965), i. 44.

A century later the *Westminster Review* revised this estimate to thirty.[2] The unstamped press of the early nineteenth century was particularly variable in this respect, with levels of political interest or agitation determining both a paper's overall print-run and the numbers of people who read each copy. Estimates of the degree of multiple readership which took place may have varied a good deal, but commentators were not divided concerning the frequency with which newspapers were shared.

There is little doubt that the proportion of newspaper readers was higher in the capital than anywhere else during the eighteenth and nineteenth centuries. In the later eighteenth century, the political agent Dennis O'Bryen believed that there were 250,000 newspaper readers in the capital, that is ten readers for each paper.[3] O'Bryen's figure constitutes one third of the London population. Looking back even earlier, Michael Harris has calculated that by the middle of the eighteenth century there were 100,000 newspapers sold every week in the capital,[4] or about 16,500 a day. Using the same multiplier of ten, this suggests that one quarter of the capital's residents read a newspaper in 1750, compared with a third in the 1780s. This proportion does not appear to have increased much by the turn of the century, but by 1840 the situation was very different. Although the population of the capital had doubled, perhaps five times as many papers were sold here, suggesting a London readership of around five-sixths of the population.[5]

Estimating the number of newspaper readers in the provinces is equally problematic and speculative. In 1750, there were at least forty provincial newspapers produced in England. If we assume a weekly print-run of 1,000 copies for each, this means that an estimated 40,000 copies of provincial newspapers appeared every week. The number of people who read each paper was probably lower in the provinces than in the capital, so if we use a multiplier of five, then the estimated size of the provincial newspaper readership is 200,000, or about 4 per cent of the population in England outside London. By 1780, this figure had probably doubled to 8 per

2. Arthur Aspinall, *Politics and the Press: c. 1780–1850* (London, 1949), pp. 24–5.

3. Dennis O'Bryen to Edmund Burke, March 1782, Wentworth Woodhouse Muniments, Sheffield City Archives, BK 1/1557.

4. Michael Harris, *London Newspapers in the Age of Walpole: A Study in the Origins of the Modern English Press* (London, 1987), p. 190.

5. On population, see C.M. Law, 'Some notes on the urban population of England and Wales in the eighteenth century', *Local Historian*, **10** (1972), p. 24; B.R. Mitchell, *British Historical Statistics* (Cambridge, 1988), p. 30.

cent; during the 1830s it may have been 16 per cent; and ten years later as high as 30 per cent.[6] This suggests a much lower level of readership than in the capital, but one which was growing quickly. However, these calculations do not take into account the degree of penetration by London newspapers in the provinces, nor do they show the undoubted importance of regional variation and, in particular, the difference between urban and rural readerships. It was certainly the case that a far greater proportion of provincial newspaper readers came from towns and their immediate environs, and that readership was spread more thinly in rural areas. James Lackington's optimistic account of widespread reading amongst the rural poor in the eighteenth century was probably a gross overstatement.[7] William Cobbett, who spent his childhood in Farnham, wrote in 1796: 'I do not remember ever having seen a news-paper in the house.'[8] However, other records of country life, such as the diaries of the Sussex shopkeeper Thomas Turner, and those of Elizabeth Shackleton, wife of a Lancashire woollen merchant, suggest a familiarity with newspapers and regular reading habits amongst at least a section of the rural community.[9]

The correspondence, diaries and memoirs of the upper classes in eighteenth- and nineteenth-century England leave us in no doubt that newspapers provided a constant source of information, debate and concern for the ruling elite throughout our period. However, since this group was both small and changed very little in size, what is open to question is the identity of those new readers who prompted the rise in newspaper sales. The pattern of newspaper proliferation between 1695 and 1855 makes it tempting to link the growth in newspaper readership to the expanding middle classes: the mostly urban, consuming and socially ambitious men and women who have recently received much historical attention. Indeed, Bob Harris maintains that the upper and middle classes formed the backbone of newspaper readership during the

6. On population, see E.A. Wrigley and R.S. Schofield, *The Population History of England 1541–1871: A Reconstruction* (Cambridge, 1989), pp. 333–5 and appendix 3; Law, 'Some notes on the urban population of England and Wales in the eighteenth century', pp. 22 and 24; Mitchell, *British Historical Statistics*, pp. 15, 25–7 and 30.

7. James Lackington, *Memoirs of the First Forty-Five Years of the Life of James Lackington* (London, 1792), p. 254.

8. M.J. Smith, 'English radical newspapers in the French revolutionary era' (London University PhD thesis, 1979), p. 151.

9. *The Diary of Thomas Turner 1754–1765*, ed. David Vaisey (Oxford, 1985), pp. 6, 43, 62, 80–1, 99, 124, 153–4, 191; Amanda Vickery, *The Gentleman's Daughter: Women's Lives in Georgian England* (New Haven, Conn., 1998), p. 260.

eighteenth century.[10] Cranfield has noted that the diaries and correspondence of local gentry, clergymen and town magnates typically recorded contact with both London and provincial newspapers in the first half of the eighteenth century,[11] whilst in his study of the 1760s, John Brewer has argued that London readers were also drawn largely from the elite.

Brewer has shown from the accounts of the *Public Advertiser* between 1765 and 1771 that fluctuations in the circulation within the calendar year corresponded with the London season: sales thus reached a peak in February and March, just before parliament ended its business for the year, and did not pick up again until October or November with the new parliamentary session.[12] Brewer concludes that these fluctuations are a sign that most newspaper readers came from those classes whose members followed the social season, and were thus only in London at certain times of the year. However, this does not appear to have been the case two decades later. An examination of the sales of the *Gazetteer* between 1784 and 1795 is less indicative of an elite readership. A declining importance of the London season to newspaper sales, coupled with a boom in newspaper circulation which outstripped the growth of the middle classes, might suggest a broadening of the newspaper-reading public during the eighteenth century as it became both larger and more socially mixed.[13] How far this development was repeated outside London is less clear. When the radical *Northern Star* appeared in 1838, it claimed to serve a largely working-class readership, which had previously found 'no single provincial organ through which their wants and wishes could be adequately expressed, and by which their rights could be duly asserted and their interests maintained'. It was, the paper asserted, 'an entirely new class of readers'.[14] Yet Patricia Hollis has shown that the unstamped press circulated widely throughout the provinces from 1831 onwards,[15] and it is also probable that many

10. Bob Harris, *Politics and the Rise of the Press: Britain and France, 1620–1800* (London, 1996), p. 15.

11. G.A. Cranfield, *The Development of the Provincial Newspaper* (Oxford, 1962), pp. 181–2.

12. John Brewer, *Party Ideology and Popular Politics at the Accession of George III* (Cambridge, 1976), p. 143.

13. Hannah Barker, *Newspapers, Politics, and Public Opinion in Late Eighteenth-Century England* (Oxford, 1998), pp. 22–42.

14. J.A. Epstein, 'Feargus O'Connor and the *Northern Star*', *International Review of Social History*, **xxi** (1976), pp. 71–2.

15. Patricia Hollis, *The Pauper Press: A Study in Working-class Radicalism of the 1830s* (Oxford, 1970), pp. 108–16.

of the provincial labouring classes were reading newspapers before the 1830s.

Indeed, in London and the provinces, there is much anecdotal evidence to suggest that those fairly low on the social scale might have had access to newspapers, although more was made of this phenomenon in the capital. In the early eighteenth century, contemporary reports concerning the social composition of London's newspaper readership usually emphasised its diversity. In 1726, César de Saussure remarked that 'all Englishmen are great newsmongers. Workmen habitually begin the day by going to coffee-rooms in order to read the latest news. I have often seen shoeblacks and men of that class club together to purchase a farthing paper.'[16] In his *Notes sur Angleterre*, written during the 1730s, Montesquieu was struck not only by the number and licentiousness ·of newspapers, but also by the fact that working men read them, to such a degree that 'the very slaters had the newspapers brought to the roofs of the houses on which they were working, that they might read them'.[17]

From the mid-century onwards, the lower orders' interest in news seems to have increased, thus in 1757, John Newbery set up the *Universal Chronicle*, eager to take advantage of 'that rage for intelligence which the successes of the war had excited in even the lower orders of the people'.[18] A year later, Dr Johnson noted that 'all foreigners remark, that the knowledge of the common people of England is greater than that of any other vulgar. This superiority we undoubtedly owe to the rivulets of intelligence, which are continually trickling among us, which every one may catch, and of which every one partakes.'[19] One such foreign writer, Johann Wilhelm von Archenholz, described reading the daily papers to be 'actually an epidemical passion among the English', and noted that 'sometimes a politician will insert an essay on a subject which concerns the welfare of the whole nation, and everybody, even a fish-woman, is able to comprehend it. It is not at all uncommon to observe such persons reading and comment-ating on the public prints.'[20] Of course, writers such as von

16. César de Saussure, *A Foreign View of England in the Reigns of George I and George II* (London, 1902), p. 162.
17. A. Aspinall, 'The circulation of newspapers in the early nineteenth century', *Review of English Studies* **xxii**, 85 (1946), p. 29.
18. J.P. Thomas, 'The British Empire and the press, 1763–1774' (Oxford DPhil thesis, 1982), p. 37.
19. Harris, *London Newspapers in the Age of Walpole*, p. 195.
20. J.W. von Archenholz, *A Picture of England* (Dublin, 1791), pp. 44 and 39.

Archenholz and Montesquieu were far from objective in their descriptions of English life. Both had agendas which made them keen to present the English constitution and its famously free press in a favourable light. The same may also be said of Johnson. However, this does not negate the usefulness of such comments to the historian, particularly when the sentiments they expressed appear so often elsewhere.

The reading habits of the lower orders were often reflected in contemporary prints. Hogarth's 'Beer Street' shows a butcher and a blacksmith reading a newspaper. Other satirical prints from the 1760s and 1770s, such as 'St. Monday', 'The Blacksmith lets his Iron grow cold attending to the Taylor's News', 'The Morning News' and a 'Meeting of City Politicians', depict all sorts of working men reading, or listening to newspapers being read, several prints being openly critical of the way the working day is disrupted as a result.[21] Other commentators were also damning about the effect that printed material in general, and newspapers in particular, could have on the lower orders. Vicesimus Knox, for example, spoke in the 1790s of newspapers deceiving 'the more ignorant classes'.[22] Even the author and publisher John Trusler reflected general anxieties about the spread of reading in the eighteenth century, and worried that printed matter was becoming so cheap that everyone would be able to afford it. In the country, where he claimed all men were learning to read, Trusler believed that they had started to 'sacrifice the wholesome food of the body for the pernicious poison of the mind'.[23] In the early nineteenth century, the Lancashire reformer Samuel Bamford reported that the *Political Register* was read on nearly every cottage hearth in the manufacturing districts of south Lancashire, Leicester, Derby and Nottingham, whilst Henry Bankes wrote of his regret concerning 'the universal rage for spreading education among the poor', which caused them to absorb 'ill impressions' from newspapers.[24] An anonymous letter to Lord Eldon written in 1819 complained that in a northern

21. John Brewer, *The Common People and Politics 1750–1790s* (Cambridge, 1986), pp. 69, 73, 75 and 160.

22. Vicesimus Knox, *The Works of Vicesimus Knox* (7 vols., London, 1824), v. 176.

23. Trusler's memoirs cited by James Raven in 'From promotion to proscription: arrangements for reading and eighteenth-century libraries', in Helen Small, Naomi Tadmor and James Raven, eds., *The Practice and Representation of Reading in England* (Oxford, 1992), p. 193.

24. Aspinall, *Politics and the Press*, pp. 10 and 30.

colliery district the radical *Black Dwarf* was to be found 'in the hat-crown of almost every pitman you meet'.[25]

Trusler's rather optimistic belief in the universality of literacy was echoed in 1791 by the London publisher James Lackington, who described reading amongst 'the poorer sort of farmers, and even the poor country people in general ... in short, all ranks and degrees now READ'.[26] This contemporary perception of increasing literacy is not necessarily supported by modern historical research, which suggests that even by the mid-nineteenth century half of the English population could not write (with women less likely to be literate than men).[27] Indeed, James Raven is keen to stress that the boom in print in the eighteenth century did not represent a major increase in new readers, but rather that those already reading books were buying or borrowing more. 'If readership was a "widening circle", stimulated and supported by the prodigious growth in newspapers and circulating libraries', he argues, 'then it was restricted by literacy rates and even more by levels of household income.'[28] Raven appears to contradict the work of Margaret Spufford on chapbook literature in the seventeenth century, in which she points out that the existence of very large numbers of these cheap publications presupposed a large and 'humble' reading public.[29] Moreover, David Cressy's work demonstrates high levels of literacy amongst London craftsmen and traders during the eighteenth century. He claims that by the early eighteenth century almost all of those who constituted the commercial classes in the capital were literate.[30] But his work on Norwich also shows that literacy was declining amongst some social groups between the 1660s and 1720s.[31] Historians are increasingly wary of presenting

25. Anonymous letter to Lord Eldon, 25 October 1819, cited in W.H. Wickwar, *The Struggle for the Freedom of the Press 1819–1832* (London, 1928), p. 57.

26. Lackington, *Memoirs of the First Forty-Five Years*, p. 254.

27. Roger Schofield, 'Dimensions of illiteracy in England 1750–1850', in H.J. Graff, ed., *Literacy and Social Development in the West* (Cambridge, 1981), p. 207; L. Stone, 'Literacy and education in England 1640–1900', *Past and Present* 42 (1969), 105; David Vincent, *Literacy and Popular Culture: England 1750–1914* (Cambridge, 1989), pp. 22–4.

28. James Raven, *Judging New Wealth: Popular Publishing and Responses to Commerce, 1750–1800* (Oxford, 1992), p. 56. Cf. R.M. Wiles, 'The relish for reading in provincial England two centuries ago', in Paul J. Korshin, ed., *The Widening Circle: Essays on the Circulation of Literature in Eighteenth-Century Europe* (Philadelphia, Pa., 1976).

29. Margaret Spufford, *Small Books and Pleasant Histories: Popular Fiction and its Readership in Seventeenth-Century England* (London, 1981).

30. David Cressy, *Literacy and the Social Order* (London, 1975), p. 154.

31. David Cressy, 'Levels of illiteracy in England 1530–1730', in Graff, ed., *Literacy and Social Development in the West*, p. 113.

the growth of literacy in the eighteenth and nineteenth centuries as either inevitable or constant. Roger Schofield has estimated that literacy levels in England as a whole remained static between 1750 and 1815, after which they did start to increase, but he also notes large regional diversities in the 1830s and 1840s. In addition, Schofield argues that those who lived in towns were more likely to be literate than those who did not, and that throughout the eighteenth and nineteenth centuries there was an occupational hierarchy of illiteracy, with those at the lower end of the social scale far more likely to be illiterate than those at the upper end. According to his evidence, even by 1844 most labourers and servants remained illiterate, and high levels of illiteracy were also prevalent amongst the armed forces and within the mining and construction trades.[32] However, it must be remembered that even if labourers were far less likely to read than lawyers, there were still many more literate labourers than lawyers, in absolute numbers.

Of course, judging literacy levels amongst any social group is notoriously difficult, particularly as the ability to read may not have been dependent upon the ability to write. In her study of late seventeenth-century spiritual autobiography, Margaret Spufford claimed that reading was a more socially diffused skill than writing.[33] Moreover, the audience for newspapers was not limited to those who could read, since papers could be, and often were, read aloud. Indeed, David Vincent's work on literacy and popular culture in England between 1750 and 1914 has shown how familial and community networks ensured that most illiterate people knew others who were literate. Vincent argues that 'the skill of reading . . . was at once a personal and a collective possession':[34] in other words, those who could read were expected to read aloud to those who could not. Naomi Tadmor's study of household reading in the eighteenth century demonstrates how reading was frequently sociable rather than solitary, and involved individuals reading to family members and guests.[35] Charles Leslie, author of *The Rehearsal*, noted

32. Schofield, 'Dimensions of illiteracy in England 1750–1850', pp. 206–13.

33. Margaret Spufford, 'First steps in literacy: the reading and writing experiences of the humblest seventeenth-century spiritual autobiographies', *Social History*, 4 (1979).

34. Vincent, *Literacy and Popular Culture*, pp. 23 and 49.

35. Naomi Tadmor, 'In the even my wife read to me: women, reading and household life in the eighteenth century', in Raven, Small and Tadmor, eds., *The Practice and Representation of Reading in England*. See also John Brewer, 'Reconstructing the reader: prescriptives, texts and strategies in Anna Larpent's reading', in Raven, Small and Tadmor, eds., *The Practice and Representation of Reading in England*.

at the very beginning of the eighteenth century that 'the greatest part of the people do not read books, most of them cannot read at all. But they will gather together about one that can read, and listen to an *Observator* or *Review* (as I have seen them in the streets) where all the principles of rebellion are instilled into them.'[36]

Such practices were still common in the nineteenth century. Cobbett referred to the audience for his *Political Register* as 'my readers, or hearers',[37] and in 1831 the *Spectator* claimed that 'in most towns of the kingdom, there are public houses, the landlords of which retain readers in their pay, who sit in the place of common resort, and read all the most interesting parts of the newspapers aloud'.[38] The practice of reading aloud was particularly well recorded in the case of the Chartist press. W.E. Adams wrote in his memoirs that a local shoemaker would appear at his home with the *Northern Star* every Sunday morning in order for a member of the household to read sections of the paper to him and his friends.[39] Ben Brierley, in his youth a handloom weaver of velvet in the south Lancashire village of Failsworth, recorded reading the *Star* to his father and five others who jointly subscribed to the paper: 'It was my task to read aloud so that all could hear at the same time', and so that comments and joint discussion could follow. Likewise, Ben Wilson of Halifax recalled that: 'it was common practice, particularly in the villages to meet at friends' houses to read [the *Northern Star*] and talk over political matters.'[40]

Reading newspapers aloud was also a common theme in eighteenth-century prints. In 'A Meeting of City Politicians' from 1779, for example, a large group of men sit around the table of a public house. Some read newspapers to themselves, at least one reads aloud to his companions and several look over others' shoulders.[41] Here newspaper reading is presented as a form of communal activity which could extend far beyond the limits of the literate, or indeed the purchasers of newspapers. There may, however, have

36. J.A. Downie, *Robert Harley and the Press: Propaganda and Public Opinion in the Age of Swift and Defoe* (Cambridge, 1979), p. 6.

37. Kevin Gilmartin, *Print Politics: The Press and Radical Opposition in Early Nineteenth-Century England*, (Cambridge, 1996), p. 103.

38. G.A. Cranfield, *The Press and Society: From Caxton to Northcliffe* (London, 1978), p. 119.

39. Brian Harrison, in 'Press and pressure group in modern Britain', in Joanne Shattock and Michael Wolff, eds., *The Victorian Periodical Press: Samplings and Soundings* (Leicester, 1982), pp. 283–4.

40. Epstein, 'Feargus O'Connor and the *Northern Star*', pp. 73–4.

41. 'A meeting of city politicians', July 1779, British Museum DG 5613.

been differences between the town and the countryside in the degree to which such behaviour was acceptable in public. The *Country Spectator* noted in 1792 that whilst in the countryside people were happy to listen to newspapers being read aloud and to public discussion of their contents, in London 'coffee-house orators' were interrupted by those who wished to read, not listen.[42] More than likely this reflected differing levels of general literacy in the capital and in rural areas. When William Lovett opened a coffee-house in 1834 he got round this problem by setting one room aside as a 'conversation-room' in order to separate talkers from readers.[43]

By the late eighteenth century, reading newspapers aloud was common amongst radical groups such as the London Correspond-ing Society and the Manchester Reformation Society, and the practice was even blamed for the disaffection which had culminated in the naval mutinies of 1797.[44] In 1798, at least one branch of the United Englishmen subscribed to the *Courier*. Consisting mostly of shoemakers and weavers, this group met at various public houses in the East End of London and always began their meetings by reading the paper aloud.[45] In 1817, Southey complained to Lord Liverpool that newspapers such as *Cobbett's Register* and *Hone's Register* were 'read aloud in every ale-house' and wherever soldiers met.[46] Public readings were also organised on a much greater scale. The Birmingham Political Union, for example, arranged news-paper readings at its large public meetings; and during the reform agitation of the early 1830s, large numbers of Birmingham people used to congregate in their dinner hour and in the evenings to hear the news of the day. In 1839, the town witnessed Chartist meetings of up to 80,000 in the Bull Ring, where Lovett noted that the crowd 'paid very polite attention to a person reading a newspaper'.[47] Indeed, Epstein claims that the Chartist *Northern Star* was written with public readings very much in mind: 'It is obvious from the highly rhetorical style of the *Star*'s leading articles that the paper was designed to be read aloud.'[48] Moreover, readings of radical

42. Black, *English Press*, p. 302.
43. Aspinall, 'The circulation of newspapers in the early nineteenth century', p. 36.
44. Aspinall, 'The circulation of newspapers in the early nineteenth century', p. 34.
45. Smith, 'English radical newspapers', pp. 110 and 164.
46. Aspinall, *Politics and the Press*, p. 29.
47. Aspinall, 'The circulation of newspapers in the early nineteenth century', p. 34; Asa Briggs, 'Press and public in early nineteenth-century Birmingham', *Dugdale Society Occasional Papers*, **8** (1949), p. 14.
48. Epstein, 'Feargus O'Connor and the *Northern Star*', p. 70.

papers were not met with reverential silence, but formed the basis of listeners' subsequent discussions, as Brierley and Wilson's comments show, and as is evident in the announcement made in 1838 by the Mossley Working Men's Association that they had procured their own reading room 'where they assemble to read the *Northern Star* and other newspapers' and where 'we read the news of the week, and discuss it paragraph by paragraph, as it is read'.[49] Public newspaper reading was thus an active, participatory experience. As Gilmartin has argued, such forms of collective reception, which radical papers themselves encouraged, were important forms of politicisation, which led readers 'to understand their own experience as part of a collective historical process, and to perceive common interests among individuals widely separated in time and space'.[50]

It has already been noted that the relatively high price of newspapers restricted sales, but as we have seen, this does not necessarily mean that they were out of range of the lower classes. In addition to reading papers aloud, sharing newspapers appears to have become increasingly common during our period. As early as 1746 there was a 'Friendly Society of neighbours' which met in Cambridgeshire every week to read and discuss the news.[51] By 1821 the *Monthly Magazine* reported that there were no fewer than 5,000 'newspaper societies' comprising six to a dozen families across the country.[52] Aspinall's work on the circulation of newspapers in the early nineteenth century contains many instances of shared newspaper purchase. For example, he cites the Tory MP Henry Goulburn, who in 1836 described how the working classes would come together for the purposes of reading newspapers, whilst an employer's papers were often read by the whole household and his employees. Radical movements, and Chartism in particular, clearly boosted the trend further. In 1818, Wooler's *Black Dwarf* noted the appearance of a number of short-lived Political Protestant Associations, a reform group which began in Hull and planned weekly meetings in classes of not more than twenty with a penny a week subscription to buy newspapers.[53] Viscount Snowden

---

49. Epstein, 'Feargus O'Connor and the *Northern Star*', p. 76.

50. Gilmartin, *Print Politics*, pp. 106–7.

51. Cranfield, *The Development of the Provincial Newspaper*, p. 177.

52. Richard D. Altick, *The English Common Reader: A Social History of the Mass Reading Public 1800–1900* (Chicago, Ill., 1957), p. 323.

53. Cited in Aspinall, 'The circulation of newspapers in the early nineteenth century', p. 33.

was told by his father that during the Chartist period, a number of Yorkshire handloom weavers contributed a halfpenny per week to buy copies of the sympathetic *Leeds Mercury* which he travelled four miles to collect, and that they then met in a cottage where he would read them the news. The autobiography of another Chartist, Thomas Cooper, recorded how groups of brushmakers in his native town of Gainsborough would club together to buy papers such as *Black Dwarf* and *Cobbett's Political Register*.[54] The publishers of the *Anti-Jacobin* even suggested that readers lent their copies to their poorer neighbours.[55] Yet it was not only the poor who shared newspapers. In Tiverton in 1799, the London *Courier* was reportedly circulated amongst a surgeon, Congregational minister, druggist, undermaster of a local school and a French émigré, before being passed on to a sergemaker and then to 'the common people'. Another copy was said to have been passed around fifteen pairs of hands, and was finally sold to a Parson Lewis of Clayhanger, according to a hostile observer, 'to poison the honest country-men'.[56]

For those without the opportunity or inclination to organise the shared purchase of a newspaper, other options existed which were cheaper than bearing the whole cost alone. For the price of a drink, coffee and public houses provided easy access to newspapers for those who could not afford to buy their own. However, it should be noted that many coffee-houses had a more select clientele than other venues in terms of social class, and that coffee-houses were also likely to be male-dominated spaces, unlike alehouses and taverns, where the company was more likely to be mixed.[57] Reading newspapers in coffee-houses had been a theme of satirical prints since the early eighteenth century.[58] Christie estimates that there were around 200 coffee-houses in London by the late eighteenth century, and that by 1820 this figure had risen to around 300, with large numbers of inns, alehouses and gin-shops also keeping

54. Aspinall, *Politics and the Press*, p. 26; Aspinall, 'The circulation of newspapers in the early nineteenth century', p. 35.
55. Aspinall, 'The circulation of newspapers in the early nineteenth century', p. 32.
56. Smith, 'English radical newspapers', p. 165.
57. Brewer, *Party Ideology and Popular Politics*, pp. 148–50; Kathleen Wilson, *The Sense of the People: Politics, Culture and Imperialism in England, 1715–1785* (Cambridge, 1995), p. 47. See also Aytoun Ellis, *The Penny Universities* (London, 1956); Bryant Lillywhite, *London Coffee Houses* (London, 1963).
58. Brewer, *The Common People and Politics*, pp. 126–9.

newspapers for their customers.[59] However, Michael Harris claims that even in 1739 there were over 550 coffee-houses in London, and places such as chandlers and barbers had been supplying newspapers for their customers from the early eighteenth century.[60] A writer in *Lloyd's Evening Post* in 1780 commented: 'Without newspapers our Coffee-houses, Ale-houses, and Barber shops would undergo a change next to depopulation.'[61] According to Cobbett, newspapers were an even bigger draw for publicans than the beer they served:

> Ask the landlord why he takes the newspapers. He'll tell you that it attracts the people to his house, and in many cases its attractions are much stronger than those of the liquor there drunk, thousands upon thousands of men having become sots through the attraction of these vehicles of novelty and falsehood.[62]

The evidence of a labourer to the Select Committee on Newspaper Stamps in 1851 made a similar point, if perhaps somewhat disingenuously:

> I tell you, Sir, I never go to the public-house for beer, I go for the news; I have no other way of getting it; I cannot afford to pay five-pence, but unfortunately I go on drinking till I have spent a shilling, and I might as well have bought the paper in the first instance; still, that is my reason, my only reason for going to the public house; I hear people read the paper, and say what is going on in London, and it is the only place where I get the news.[63]

Godwin was less critical of pubs, which he described as the labourer's university and a place where men were educated into citizenship.[64]

By the late eighteenth century, in addition to inns and pubs where newspapers were available, many provincial towns also had

59. I.R. Christie, 'British newspapers in the later Georgian age', in I.R. Christie, *Myth and Reality in Late-Eighteenth-Century British Politics and Other Papers* (London, 1970), p. 325.

60. Michael Harris, 'The structure, ownership and control of the press, 1620–1780', in George Boyce, James Curran and Pauline Wingate, eds., *Newspaper History from the Seventeenth Century to the Present Day* (London, 1978), p. 91; Harris, *London Newspapers in the Age of Walpole*, p. 47.

61. Solomon Lutnick, *The American Revolution and the British Press 1775–1783* (Columbia, Mo., 1967), p. 1.

62. Aspinall, *Politics and the Press*, p. 11.

63. Joel H. Wiener, *The War of the Unstamped: The Movement to Repeal the British Newspaper Tax, 1830–1836* (Ithaca, NY, 1969), p. 35.

64. Cited in Aspinall, 'The circulation of newspapers in the early nineteenth century', p. 38.

coffee-houses where papers could be read. Clare has noted that Manchester, Sheffield and Leeds all boasted coffee-houses which supplied their customers with newspapers; and often set aside a special newspaper reading room.[65] In Liverpool, large news-rooms were established in the St George's and Pontack's coffee-houses by the 1760s.[66] John Money's study of eighteenth-century Birmingham reveals a network of coffee-houses and newspaper outlets which served a growing demand for 'information on all matters of general and particular interest'.[67] Even a town the size of Knaresborough, with under 3,000 inhabitants, had its own coffee-house by the 1760s, whilst a small town such as Loughborough with a population of only 4,000 could support 43 inns in 1770.[68]

The eighteenth century also witnessed the rise of libraries and subscription reading rooms, where members paid a fee to gain access to several newspapers. These had been growing in number since the mid-eighteenth century. Paul Kaufman has estimated that, by 1800, 112 circulating libraries had been established in London and 268 in the provinces. However, as John Brewer has pointed out, early libraries were not cheap to join, and their cost probably restricted membership to all but the 'gentle and professional or merchant classes'.[69] This situation was to change somewhat in the nineteenth century. Aspinall notes that by the early 1800s, every large, and many small, towns had their own subscription reading rooms, usually charging a guinea a year. The Bristol Institution for the Advancement of Science and Arts, for example, subscribed to over 300 papers in 1837,[70] whilst by the 1840s, the Manchester

65. D. Clare, 'The growth and importance of the newspaper press in Manchester, Liverpool, Sheffield and Leeds between 1780 and 1800' (University of Manchester MA thesis, 1960), p. 17.

66. Richard Brooke, *Liverpool as it was during the Last Quarter of the Eighteenth Century: 1775 to 1800* (Liverpool, 1853), pp. 163 and 269.

67. John Money, 'Taverns, coffee houses and clubs: local politics and popular articulacy in the Birmingham area in the age of the American Revolution', *Historical Journal*, **xiv**, 1 (1971), p. 24.

68. Brewer, *Party Ideology and Popular Politics*, p. 150; Law, 'Some notes on the urban population of England and Wales in the eighteenth century', p. 26; Alan Everitt, 'The English urban inn, 1560–1760', in Alan Everitt, ed., *Perspectives in English Urban History* (London, 1973), p. 94. For a discussion of the place of coffee-houses in provincial urban culture, see Peter Borsay, *The English Urban Renaissance: Culture and Society in the Provincial Town 1660–1770* (Oxford, 1989); and Ellis, *The Penny Universities*.

69. Paul Kaufman, *Libraries and Their Users* (London, 1969), p. 192; Brewer, *Party Ideology and Popular Politics*, p. 151.

70. Aled Jones, *Powers of the Press: Newspapers, Power and the Public in Nineteenth-Century England* (Aldershot, 1996), p. 184.

Exchange had over 1,800 subscribers and took 130 papers a day, including multiple copies of the most popular ones.[71]

For those less well off, there were smaller scale penny-a-week subscription rooms, generally run by radicals, such as the Union Rooms in Prescot. At the end of the Napoleonic Wars, a Manchester brushmaker and one of 'Orator' Hunt's associates, Joseph Johnson, was using his shop as a working-class reading room.[72] In the 1830s, Thomas Grundy of Bury organised 100 subscribers in order to buy three daily and eight weekly papers.[73] Poorer readers could also hire newspapers for a fraction of the cover price from hawkers, who would then return the papers to the publishers as unsold. In 1724, this prompted Nathaniel Mist to complain that hawkers were allowing people to look at his paper for a third of the cover price.[74] Although this practice was made illegal in 1789 it appears to have continued unchecked, and copies of *The Times* were reported to have been hired for 1d an hour by newsmen in the 1830s.[75]

It has already been noted that contemporary accounts of readership are not necessarily reliable, and almost always both impressionistic and politically motivated (either praising the 'enlightening' effect of newspapers or more commonly damning their 'pernicious' influence). For some historians, the key to discovering the identity of newspaper readers lies not in the accounts of contemporary observers, but in the newspapers themselves. Text-based approaches assume that what appears to be a paper's targeted audience and what constituted its actual readership are closely related. Schweizer and Klein have used this method in a study of London newspaper advertisements in the early 1790s. From this they have concluded that newspapers were 'a vehicle for the expression of the sentiments of the new moneyed class who comprised a vital segment of the reading public'.[76] It is true that for much of the eighteenth and early nineteenth centuries, newspapers carried a range of advertisements which appear to support the

71. A.P. Wadsworth, 'Newspaper circulations, 1800–1954', *Transactions of the Manchester Statistical Society* (1955), pp. 4–6; D. Read, *Press and People 1790–1850: Opinion in Three English Cities* (Aldershot, 1993), p. 202.

72. Aspinall, 'The circulation of newspapers in the early nineteenth century', pp. 25–31.

73. Jones, *Powers of the Press*, p. 184.

74. James Sutherland, *The Restoration Newspaper and its Development* (Cambridge, 1986), p. 224.

75. *The History of The Times*, vol. I: *'The Thunderer' in the Making: 1785–1841* (London, 1935), p. 435.

76. K. Schweizer and R. Klein, 'The French Revolution and the developments in the London daily press to 1793', *Publishing History*, **XVIII** (1985).

thesis linking newspapers to a growing commercial, consumerist 'middle class'. Thus, for example, one finds a concentration of advertisements for goods and services at the 'luxury' end of the market. But whilst an examination of newspaper advertisements does suggest a certain type of reader, it is an approach which places great weight upon the ability of advertisers to gauge the effectiveness of advertising, and, more importantly, it assumes that advertisers catered for the bulk of newspaper readers. Both assumptions are open to question. There is evidence to suggest that eighteenth-century advertisers at least intended to appeal to only a select and richer proportion of newspaper readers.[77]

Other types of advertisement lead us to different conclusions. For example, in the late eighteenth century, the *Morning Herald* seems to have specialised in advertising for servants wanted and in publishing advertisements placed by servants seeking employment, suggesting a readership from amongst the servant class. Advertisements for prosecution associations in the late eighteenth century also indicate that contemporaries perceived a readership for provincial newspapers that reached quite far down the social scale. Peter King's research on these associations suggests that they were generally formed by farmers and small freeholders in rural areas, and by manufacturers and tradesmen such as butchers, bakers, brewers and millers in towns.[78] Newspapers also carried adverts placed by hopeful candidates for parliamentary election, addressed to their prospective constituents. This suggests that those who could vote comprised at least a section of the newspaper-reading public, which in places such as Middlesex and the City could mean a very broad constituency. However, since from the 1760s onwards many newspapers were forceful proponents of electoral reform, it also seems likely that papers were read by those who could not vote, but might be persuaded they had a right to do so, which could conceivably constitute an extremely large proportion of the country's male population.

Bob Harris has rightly taken issue with the contention of Stephen Botein, Jack Censer and Harriet Ritvo that British newspapers in the eighteenth century adopted a particularly bourgeois tone and perspective. English newspapers increasingly addressed a more socially diverse audience than this. The criticism of the aristocracy

77. Barker, *Newspapers, Politics, and Public Opinion*, pp. 32–3.
78. Harris, *Politics and the Rise of the Press*, p. 21; Peter King, 'Prosecution associations and their impact in eighteenth-century Essex', in Douglas Hay and Francis Snyder, eds., *Policing and Prosecution in Britain, 1750–1850* (Oxford, 1989).

in newspapers, on which much of the Botein/Censer/Ritvo thesis rests, was not necessarily 'bourgeois' or middle-class in origin; nor was it consistent, since newspapers would frequently praise aristocrats and endorse the existing social hierarchy.[79] As we saw in chapter 1, newspaper appeals to 'the people' became more common and definitions of 'the public' more broad as time went on, suggesting a readership which not only increasingly stretched further down the social scale, but was not conceived of in a narrow, 'class'-based manner.

Newspapers have also been linked to the middle classes because of their interest in the world of trade and commerce. In his examination of the creation of a fiscal-military state in seventeenth- and eighteenth-century England, Brewer suggests that the English public followed the progress of hostilities during wartime 'with an assiduity worthy of Tristram Shandy's Uncle Toby', because of their interest in its economic repercussions.[80] Brewer stresses the importance of narrowly defined commercial and trading interests in the public's interest in 'world' events and links the desire for news with middle-class concerns. But once again, we should be wary of assuming that newspaper interests reflected the concerns of the growing commercial classes alone, since foreign news had occupied a prominent place in English newspapers throughout the eighteenth century. De Saussure, writing about newspaper readership in 1726, remarked with surprise that 'you often see an Englishman taking a treaty of peace more to heart than he does his own affairs'.[81] In addition, foreign news would have appealed to more than just those interested in the economic repercussions of war. In the case of Anglo-American relations in the 1770s, for example, the capital's radicals would have had political, rather than commercial, motives for their interest in the progress of events (although in the case of many London merchants, the 'commercial' and the 'political' are not easy to disentangle). Richard Wilson also casts doubt on the importance of newspapers to traders and manufacturers, and has argued that although the amount of specifically business and trade-oriented news in papers increased from around

79. Harris, *Politics and the Rise of the Press*, pp. 94–6; Stephen Botein, Jack R. Censer and Harriet Ritvo, 'The periodical press in eighteenth century English and French society: a cross-cultural approach', *Comparative Studies in Society and History*, **23** (1981).

80. John Brewer, *Sinews of Power: War, Money and the English State, 1688–1783* (London, 1989), p. xxi.

81. Saussure, *Foreign View of England*, p. 162.

1760, other sources of information, and particularly correspondence with suppliers, agents and customers, continued to be more
important until the development of trade journals in the late
nineteenth century.[82]

Conclusion

Although the evidence is patchy, it seems clear that newspaper
readers became both more numerous and more socially diverse
between 1695 and 1855. In London in particular, it appears that
those fairly low down the social scale would have had some contact
with the press. This was also increasingly true of the provinces, in
part because of the growth of radicalism in the nineteenth century,
which encouraged the labouring classes to read newspapers as a
means of politicisation. Neither the inability to read nor the high
cost of newspapers necessarily prevented the bulk of the population
from discovering their contents. Reading aloud – either in private
homes or at public meetings – was a common activity, and the
shared purchase and hire of newspapers, coupled with their
presence in coffee-houses, pubs and shops, as well as in increasing
numbers of subscription reading rooms (both genteel and lowly)
and circulating libraries, made them accessible to many. The
attempts of some historians to link the growth in newspaper
readership with the rising middle classes is not wholly unconvincing, but examinations of advertising, nascent 'class consciousness'
or commercial interests have not proved conclusive, and readers of
newspapers in the eighteenth and nineteenth centuries were likely
to have come from a much wider section of society.

It has also become apparent that when assessing the influence of
newspapers, it is important to know not just who read them, but *how*
they were read. In other words, it must be remembered that
readers' response to newspapers and the cultural and political
meanings they ascribed to newspaper contents were dependent
upon the conditions in which they were read. There is a great deal
of difference between the solitary and leisurely perusal of a paper
and hearing excerpts read aloud as part of a group, when what was
read was decided by others and the text was almost certainly

---

82. Richard Wilson, 'Newspapers and industry: the export of wool controversy in
the 1780s', in Michael Harris and Alan Lee, eds., *The Press in English Society from the
Seventeenth to the Nineteenth Centuries* (London, 1986), p. 82.

accompanied by the comments and discussion of one's fellow listeners. No doubt the success of the newspaper press owed much to the flexibility with which newspapers could be read – either alone or in company, and from start to finish or in part (a practice to which the provision of news in short paragraph-form lent itself). This, coupled with the sense of immediacy and reader interaction which newspapers offered by way of their letter pages, their frequent publication and because they appeared to represent their readers, seems to have fuelled their popularity. However, for historians, the very scale of the newspaper's success in the eighteenth and early nineteenth centuries must serve to complicate the contemporary meanings of its contents and the identity of its readers.

CHAPTER FOUR

Politicians and the Press

Taxation and Legislation

As the newspaper press grew in size and influence during the eighteenth and nineteenth centuries, it faced a variety of state controls and political influences. As has been noted, the lapsing of the Printing Act in 1695 freed the press from considerable legal restraints. According to Schwoerer, this was not the result of deliberate planning on the part of the government, but reflected instead its preoccupation with other matters. Downie, on the other hand, maintains that the licensing system ended because of its fundamental inefficiency.[1] Even after concerns had been raised by MPs about the dangers of an unregulated press in the years following 1695, parliament was neither sufficiently united nor committed enough to reimpose the kind of laws which had governed printing in the seventeenth century. This attitude remained despite calls from London printers who were keen for regulation to continue in order to protect their trade.[2] But whilst the government failed to keep the press under as tight a grip as it had previously, newspapers were not free from governmental constraints, and the eighteenth and nineteenth centuries witnessed the enactment of a variety of controlling and containing measures.

1. Lois G. Schwoerer, 'Liberty of the press and public opinion: 1660–1695', in J.R. Jones, ed., *Liberty Secured? Britain before and after 1688* (Stanford, Calif., 1992), p. 199; J.A. Downie, *Robert Harley and the Press: Propaganda and Public Opinion in the Age of Swift and Defoe* (Cambridge, 1979), p. ix; see also Raymond Astbury, 'The renewal of the Licensing Act in 1693 and its lapse in 1695', *Library*, 5th ser., **xxxiii**, 1 (1978).

2. Frederick Seaton Siebert, *Freedom of the Press in England 1476–1776: The Rise and Fall of Government Control* (Urbana, Ill., 1965), p. 307.

One of these was taxation, first imposed on newspapers in 1712. It is a matter of historical debate what motivated successive governments in their taxation policies, but it is probably a mistake to see newspaper taxes simply as a form of state repression. Michael Harris has stated that Lord Bolingbroke first introduced the system of newspaper taxes 'as an indirect curb on production'.[3] But an allied, and arguably more important, motivation for the government was the desire to raise money at a time when Land Tax was high and a general war-weariness was widespread.[4] Although the 1712 Act failed to raise much revenue for the Treasury initially, as taxes increased and newspaper publication grew this situation was to change, and for much of the remainder of our period, newspaper taxation policy seems to have been driven largely (although not wholly) by the revenue needs of the state, rather than by a desire to keep the press within bounds. Thus newspaper taxation, like many other forms of taxation, was at its height at the end of the Napoleonic Wars in 1815, after two decades during which government expenditure had been driven steadily upwards by a war effort of unprecedented scale.[5]

Taxes on newspapers – in the form of stamp duty paid for every paper printed, and advertisement duty payable for each advertisement which a publisher accepted – rose steadily throughout the eighteenth and early nineteenth centuries, before declining and finally lapsing, after 1855. In 1712, newspaper stamp duty was 1d and advertising duty 1s; by the late 1780s, stamp tax had risen to 2d and advertising tax was charged at 3s; by the end of the Napoleonic Wars, both stamp tax and advertisement duty were at their peak with stamp duty at 4d and advertising duty at 3s 6d. In 1833, advertising duty was reduced to 1s 6d, and in 1836 stamp duty fell to 1d. By 1855 both had been abolished. The benefits which the government reaped from taxation rose steadily. According to Siebert, the first recorded yield of the Stamp Tax was £16,500 for the year 1749.[6] Before that, Snyder has estimated that the tax yielded £6,000 a year when it was first introduced in 1712.[7] By the late eighteenth century the sums were more substantial. Pitt was

3. Michael Harris, *London Newspapers in the Age of Walpole: A Study in the Origins of the Modern English Press* (London, 1987), p. 19.

4. Downie, *Robert Harley and the Press*, pp. 157–8.

5. Patrick K. O'Brien, 'The political economy of British taxation, 1660–1815', *Economic History Review*, 2nd ser., **xli**, 1 (1988).

6. Siebert, *Freedom of the Press in England*, p. 320.

7. Henry L. Snyder, 'The circulation of newspapers in the reign of Queen Anne', *Library*, 5th ser., **xxiii** (1969), p. 219.

reported to have raised an additional £70,000 for the Treasury by raising Stamp Tax by $\frac{1}{2}$d in 1788, and over £100,000 by increases a decade later.[8]

As with many other legal pressures facing the press, enforcement of the taxation laws could be haphazard. In the early part of the eighteenth century, the government seemed unable to control the growth of an unstamped, and thus untaxed, press. It was not until 1740 that the authorities took concerted action against such papers, and particularly against the hawkers and mercuries (small print-sellers) who sold them. A 1743 Act allowed for heavy fines and imprisonment for selling unstamped newspapers. These measures appear to have had a significant impact, for most 'popular', cheaper papers went out of print.[9] However, the problems for the government of an unstamped press never went away completely, and emerged again most strikingly in the early nineteenth century. As we shall see in chapter 9, from the late 1810s until the mid-century the country was flooded with cheap, unstamped news-papers, most of which espoused radical political ideas, including calls for the removal of stamp duty.

Despite concerted attempts on the part of the government to suppress such papers, their numbers did not decline. In part, this was due to the way they were sold. The publishers of unstamped papers deployed an army of distributors who were often politically, as well as commercially, motivated. They also attempted to evade the law by claiming that their publications were not newspapers: either because they did not contain what was technically classed as 'news', or, more inventively, because they did not contain paper. Thus the *Political Touchwood* appeared on a sheet of shaving-thin plywood; Cousins's *Duster for Whigs* was printed on calico; and Berthold produced a similar calico *Political Hankerchief*.[10] However, such gimmicks did not generally catch on and the producers of unstamped papers relied in the main on bureaucratic inefficiency or the unwillingness of government to prosecute, coupled with their own attempts at evading detection.

Alongside the pressures imposed by taxation, an important restriction on press freedom came from the seditious libel law. This was sweeping in both its reach – in terms of who could be prosecuted – and in its definition of sedition. All those involved in writing,

8. Arthur Aspinall, *Politics and the Press c. 1780–1850* (London, 1949), p. 18.
9. Harris, *London Newspapers in the Age of Walpole*, pp. 28–30.
10. Patricia Hollis, *The Pauper Press: A Study in Working-class Radicalism of the 1830s* (Oxford, 1970), pp. 159–60.

printing, distributing and selling material could be charged when what was published was deemed likely to bring into hatred or contempt the ruler, his or her heirs or successors, government or any of the great national institutions, or to cause disaffection against them. For almost all of the period under discussion truth was not a defence, and for much of the eighteenth century the role of the jury was only to determine the fact of publication and the identity of the subject. It was the judge who decided whether the act had been done with criminal intent and if the material concerned did indeed constitute seditious libel. The power which this conferred on the judiciary was a cause of much discontent and was the motivation for Fox's Libel Act of 1792, which gave juries the right to bring in general verdicts and reduced the part played by judges. However, this change in the law may well have made little difference since the climate of the 1790s probably encouraged more convictions than previously. In 1843, a further change to the Libel Act provided that defendants could plead as an adequate defence that what they had published or written was in the public interest, thereby bringing this aspect of press law in line with current legislation.[11]

Despite the existence of such sweeping laws in the eighteenth and nineteenth centuries, the press in England was rarely subject to a system of organised government or legal repression and it certainly never experienced the kind of rigorous censorship which occurred in parts of continental Europe (hence the comments of foreign visitors in the previous chapter). Indeed, the use of royal proclamations throughout the eighteenth century at times of political crisis and when fears of popular insurrection were at their height, when magistrates were ordered to identify and prosecute the authors and publishers of seditious material, indicates the inefficiency with which the law was usually enforced. During periods of particular unrest, the government had to remind and encourage its local officials to perform their duties thoroughly. As the amount of political printed matter produced expanded on a dramatic scale, rigorous controls of the press became increasingly impractical, even if the government had been sufficiently motivated to try to implement them. At the time of the Jacobite threat in the first half of the eighteenth century, the government did pursue some sections of the press with vigour and managed to close down

---

11. H.M. Lubasz, 'Public opinion comes of age: reform of the libel law in the eighteenth century', *History Today*, **viii** (1958); Michael Lobban, 'From seditious libel to unlawful assembly: Peterloo and the changing face of political crime c. 1770–1820', *Oxford Journal of Legal Studies* **x**, 1 (1990).

several papers during the succession crisis.[12] However, such instances of government repression were more than balanced by the amount of anti-administration material which was able to flourish. Even in the midst of the anti-revolutionary paranoia of the 1790s, the state did not attempt a systematic clamp down of press freedoms (or any other freedoms), and the machinery of repression in England changed very little in the 1790s in comparison with the rest of the eighteenth century. As Clive Emsley has argued, there was no 'reign of terror' in England under Pitt,[13] and whilst in 1792 and 1799 the government discussed tighter statutory regulation of the press, such measures were never enacted.

This is not to say that Pitt's government made no moves against the press; indeed radical newspapers in particular were often harassed. The editor of the London daily, the *Argus*, was forced to flee the country in 1792 to escape a prosecution of seditious libel (only to be imprisoned by the French during the Terror, and then arrested by the British on his return to England in 1795).[14] In addition, a 1789 Act banned the hiring of newspapers from hawkers, a 1798 Act made publication of the names and addresses of printers or publishers on every paper statutory and the export of newspapers to enemy countries was banned, whilst in the following year, a register of printing presses was introduced. Furthermore, the government made use of *ex officio* informations (discussed in more detail below) and local initiatives to combat radical newspapers. Such action resulted in the closure of the *Argus* in London in 1792, and the *Leicester Chronicle* and the *Manchester Herald* in the following year,[15] whilst in 1794, the editor of the *Sheffield Register* was forced to flee the country (see below). In the case of the *Herald*, the government brought up to thirteen informations and indictments against the paper within a matter of months.[16]

These repressive measures certainly had an inhibiting influence on the more radical section of the newspaper press, but it should be

12. P.B.J. Hyland, 'Liberty and libel: government and the press during the succession crisis in Britain, 1712–1716', *English Historical Review* (1986).

13. Clive Emsley, 'An aspect of Pitt's "Terror": prosecutions for sedition during the 1790s', *Social History*, **vi**, 2 (1981); Clive Emsley, 'Repression, "terror" and the rule of law in England during the decade of the French Revolution', *English Historical Review*, **100** (1985).

14. M.J. Smith, 'English radical newspapers in the French revolutionary era, 1790–1803' (London University PhD thesis, 1979), p. 8.

15. Bob Harris, *Politics and the Rise of the Press: Britain and France 1620–1800* (London, 1996), p. 44.

16. Smith, 'English radical newspapers', pp. 229–30.

noted that the results of such action were piecemeal and scarcely uniform in their impact, particularly in the provinces. Thus in 1794, one of Christopher Wyvill's friends recommended Solomon Hodgson's *Newcastle Chronicle* to him as it was run by 'a man ... very firm to the cause of liberty & reform & ... not to be dismay'd at the threats that are constantly made to intimidate him'.[17] In addition, some of the London newspapers, most notably the *Morning Chronicle* and the *Morning Post*, continued to oppose the government throughout the 1790s. During the wars with Napoleonic France, the lack of an official or even a voluntary form of press censorship caused the government alarm on several occasions as sensitive military intelligence was divulged which – it was claimed – the enemy might have used to its advantage. Aspinall notes that whilst commanding the Peninsula War, Wellington often had cause to complain of the freedom with which the English press discussed the military situation. In March 1812 he wrote to his brother, Lord Wellesley, that the next campaign should prove a success, 'unless those admirably useful institutions, the English newspapers, should have given Bonaparte the alarm, and should have induced him to order his marshals to assemble their troops to oppose me'.[18]

Nor was the British government allowed to relax on matters of internal security once the war ended in 1815. A postwar depression and the economic hardship which it induced, coupled with renewed calls for political reform, meant that the following decades were to prove turbulent. The notorious 'Six Acts' or 'Gagging Acts' of 1819 contained two new laws which affected newspapers. One controlled more precisely the nature of blasphemous and seditious libels, the other provided a tighter definition of newspapers for taxation purposes. The same year witnessed libel trials for the publishers of the *Republican*, *Black Dwarf* and the *Deist*. For much of the 1820s, the radical press was left alone, but when the political atmosphere heated up again in the 1830s, radical newspapers came under attack once more. Richard Carlile was prosecuted for seditious libel for celebrating the activities of the 'Swing' rioters in the *Prompter* in November 1830 and was sentenced to two years' imprisonment. Cobbett too was tried, for criminal libel in the *Political Register* in December of 1830. However, unlike Carlile, he was acquitted.

17. J.E. Cookson, *The Friends of Peace: Anti-war Liberalism in England, 1793–1815* (Cambridge, 1982), p. 133.
18. Aspinall, *Politics and the Press*, pp. 34–5.

Hollis claims that although the government continued to scrutinise the radical press during the 1830s, prosecution followed in very few cases. Not only did the government find both informers and juries unreliable, but it was difficult to obtain witnesses.[19] Moreover, certain politicians were well aware of the potential for political martyrdom which prosecution could bring. As Home Secretary, Lord Russell was loathe to prosecute the Chartist press. He wrote to Harewood in 1838: 'So long as mere violence of language is employed without effect, it is better, I believe, not to add to the importance of these mob leaders by prosecutions.'[20] During the 1830s the vendors of unstamped papers seemed more liable to prosecution than the publishers or printers, with over 1,000 cases brought before London magistrates between 1830 and 1836. However, selling unstamped papers proved so profitable, and those who sold them were generally so poor, that despite the high risk of imprisonment, a majority of hawkers continued selling papers until they were arrested.[21] During the Crimean War, the government appeared even more powerless to curb the press than when fighting Napoleon. In 1854 the Secretary of State for War, at the request of the Commander-in-Chief at the Crimea, wrote to the editors of all London dailies pointing out the dangers of publishing military intelligence in war correspondents' letters. Rather than threaten them with possible legal action, the minister sought only to appeal to the newspapermen's sense of patriotism.[22]

It is clear, then, that the impact of government-sponsored prosecutions against newspapers could be mixed. Taking legal action was expensive and difficult to follow up, and invariably boosted sales of the paper under attack. However, mass arrests and harassment of leading opposition papers could have a serious impact on their organisation. The power of the general warrant in particular made a significant impact. Between 1713 and 1759, over 70 warrants were issued by Secretaries of State against the unnamed personnel of newspapers and related publications. The warrants allowed the king's messengers to arrest the authors, printers and publishers of specified publications and at the same time to search premises and seize any papers which might be useful in the prosecution for seditious libel. General warrants fell out of use in

19. Hollis, *The Pauper Press*, pp. 30–4 and 53.
20. Hollis, *The Pauper Press*, p. 61.
21. Hollis, *The Pauper Press*, pp. 171 and 189.
22. Olive Anderson, *A Liberal State at War: English Politics and Economics during the Crimean War* (New York, 1967), pp. 72–3.

the 1760s, after their legality was brought into question during a series of famous court cases in 1763 concerning issue number 45 of Wilkes's *North Briton*. On 18 November 1762, a general warrant had been issued for the arrest of the authors, printers and publishers of the paper. Yet when Wilkes challenged his imprisonment in the courts he was released and subsequently managed to turn the tables on the government by seeking legal redress against those state officials who had 'stolen' his property under the original warrant. Eventually Wilkes was awarded damages in a judgement which also condemned the use of general warrants.[23] After the furore surrounding the case, the general warrant fell out of use. Before the 1760s though, the general warrant formed a major part of any government's weaponry against newspapers thought to have over-stepped the mark. From the early 1720s until the 1740s, Nicholas Paxton, assistant to the Treasury Solicitor and then Treasury Solicitor himself, was paid a generous annual fee to check the contents of newspapers and pamphlets for the government, and as Treasury Solicitor he initiated many prosecutions against news-papers himself.[24] The effect of such government action could be disastrous for individuals. Even if acquitted, the costs of arrest, confinement, bail and seizure of property could not be recovered. Particularly unfortunate was the Bristol newspaperman Edward Farley, who died in prison after printing an attack on Walpole entitled the 'Persian Letter' which he copied from *Mist's Weekly Journal* in 1728. Twenty-five years later one of his relations, Mark Farley, was imprisoned for a year for printing what was deemed to be a seditious song on the anniversary of the Pretender's birthday.[25]

Despite the demise of the general warrant, prosecutions were still common at a much later date, and during the 1790s the govern-ment's ability to harass the press was boosted by the use of *ex officio* informations, which had also been used against Wilkesite and Jacobite publishers earlier in the century. This was a legal move which dispensed with the intermediate step of a grand jury and allowed the government to prosecute for libel more or less at will. In addition, there was no compulsion on the Attorney-General to

23. P.D.G. Thomas, *John Wilkes: A Friend to Liberty* (Oxford, 1996), ch. 3.
24. Michael Harris, 'The structure, ownership and control of the press, 1620–1780', in George Boyce, James Curran and Pauline Wingate, eds., *Newspaper History from the Seventeenth Century to the Present Day* (London, 1978), 82–97, p. 96; Harris, *London Newspapers in the Age of Walpole*, pp. 136 and 150.
25. G.A. Cranfield, *The Development of the Provincial Newpaper* (Oxford, 1962), pp. 60–1.

bring the case to trial, so that he could leave the threat hanging over a printer's head, and if he could not offer bail, the accused could be held in prison without trial.[26] Very few *ex officio* informations were filed against publishers and printers, but there is no doubt that they served to intimidate the printing community in general. Just as Nathaniel Mist had been forced into exile some seventy years earlier, Joseph Gales, editor of the radical *Sheffield Register* during the early 1790s, fled to America in 1794 as a result of threatened prosecution. His immediate successor, James Montgomery, who set up the *Sheffield Iris* as a replacement for the *Register*, was prosecuted three times in as many years, and suffered both fines and prison sentences as a result of government-initiated persecution.[27] The 1790s were also a difficult period for the printers of the radical *Manchester Herald*. Soon after it was launched in 1792, five *ex officio* informations were laid against the paper's printers, Faulkner and Birch. Like Gales, they fled the country.[28]

During the 1790s, radical newspapers also came under attack as newspaper personnel and newspaper readers suffered harassment from both private individuals and local officials. Eliza Gould, who ran a boarding school in South Molton in Devonshire, reportedly met with 'insult and persecution' from her neighbours for taking the *Cambridge Intelligencer* and was finally forced out of the area in 1794. In Manchester, there were reports of tradesmen being threatened with the withdrawal of custom because of their reading habits, whilst the readers of the *Sheffield Iris* who visited post offices in Leeds, Halifax and Wakefield to collect their papers were subjected to a barrage of insult and verbal abuse from the postmasters.[29] According to Sheridan, magistrates visited various publicans in London at the start of the war with France and threatened them with prosecution if any of the newspapers they took were found to be seditious. Provincial magistrates also threatened publicans with the removal of their licences for taking papers such as the *Manchester Herald* and the *Courier*.[30]

26. Emsley, 'An aspect of Pitt's "Terror"', p. 168.

27. M.E. Happs, 'The Sheffield newspaper press and parliamentary reform, 1787–1832' (Oxford BLitt thesis, 1973), pp. 51–80; Joseph O. Baylen and Norbert J. Gossman, eds., *Biographical Dictionary of Modern British Radicals*, vol. 1: *1770–1830* (Hassocks, 1979), pp. 183–5 and 327–30.

28. Donald Read, *Press and People 1790–1850: Opinion in Three English Cities* (Aldershot, 1993), pp. 71–2.

29. Smith, 'English radical newspapers', p. 187.

30. Smith, 'English radical newspapers', pp. 190–1.

One of the primary objectives of the Reeves Association, founded in 1792 to combat domestic Jacobinism and promote a spirit of loyalism, was 'discouraging and suppressing seditious prints'.[31] Such sentiments lay behind an assault on the office of the *Manchester Herald* in 1792 by a violent 'Church and King' mob, who 'attacked the house and shop with stones and brickbats, till the windows were destroyed and beaten in at the front', whilst local officials looked on.[32] Newspaper agents could also suffer at the hands of loyalists. A newsman who delivered the *Leicester Herald* was reported as saying that 'when he had got through Birmingham', he 'was always thankful that he had escaped a pelting'. The newsman who delivered the *Sheffield Register* in Wakefield was less fortunate in May 1794, when he failed to outrun a hostile crowd and was violently assaulted. Even more unlucky was a radical bookseller and local agent of the *Courier* from Bath, whose house was demolished by a drunken mob in 1794 to the tune of 'God save the king'.[33]

The nineteenth century saw government actions similar to those of the 1790s. In 1809, William Cobbett was convicted of a seditious libel in the *Register* for an article concerning the use of German mercenaries to flog mutinous local militiamen. He was sentenced by a corrupt, 'packed' jury to two years' imprisonment and a £1,000 fine, in what Ann Hone states was part of a government campaign to silence some of its most damaging critics. Activity was not restricted to the capital during this period and John Drakard of the *Stamford News* was sent to Lincoln gaol for eighteen months for reprinting an article from the *Examiner* which criticised the punishments doled out to soldiers in the British army.[34] Legal action could also be local in its origin, often spurred on by the proclamations issued by central government against seditious practices. One Shropshire magistrate, the Rev. Townsend Forester, wrote in February 1817 that he had prevented the circulation of *Cobbett's Political Register* in his neighbourhood by apprehending and flogging two hawkers under the terms of the Vagrancy Act.[35] Two years

31. Robert R. Rea, '"The liberty of the press" as an issue in English politics, 1792–1793', *The Historian*, **xxiv**, 1 (1961), p. 30.

32. Thomas Walker, *A Review of Some of the Political Events Which Have Occurred in Manchester During the Last Five Years* (London, 1794), p. 55; Archibald Prentice, *Historical Sketches and Personal Recollections of Manchester* (London, 1851), p. 9.

33. Smith, 'English radical newspapers', pp. 194–5.

34. J. Ann Hone, *For the Cause of Truth: Radicalism in London 1796–1821* (Oxford, 1982), pp. 197–9.

35. Aspinall, *Politics and the Press*, pp. 46–7.

after the government passed the Seditious Meetings Act of 1817, magistrates in Hanley in Staffordshire published a handbill which threatened publicans with the withdrawal of their licences if the practice of taking in 'seditious papers ... for the purpose of poisoning the minds of the ignorant and unwary' was not discontinued.[36] Landlords who stopped taking the *Black Dwarf* and the *Political Register* were a constant cause of complaint for both papers between 1816 and 1819.[37] Such activities on the part of government at both national and local levels were still apparent in the 1830s. When the radical *Cosmopolite* was launched in 1832 its publishers declared: 'We begin this paper in a spirit of warfare, and we are not to be scared by informations, or street arrests, or imprisonments.'[38] Patricia Hollis has also described instances in this period when men were sacked for reading or distributing radical papers and those who sold them were subject to other forms of harassment.[39]

Yet not only was the state not systematic in the way in which it sought to punish the press for perceived wrongdoings, but what attempts it did make were often unsuccessful, with prosecutions frequently failing. Commenting to his colleagues on Henry Crossgrove, a printer from Norwich with notoriously Jacobite sentiments in 1718, the Secretary of State noted that 'it will be better to leave these people alone than to meddle with them only to show our impotency.'[40] In the eighteenth century, it could be difficult to find a jury who would convict in libel cases. In 1731, the case against Samuel Farley for reprinting the 'Hague Letter' from *The Craftsman* in his Bristol paper collapsed. In 1770, all those who printed Junius's letters were acquitted, bar one, despite significant government attempts to secure a conviction.[41] Christie notes that Perry's *Morning Chronicle* was vigorously opposed to the government, but for thirty years had only two prosecutions brought against it (both of which were unsuccessful), and one unpleasant brush with the House of Lords in 1798, when Perry was imprisoned in Newgate on charges of libel and breach of privilege.[42] In addition, Wickwar shows that whilst an unusually high 33 *ex officio* informations were

36. Aspinall, *Politics and the Press*, p. 44.
37. Hollis, *The Pauper Press*, p. 38.
38. Hollis, *The Pauper Press*, p. 25.
39. Hollis, *The Pauper Press*, p. 159.
40. Cranfield, *The Development of the Provincial Newspaper*, p. 145.
41. Black, *English Press*, p. 177.
42. I.R. Christie, 'British newspapers in the later Georgian age' and 'James Perry of the *Morning Chronicle*, 1756–1821', in I.R. Christie, *Myth and Reality in Late-Eighteenth-Century British Politics and Other Papers* (London, 1970), pp. 328 and 352.

laid against printers and publishers in 1819, only a third were prosecuted to conviction.[43]

The government was also well aware that the publicity which such prosecutions brought could increase the popularity of publications and promote their sales. An anonymous correspondent informed the government in the 1720s that 'there never was a Mist or any other person taken up or tryed but double ye number of papers were sold upon it, beside ye Irritating the people from ye false notion of Persecution'.[44] William Arnall described government prosecutions as 'very considerable *Acts* of *Favour*', since 'A *Messenger* of State dispatch'd after [*The Craftsman*] will greatly *promote* the *Circulation* of his *Papers*; and when an *Information* is granted against him, scarce a *Corner* of the Kingdom will be without them'.[45] Michael Harris cites Walpole's prosecution of *The Craftsman* in 1731, which turned into a *cause célèbre* and greatly boosted the paper's sales.[46] Sales of William Hone's *Reformist Register* were also said to have increased dramatically after a failed attempt to prosecute him in 1819. Hone then profited further by selling accounts of his trial.[47] Hetherington benefited similarly from his prosecution over the publication of the *Poor Man's Guardian* in the same year.[48]

As has been shown, governments, politicians and magistrates could react harshly to criticism in newspapers. For much of the eighteenth century, most politicians were also keen to guard the privacy of parliament. Both houses of parliament claimed the authority to summon, interrogate and punish those charged with disseminating writing which was deemed to be in breach of parliamentary privilege, and until the late eighteenth century the press was strongly discouraged from publishing parliamentary proceedings. In addition, parliament felt it had a part to play in punishing the printers or authors of publications thought to libel an individual member, or to be either blasphemous or obscene.[49] Those printers or authors who offended in this way could be

---

43. William H. Wickwar, *The Struggle for the Freedom of the Press 1819–1832* (London, 1928), p. 38.

44. James R. Sutherland, 'The circulation of newspapers and literary periodicals, 1700–30', *Library*, 4th ser., **15** (1934), p. 118.

45. Simon Targett, 'Sir Robert Walpole's newspapers 1722–42: propaganda and politics in the age of Whig supremacy' (Cambridge PhD thesis, 1991), p. 76.

46. Harris, *London Newspapers*, p. 150.

47. Wickwar, *The Struggle for the Freedom of the Press*, p. 58.

48. Hollis, *The Pauper Press*, p. 117.

49. Siebert, *Freedom of the Press*, p. 369.

brought before the bar of either house and heavily fined. According to Siebert, the House of Lords was particularly zealous in protecting the personal reputation of its members and made frequent use of its powers in this respect. Such cases were ordinarily raised by the member who claimed to be defamed. Thus the Earl of Sandwich won £2,000 in damages in 1772 from John Miller, printer of the *London Evening Post*, for publishing a letter which accused him of attempting to sell an Admiralty post.[50]

When it came to publishing parliamentary debates, action against provincial printers was relatively rare compared to the frequency with which the London press was punished. However, in 1718 and 1719, the Commons summoned the printers of all three Exeter newspapers to the bar of the house for publishing such reports, and in 1728 Robert Raikes of the *Gloucester Journal* received punishment for a similar offence. Again in 1745 and 1746 both York printers were obliged to appear before the Commons.[51] In London, where prosecutions were more common and consumer demand for debate reporting arguably greater, the stakes appeared to be higher. Between 1703 and 1729, Abel Boyar published parliamentary proceedings in his magazine, *The Political State of Great Britain*. However, to escape prosecution, debates were published some time after they took place and were presented as history rather than news.[52] Charles Knight noted how Edward Cave of the *Gentlemen's Magazine* began publishing some form of record of debates at the end of each session in 1736, using only the initials of the speakers, although this ruse had to be made even more covert in 1738, after a resolution of the Commons expressly forbade the practice, and thereafter the debates appeared as those of 'the Great Senate of Lilliput'.[53] The *London Magazine* took similar action and began to report the proceedings of an imaginary club. However, like Boyer's productions, such reporting was always dated. Both publications were called to account in 1747 by the House of Lords for publishing reports of the trial of Simon Lord Lovat for high treason during the Jacobite rebellion of 1745, and Cave then ceased publishing parliamentary reports altogether, although the *London Magazine* continued to print carefully disguised accounts of a 'political club'.[54]

50. Robert R. Rea, *The English Press in Politics 1760–1774* (Lincoln, Nebr., 1963), pp. 219–20.

51. Cranfield, *The Development of the Provincial Newspaper*, pp. 156–8.

52. Siebert, *Freedom of the Press*, p. 347.

53. Charles Knight, *Shadows of the Old Booksellers* (London, 1865), pp. 175–6.

54. Siebert, *Freedom of the Press*, pp. 351–4.

Devices such as Cave's 'Lilliputian' debates were common. The threat of prosecution meant that newspapers and magazines became increasingly adept at using allusion, allegory and innuendo, rather than risk directly libelling someone or openly breaching parliamentary privilege. In addition, the use of code and partial words was common. For the historian this can make it more difficult to discern meanings, although the use of dashes in particular is rarely an effective disguise. Thus complaints about the 'K--g' or his Prime Minister 'P--t' are far from opaque, although some nicknames could be. Of course, contemporary readers were unlikely to have had such problems; indeed, the use of complex codes, rather than alienating readers, was likely to have flattered them by encouraging them to consider themselves some-how 'in the know' and privy to a secret political language.

The late 1750s and 1760s witnessed an increasing number of London newspapers covering parliamentary debates and quickly overtaking magazines as the main source of parliamentary news. In his memoirs, John Almon described his own parliamentary report-ing in the late 1760s and linked its growth to the emergence of popular radicalism.[55] Parliament reacted by prosecuting several offenders, but the newspapers appeared undeterred. In 1770 London papers began to publish extended reports of debates, as opposed to the much briefer summaries and lists of speakers which had gone before. It was at this point that William Woodfall (who came to be known as 'Memory' Woodfall thanks to his capacity to memorise debates) came to prominence. By the end of November 1770, he was producing reports of over 17,000 words, which other papers often copied. The parliamentary anger that this incited led to the prosecution of eight printers in the Commons during February and March 1771. A crisis was then provoked by the calculated refusal of some City of London officials to allow messengers from the House of Commons to apprehend three printers who took refuge in the City, where an exclusive right of arrest was claimed. The Mayor of London and an alderman were sent to the Tower, but the London press continued to publish debates. Eventually the Commons backed down and parliament effectively gave up its right to prosecute the press for publishing its debates.[56]

55. John Almon, *Memoirs of a Late Eminent Bookseller* (London, 1790), p. 119.
56. P.D.G. Thomas, 'John Wilkes and the freedom of the press (1771)', *Bulletin of the Institute of Historical Research* (1960).

Not surprisingly, this decision resulted in the proliferation and lengthening of reports. However, during the 1770s parliament still made regular use of its power to exclude strangers from the gallery during 'sensitive' debates, such as those in the 1770s on the Royal Family Marriage Bill and on American legislation. Note-taking was not allowed until after 1783,[57] and before the late nineteenth century any member of the house might order the gallery to be cleared (although this right was unlikely to be exercised in mid-debate) and up to mid-century the gallery was often cleared for divisions as a matter of course.[58] On top of all these restrictions, the life of a parliamentary reporter was made even more irksome by the absence of a reporters' gallery. Journalists were forced instead to cram themselves in with the general public in conditions which were uncomfortable and, more-over, not conducive to accurate reporting. One reporter, James Stephen, outlined a series of complaints about his experiences in the 1780s:

> No man was allowed to take a note for the purpose. – We were obliged therefore to depend on memory alone and had no assistance in the work, one Reporter for each house being all that any Paper employed. – We were obliged to sit in the Gallery from the sitting of the House till its adjournment, and afterwards, however late, to begin and finish our work before we retired to rest.[59]

Little had changed by 1812, when it was noted that reporters could become so fatigued after several nights of long debates, or so hot in a crowded gallery, that it was impossible for them to do justice to the speeches.[60] However, by 1824, reporters were allowed to enter the gallery after it had been locked against strangers and had been given a private entrance so that they could avoid the crowds.[61]

57. P.D.G. Thomas, 'The beginning of parliamentary reporting in newspapers, 1768–1774', *English Historical Review*, **LXXIV** (1959), pp. 623–31.

58. Aspinall, *Politics and the Press*, p. 36.

59. *The Memoirs of James Stephen Written By Himself for the Use of His Children*, ed. Merle M. Bevington (London, 1954), p. 291.

60. Ivon Asquith, 'James Perry and the *Morning Chronicle* 1790–1821' (London University PhD thesis, 1973), pp. 287–8.

61. A. Aspinall, 'The reporting and publishing of the House of Commons' debates 1771–1834', in Richard Ares and A.J.P. Taylor, eds., *Essays Presented to Sir Lewis Namier* (London, 1956), p. 251.

Covert Political Manipulation

Laws, taxes and prosecutions were not the only ways in which governments and politicians could influence the press. Other, more subtle means were also available. These included the payment of 'subsidies' or bribes, manipulation of the postal system and the use of privileged intelligence. 'High' political involvement in the press was nothing new. Both Charles II and his brother James II had tried to impose censorship, and William III had pursued a vigorous press campaign. Yet political interference in the press – or 'corruption' – during the eighteenth century became a dominant theme for many historians from the second half of the nineteenth century onwards. Works such as Hunt's *The Fourth Estate* traced the emergence of 'press freedom' and compared the independence of the nineteenth-century press with its earlier political 'subservience', thereby depicting its establishment as the 'bulwark' of British democracy: the 'fourth estate' of the constitution.[62] The work of many press historians of this century continues to be dominated by this Whig thesis, mapping the rise of English newspapers from the mire of eighteenth-century corruption to the glorious independence of the Victorian age.[63] This model of newspaper history is misleading. In particular, the underlying assumption that newspapers in the eighteenth and early nineteenth centuries had been rendered impotent by political corruption and manipulation is in need of extensive revision.

Part of the blame for this misrepresentation of newspapers must rest with the press itself, for during much of the period under discussion it was common for individual papers to accuse rival publications of corruption. However, as proof of high political manipulation, such claims must be read with extreme caution. Although some of those involved in newspapers no doubt did

62. F.K. Hunt, *The Fourth Estate: Contributions towards a History of Newspapers, and the Liberty of the Press* (London, 1850). See also Alexander Andrews, *The History of British Journalism, from the Foundation of the Newspaper Press in England, to the Repeal of the Stamp Act in 1855, with Sketches of Press Celebrities* (2 vols., London, 1859); Charles Pebody, *English Journalism, and the Men who Have Made it* (London, 1882); H.R. Fox Bourne, *English Newspapers: Chapters in the History of Journalism* (2 vols., London, 1887); James Grant, *The Newspaper Press: Its Origin, Progress, and Present Position* (London, 1871).

63. Examples include: Wickwar, *The Struggle for the Freedom of the Press*; Laurence Hanson, *Government and the Press, 1695–1763* (Oxford, 1936); Aspinall, *Politics and the Press*; Harold Herd, *The March of Journalism: The Story of the British Press from 1622 to the Present Day* (London, 1952); Siebert, *Freedom of the Press*.

receive political bribes (as will be discussed), the constant barrage of accusation and counter-accusation which appeared, particularly in the London press, was almost certainly based more upon rumour and attempts to discredit rivals than upon a fair representation of the degree of high political control. Yet this view of political corruption is one which historians have perpetuated into the twentieth century. Perhaps the most influential of these was Arthur Aspinall, whose work depicts eighteenth-century newspapers as victims of the rampant and pervasive corruption of the period:

> During the last decades of the eighteenth century when newspapers were beginning to play an important part in politics, they were not independent and responsible organs of public opinion. There were Gatton and Old Sarum newspapers as well as Gatton and Old Sarum boroughs. The great majority of the London newspapers accepted subsidies either from the Government or from the Opposition, and were tied in various ways to the Party organisations.[64]

Aspinall's views were based largely on politicians' correspondence and government papers, and the resultant high political vision is too narrow to show fully the relationship between newspapers and the political world. Aspinall asserted that the sale of newspapers in the eighteenth century was too restricted to make them self-supporting, and that they were therefore dependent for their survival on political subsidy. Yet this was unlikely to have been the case. As will be shown in chapter 5, newspapers became increasingly profitable between 1695 and 1855. Whilst it is conceivable that the £200 a year which the *London Journal* received from Walpole's government in the 1730s might have dictated the paper's politics,[65] it is far less likely that the £100 given to various London papers by Pitt's ministry during 1784 would have had the same impact.[66] Indeed, one of these papers, the *Morning Herald,* remained vociferous in its support for Fox.

Archenholz described the newspaper business in the 1780s as 'extremely lucrative, and maintains, in the city of London alone, a prodigious multitude of persons...'.[67] In the early 1780s, the *Morning Post* paid out dividends of £1,500 and made returns for its owners of 18 per cent,[68] whilst in 1788, a third share in *The World*

---

64. Aspinall, *Politics and the Press,* p. v.

65. Harris, *London Newspapers in the Age of Walpole,* p. 108.

66. *The Later Correspondence of George III,* ed. A. Aspinall (5 vols., Cambridge, 1962), i, 116–18.

67. J.W. von Archenholz, *A Picture of England* (Dublin, 1791), p. 42.

68. Aspinall, *Politics and the Press,* p. 72.

was worth £4,000.[69] Christie has shown that by the 1810s a successful paper such as the *Morning Chronicle* could make an annual profit of £12,000.[70] Indeed, Aspinall himself argues that by around 1815 newspapers were becoming so profitable, and governments so poor by comparison, that full-scale 'corruption' was no longer an option. Even when the *Courier* was struggling in the late 1820s, it was still valued at over £30,000, whilst *The Times* was said to be worth at least £500,000 in 1839. As Lord Liverpool wrote to Castlereagh in 1815, 'no paper that has any character, and consequently an established sale, will accept money from the Government; and, indeed, their profits are so enormous in all critical times, when their support is most necessary, that no pecuniary assistance that Government could offer would really be worth their acceptance'.[71] In fact, on the contrary, newspapers were not wholly, or even largely, open to control by political subsidy before the nineteenth century. The relationship between politicians and newspapers throughout the period under discussion was a complex one, but, by and large, subsidy was not the controlling force in newspaper politics. For the most part newspapers depended on advertising revenue and, more importantly, sales to make money. Newspapers in Britain were, above all, commercial enterprises. Given the basis of newspaper profitability, newspapermen concentrated on increasing readership and advertising revenue as the means to ensure financial security, rather than chasing relatively small political bribes. In his book *A Stranger in England; or, Travels in Great Britain*, published in 1807, Goede maintained that 'editors are not a set of hungry scribblers, ready to barter their reputation for a mess of porridge, but mostly men of considerable fortune'.[72] It was the profitability of newspapers, not the availability of politicians' money, which led to an increase in titles as the period progressed. This development was not, of course, limited to the capital; the growth of the provincial press was also prolific (with less question here of political subsidy, at least in the eighteenth century). Yet there is no doubt that political 'corruption' was not uncommon. What we need to remember is

69. Aspinall, *Politics and the Press*, p. 72.

70. Christie, 'British newspapers in the later Georgian age', pp. 318–22.

71. Cited in Tom Morley, '"The Times" and the concept of the fourth estate: theory and practice in mid-nineteenth century Britain', *Journal of Newspaper and Periodical History* **i**, 3 (1985), pp. 12–13.

72. C.A. Goede, *The Stranger in England: Or, Travels in Great Britain* (3 vols., London, 1807), i. 222.

that the relationship between newspapers and politicians was complicated: that politically inspired plans often failed or even backfired, and that for every 'corrupt' paper sold, many others opposed to the government (the main briber of newspapers) were consumed by the public. As we saw in chapter 1, public opinion, not political influence, was the driving force behind newspaper politics.

However, there is no doubt that there are numerous examples of newspapers being bribed, 'assisted' or otherwise influenced by politicians in our period. But the success with which they did so, and the influence which they achieved, could be very mixed. Ministerial sponsorship of the press remained sporadic, reflecting differing political circumstances and the attitude of individual politicians. In the first two decades of the eighteenth century, Robert Harley, Earl of Oxford, created several 'unofficial' government publications alongside the government-sponsored *London Gazette*. The opposition were slow to respond to this bold ministerial initiative, but by 1714, under the leadership of Richard Steele and Samuel Buckley, they succeeded in doing so.[73] As Harley's influence declined after 1714, the structure of press influence which he created lost much of its power, but it was resurrected under Walpole as he began to respond to the opposition press.[74] According to Simon Targett, historians have overemphasised Walpole's policy of proscription, and ignored the money (nearly £50,000 between 1731 and 1741) and effort put into pro-government propaganda.[75] Under Walpole, the government appears to have nurtured a whole family of ministerial writers. Men such as William Arnall came under the direct oversight of Walpole himself. He was recruited in 1728 and worked until his premature death in 1736 on a series of newspapers, particularly the *Free Briton* and the *Daily Gazetteer*. However, his position seems to have been unusual, and neither of the other principal ministerial journalists – James Pitt, who wrote for the *London Journal*, or Ralph Courteville, who took over from Arnall – appears to have had such direct dealings with the Prime Minister. In general the work of ministerial writers was co-ordinated by the Treasury Solicitor, Nicholas Paxton.[76] By the early 1730s, the government was funding at least four newspapers,

---

73. Downie, *Robert Harley and the Press*, pp. 2–3.
74. Harris, *London Newspapers in the Age of Walpole*, p. 113.
75. Simon Targett, 'Sir Robert Walpole's newspapers', pp. 30–1.
76. Harris, *London Newspapers in the Age of Walpole*, pp. 102–3.

which in 1735 were merged into a single publication, the *Daily Gazetteer*.[77] However, opposition papers, such as *Fog's Weekly Journal*, *The Craftsman* and *Common Sense*, were far more successful. Whilst *The Craftsman* sold perhaps 10,000 per week in 1730, the most popular 'ministerial' paper, the *London Journal*, reached sales of only 2,000–3,000.[78]

After Walpole's fall, the scale of government sponsorship contracted dramatically. This, claims Bob Harris, was all the more surprising given the volume and influence of the anti-Hanoverian press campaign of 1742–4. In part, we can attribute this change in governmental behaviour to the fall of Nicholas Paxton and Joseph Bell, two men who had been at the heart of the Walpolian press empire. In addition, Pelham, unlike Walpole, appears to have been far less disturbed by press comment. In 1753 he wrote to Newcastle about newspaper attacks made by James Ralph in the opposition essay paper, the *Protestor*. 'I am satisfied, the less notice is taken of him the better; it has been my doctrine always, and I think experience shews I am in the right.'[79] However, Black has described how Ralph and others were paid by the government for their silence during the 1740s and 1750s,[80] for even though many politicians were wary of involvement in the press around the mid-century, few could ignore it altogether by this time. It is not surprising that the Duke of Newcastle spent £4,000 on pensions for journalists and pamphleteers in the 1750s.[81]

Famously, the Earl of Bute's attempts to influence public opinion in the 1760s largely backfired. Although he hired men such as Tobias Smollett, Arthur Murphy and Hugh Kelly to sing the administration's praises, their efforts made little difference in the face of hugely popular papers such as the *North Briton* and the *Monitor*.[82] Even the support of a cohort of pensioners and literary hacks to write pamphlets and letters to the newspapers on Bute's

77. William Speck, 'Politics and the press', in Michael Harris and Alan Lee, eds., *The Press in English Society From the Seventeenth to Nineteenth Centuries* (London, 1986), p. 49.

78. Harris, *London Newspapers in the Age of Walpole*, p. 117.

79. Bob Harris, *A Patriot Press: National Politics and the London Press in the 1740s* (Oxford, 1993), p. 37.

80. Black, *English Press*, p. 149.

81. Sir Lewis Namier, *The Structure of Politics at the Accession of George III* (London, 1963), p. 229.

82. J.P. Thomas, 'The British empire and the press, 1763–1774' (Oxford DPhil thesis, 1982), p. 2.

behalf did not improve his standing in the country.[83] A broadside from 1762 mocked the futility of Bute's press activities:

> When his Lordship from Nothing was call'd into Power,
> Conscious Wits wou'd be squirting, and Writers wou'd lour;
> He got *this* a pension: and he gave *that* a bribe.
> But this fortune can't silence the ill-natur'd Tribe.[84]

Brewer has described Bute's failure to secure a positive public image, despite expending a great deal of money and energy, as 'one of the greatest ironies of the 1760s'.[85] Yet Bute was not alone. Diary entries show Thomas Hollis making regular payments to news-papermen in the 1760s to support his cause, whilst both Sandwich and Grenville kept paid apologists and attacked the press when it libelled them.[86] Of course, at the same time that Bute was failing in his efforts to win public support, John Wilkes, the maverick radical politician and Bute's antagonist, was proving himself a skilful journalist, capable of producing devastating attacks on the Prime Minister. Wilkes wrote first in the *Monitor*, and then founded his own paper, the *North Briton*, in 1762.[87] As Brewer has shown, the 1760s saw all three main political groups – the followers of Bute, the Rockingham–Newcastle connection and the Grenvillites – demonstrating fairly high levels of press activity despite their distaste for the press and the anxieties which it caused them.[88] Such involvement was increasingly seen as a necessary evil. In response to attacks in the opposition papers, Lord Hardwicke wrote to his son in 1761: 'I agree with every word you say as to the neglect and obstinacy in not publishing proper answers to the ribaldry with which the papers abound against the administration, nor proper defences of their own conduct...'[89]

Lutnick claims that in 1781, the Rev. Henry Bate received over £3,000 from Secret Service accounts in return for backing North at a time when most newspapers were highly critical of his ministry. North wrote to the King in 1782 that Bate kept his newspaper 'open for all writings in favour of Government ... to do Mr. Bate justice,

83. John Brewer, *Party Ideology and Popular Politics at the Accession of George III* (Cambridge, 1976), pp. 223–6.

84. Cited in Rea, *The English Press in Politics*, p. 24.

85. Brewer, *Party Ideology and Popular Politics*, p. 221.

86. Thomas, 'The British empire and the press', pp. 55 and 80.

87. Thomas, 'John Wilkes', pp. 19–20.

88. Brewer, *Party Ideology and Popular Politics*, pp. 227–35.

89. Cited in Karl W. Schweizer, 'Lord Bute and the press', in *Lord Bute: Essays in Re-interpretation* (Leicester, 1988), p. 86.

he was a very constant, diligent, zealous and able, though perhaps too warm a writer on the part of the government'.[90] Yet Bate was no servant of the government, and his paper, the *Morning Herald* – widely regarded as the best selling in London – was famous for the virulence of its attacks on politicians of all political persuasions.[91] Government Secret Service accounts show that several thousand pounds were given to newspapers and writers during the early 1780s, yet both North's ministry, and that of the Rockingham Whigs which succeeded it, proved singularly unsuccessful at arranging support from a majority of the capital's newspapers.[92] A decade later, Aspinall has calculated that the government spent just under £5,000 a year on the press during the early years of the French Revolution.[93] Pitt and his Treasury were also supposed to have had a hand in the formation of both the *True Briton* and the *Sun* in 1792, although no record of Secret Service expenditure seems to have survived.[94] Pitt did receive much favourable publicity, but as will be shown in chapter 8, the support given to his ministry was not bought from the press.

The problem of bribing newspapers in the nineteenth century, given their increased profitability, has already been noted. However, Patricia Hollis argues that the government was behind the launch of several papers in 1817 and 1818 in an attempt to counteract various radical publications. Thus Cobbett's *Register* was met with the *Anti-Cobbett*, and Wooler's *Black Dwarf* with Merle's *White Dwarf*.[95] But despite the existence of political backers, newspapers struggled if they did not attract readers. In 1811, the bi-weekly *National Adviser* was started in London with the support of some politically motivated 'gentlemen of respectability' who were eager to counter 'Jacobinical principles'. However, as the editor was to relate to Lord Sidmouth in 1813, low sales meant the paper proved too expensive to continue based only on 'the most distinguished and flattering support from a highly respectable, if not a numerous body of readers'.[96] This was also the fate of another London newspaper, the *Representative*, which was launched in 1826

90. North to George III, 18 April 1782, *Correspondence of King George III*, ed. Sir John Fortescue (6 vols., London, 1927–8), v. 471.
91. Hannah Barker, *Press, Politics, and Public Opinion in Late Eighteenth-Century England* (Oxford, 1998), ch. 2.
92. Barker, *Press, Politics, and Public Opinion*, ch. 2.
93. Aspinall, *Politics and the Press*, pp. 68–9.
94. Aspinall, *Politics and the Press*, pp. 78–9.
95. Hollis, *Pauper Press*, p. 136.
96. Aspinall, *Politics and the Press*, p. 89.

by a group of Tories who included the publisher John Murray. Murray's hopes of challenging the dominance of *The Times* were soon dashed, and £26,000 was sacrificed in the process.[97] The Conservatives were also involved in plans to set up their own papers in the provinces. According to the biographer of Alaric Watts, one-time editor of the *Standard*, he was given £10,000 by the Carlton Club between 1832 and 1833 to spend on the development of provincial conservative papers. These were prepared in London and then distributed, with additional local matter, to various districts. The venture was not particularly successful, and Watts was described by his successor at the *Standard* as 'head nurse of a hospital of rickety newspaperlings, which breathe but to die'.[98]

Despite the increasing futility of offering newspapers bribes in the nineteenth century, politicians were still able to manipulate the press in other ways. Lord Holland claimed that on the eve of the general election in 1807, Lord Henry Brougham organised an extensive press campaign in support of the Whigs by writing paragraphs for the newspapers as well as pamphlets and handbills for national distribution.[99] Indeed not only Broughton, but Lord Holland and John Allen kept in close touch with James Perry, editor of the *Morning Chronicle*, and kept him supplied with political squibs and paragraphs as part of a widespread newspaper campaign.[100] In 1827 the Marquess of Londonderry contributed letters to the *Morning Herald* attacking the Canning ministry under a pen name (although it appears that he was not a particularly skilled propagandist),[101] whilst the diarist Charles Greville claimed that Whig politicians deserved the credit for re-establishing the prosperity of the *Morning Chronicle* in the 1830s: 'Hobhouse, Normanby, Poulett, Thomson, Le Marchant and several others, wrote day after day a succession of good articles, which soon renovated the paper and set it on its legs.'[102] Yet despite such bursts of energy, the Whig Party machinery was never sophisticated enough to produce anything like a systematic press campaign.[103]

97. Stephen Koss, *The Rise and Fall of the Political Press in Britain*, vol. 1: *The Nineteenth Century* (London, 1981), pp. 46–7.

98. Lucy Brown, *Victorian News and Newpapers* (Oxford, 1985), pp. 65–9.

99. Aspinall, *Politics and the Press*, p. 284.

100. I.R. Christie, 'James Perry of the *Morning Chronicle, 1756–1821*', p. 353.

101. Aspinall, *Politics and the Press*, p. 328.

102. Cited in Aspinall, *Politics and the Press*, p. 241.

103. Ivon Asquith, 'The Whig Party and the press in the early nineteenth century', *Bulletin of the Institute of Historical Research* (1976).

Not all politically inspired newspaper activities stemmed from Westminster. From the late eighteenth century onwards, provincial newspapers were increasingly likely to receive political subsidies. In 1791 the Manchester Constitutional Society was behind the establishment of a new paper in the town, since of the two already in existence, one was 'most decidedly and virulently aristocratic' and the other, although 'generally moderate', would not print the Society's material.[104] Ivon Asquith has noted an increasing trend at the beginning of the nineteenth century for politically motivated groups in the provinces to launch newspapers. For example, in 1810 a committee of fifteen opposed to the local Anglican-Tory corporation raised £750 to found the *Leicester Journal*. Several local Whigs financed the establishment of the *Chester Guardian* in 1817, and Tory gentlemen in Kendal raised £1,200 to start the *Westmorland Gazette* in 1818. The *Sheffield Independent* was helped out of financial difficulty in 1820 by a group of local manufacturers and Unitarians, whilst eleven middle-class reformers – a mixture of Unitarians and cotton manufacturers, including three MPs – subscribed £1,050 to start the *Manchester Guardian* in 1821. According to Asquith, this pattern continued to the mid-nineteenth century.[105]

Yet, as in London, the fate of politically backed papers such as these was not always happy. The gentlemen of Kendal who joined together in 1818 were, according to one of their members, hoping to counteract the 'vile effects' upon the 'lower orders' of the established *Kendal Chronicle*. But, like many other papers produced from political rather than commercial motives, the *Westmorland Gazette* was never a great success. It suffered from low sales and failed to make a profit, although, propped up by local political interests, it did not go out of business.[106] A similar example can be found in Birmingham, where in 1825 a group of local Tories set up the *Birmingham Journal*, with, it appears, the express purpose of challenging the anti-conservative stance adopted by *The Times*. However, the *Journal* quickly changed hands, and despite a brief period as an ultra-Tory organ, it was to emerge far more successfully by the 1830s as the 'political clarion' of the radical Birmingham Political Union.[107] This is not to say that all papers launched

104. Aspinall, *Politics and the Press*, p. 270.
105. Ivon Asquith, 'The structure, ownership and control of the press, 1780–1855', in Boyce, Curran and Wingate, eds., *Newspaper History from the Seventeenth Century to the Present Day*, pp. 105–6.
106. Aspinall, *Politics and the Press*, pp. 356–63.
107. Asa Briggs, 'Press and public in early nineteenth-century Birmingham', *Dugdale Society Occasional Papers*, **8** (1949), pp. 8–10.

primarily for political, rather than commercial, reasons were failures. The radical press of the 1830s and 1840s provides a case in point. The most successful of all Chartist newspapers, the *Northern Star*, was started with money raised by political subscriptions, mostly from Yorkshire towns: Huddersfield in particular.[108] What differentiated it from papers such as the *Westmorland Gazette*, however, was the large readership which it managed to attract.

One of the reasons why politicians could not control the press was their attitude towards it. Not all politicians were as embroiled in press activities as the likes of Walpole, Bute and Holland, and nor did they want to be. Pitt the Elder boasted of having 'contracted an indifference to newspapers' early on in his career.[109] Asquith remarks that in the summer of 1793, the conservative Whigs 'might have been willing . . . to subscribe thousands of pounds for the relief of Fox's debts, but they were not prepared to donate a few hundred towards the propagation of his opinions'.[110] The Prime Minister, Lord Grey, was also proud of his lack of experience with the press. In January 1832 he wrote to his parliamentary colleague, Lansdowne, '[I] never have had, and never will have any dealings with the newspapers.' His advice to those attacked by the press was 'as the Irish say, "to keep never minding"'. Grey was being disingenuous. He was certainly concerned in 1815 by the lack of support which the Whigs received in the papers, although he declared that 'the cause of the blame for this it is in vain to explore, as I am convinced the evil is beyond the reach of any remedy that I can apply'.[111] Wellington was no fan of newspapers either, particularly following their reports of the war against Napoleon which he claimed undermined the British position. But, like Grey, his relationship with newspapers was ambivalent. He wrote to the Tory politician, John Croker, on 14 September 1828, 'I hate meddling with the Press', whilst admitting that his predecessors had depended on such activities and complaining that the current Secretary of the Treasury was not meddling 'with that degree of intelligence which might be expected from him', finally noting that 'I must put this to rights'.[112] For his part, the Conservative leader Sir Robert Peel was reported to have expressed a horror

---

108. Eric Glasgow, 'The establishment of the *Northern Star* newspaper', *History* (1954), p. 63.
109. Rea, *English Press in Politics*, p. 15.
110. Asquith, 'James Perry and the *Morning Chronicle* 1790–1821', p. 43.
111. Aspinall, *Politics and the Press*, pp. 198 and 294.
112. Aspinall, *Politics and the Press*, p. 232.

of money transactions with newspaper proprietors and refused to support the ailing *Conservative Journal* in 1840 with party funds.[113]

Even those politicians who professed a desire to involve themselves with newspapers could be singularly negligent in their dealings with them. In 1794, the newspaper publisher John Almon wrote to the Home Secretary, the Duke of Portland, claiming that subsidies promised by Richard Brinsley Sheridan in the 1780s had not been paid: money due for 1785 and 1786 having been postponed owing to 'the Westminster scrutiny, at that time, and other great expenses happening'.[114] Even when money was given, as in the case of the *Anti-Gallican Monitor* in 1811 and 1812, payments could be erratic and a cause of complaint from those who produced the papers. The editor of the *Monitor*, Lewis Goldsmith, wrote to the Prime Minister, Lord Liverpool, in September 1812 that payment of his allowance was so uncertain that he was at a loss to know whether the Treasury meant to continue it or not.[115]

Yet despite such apparent inefficiency and lack of concern on the part of certain politicians when it came to party political propaganda, many were not so reticent when it came to their personal standing in public. Even though MPs might have criticised the publication of parliamentary debates, it is clear that from the 1740s at the latest, some of them were supplying newspapers with copies of their speeches. Harris cites several instances from this period, some involving Lord Perceval, a vocal critic of the press.[116] The papers of John Almon, publisher of the *London Courant*, provide us with other good examples, including letters from the MPs Nicholson Calvert and Lord Bristol. In 1765, Calvert wrote with a written version of one of his speeches, which he described as 'literally the same as spoken in the House'. Fourteen years later, Bristol sent one of his own, fearing he might otherwise be misrepresented to the public.[117] When Pitt the Younger visited the House of Commons in 1780, he noted the differences between the original and the newspaper versions of the speeches. On one occasion he wrote that 'Burkes Extempores have both Times exceeded his corrected Publication, which (entre nous) is in my

113. Jones, *Powers of the Press*, p. 161.
114. Aspinall, *Politics and the Press*, p. 272.
115. Aspinall, *Politics and the Press*, p. 93.
116. Harris, *Patriot Press*, pp. 22–3.
117. BL Add MS 20733 (Almon papers), fos. 16 and 28.

opinion much the worse for revision'.[118] By 1784, Pitt too was supplying newspapers with copies of his speeches.[119] During the 1790s and the early years of the nineteenth century, James Perry of the *Morning Chronicle* successfully persuaded several politicians, including Charles James Fox, Richard Sheridan, Lord Holland and Philip Francis, to revise versions of their parliamentary speeches for publication,[120] whilst the closure of the gallery during debates concerning the Princess of Wales between 1813 and 1814 prompted several Whig MPs to send the *Morning Chronicle* accounts of the proceedings.[121] Finally, in 1832, the House of Commons decided against taking action against the MPs Hume and Warburton who had taken notes of speeches delivered in the house in order to send reports to newspapers.[122]

The practice of MPs supplying newspapers with accounts of their own speeches could occasionally result in disaster. John Taylor, editor of the *Morning Post* between 1788 and 1790, recorded an incident when John Wilkes begged for permission to make a speech in the House of Commons because, he said, 'I have sent a copy to the "Public Advertiser", and how ridiculous should I appear if it were published without having been delivered'.[123] In 1828, the *Sun* published an advance copy of a speech to be delivered in the Commons by Richard Lalor Sheil on Catholic emancipation. Only after it was printed did the editor, Murdo Young, realise that the speech had not been delivered.[124] Such gross mistakes were rare, but complaints about the accuracy of published speeches were still rife (although it should be noted that many of the complainants were politicians who disapproved of the reports of their own contributions).

In addition to supplying newspapers with money and with material for publication, politicians and governments could also help or hinder the press in other ways, for example, by distributing newspapers of which they approved. Individual politicians commonly made use of a privilege which allowed them to circulate

118. John Ehrman, *The Younger Pitt: The Years of Acclaim* (London, 1969), p. 21.

119. Barker, *Press, Politics, and Public Opinion*, p. 18.

120. Asquith, 'James Perry and the *Morning Chronicle* 1790–1821', pp. 97–9.

121. Asquith, 'James Perry and the *Morning Chronicle* 1790–1821', p. 427.

122. Aspinall, 'The reporting and publishing of the House of Commons' debates 1771–1834', p. 230.

123. John Taylor, *Records of My Life* (2 vols., London, 1832), i. 114.

124. H.R. Fox Bourne, *English Newspapers: Chapters in the History of Journalism* (2 vols., London, 1887), ii. 27.

large quantities of printed matter free of charge. This practice can be seen as early as 1705, when just under 1,000 copies of the *Gazette* were being given away each week, sponsored by the administration.[125] In 1717, the government was buying up to 2,000 copies of the *Daily Courant* each week for free distribution (half of which was to officials).[126] In a particularly fraught period in 1733, the numbers of such papers reached a weekly figure of about 12,000,[127] although Targett argues that the total number distributed by the government may have been around 30,000, when other forms of distribution are taken into consideration.[128] Bourne claims that during the 1790s, Pitt's government would distribute some of the London papers free to provincial editors, with certain articles marked with red ink for republication,[129] and a libel action in 1819 revealed that copies of the *Observer* had been freely distributed in the provinces in 1817, whilst it was claimed that an article on the Derbyshire insurrection contained within it was, in fact, a government manifesto.[130]

Occasionally the government would attempt to constrict the influence of certain newspapers by preventing postal distribution. This could be a significant blow to the many London papers which relied on provincial sales. In 1728, this fate befell *Mist's Weekly Journal* and five years later, on the eve of a general election, it was the turn of the *London Evening Post*, later followed by *Common Sense* and the *Champion*, and in 1754, before another election, the *London Evening Post* was blocked over its attitude to the 'Jew Bill'.[131] However, as with prosecutions, the overall effect of such action appears to have been to make restricted papers more desirable to readers. The government could also favour or punish certain papers by the way in which it distributed advertisements from its own departments. Aspinall claimed that *The Times* received practically no advertisements in 1835 after the Whigs returned to office.[132] However, Asquith has questioned the impact of such measures. He claims that the removal of government adverts from the *Morning*

125. J.M. Price, 'A note on the circulation of the London press, 1704–1714', *Bulletin of the Institute of Historical Research*, **xxxi** (1958).

126. P.M. Handover, *A History of the London Gazette 1665–1965* (London, 1965), pp. 49–50.

127. Harris, *London Newspapers in the Age of Walpole*, p. 119.

128. Targett, 'Sir Robert Walpole's newspapers', p. 198.

129. Bourne, *English Newspapers*, i. 246.

130. Aspinall, *Politics and the Press*, pp. 151–2.

131. Cranfield, *The Development of the Provincial Newspaper*, pp. 146–7.

132. Aspinall, *Politics and the Press*, p. 133.

Chronicle in 1798 and 1799 was no great hardship for the paper, since they had constituted probably less than 2 per cent of advertising revenue.[133] Finally, government departments and ministers could support certain papers with early intelligence. This was a cause for complaint in 1793 for John Walter, editor of *The Times*, who claimed that the ministry was helping the pro-government *Sun*: 'It is notorious', he wrote, 'that scarce a dispatch comes from the Armies, or is there a Paris journal forwarded to any of the public offices, but what is immediately transmitted to the *Sun* office'.[134] In 1810, his son and successor, John Walter II, complained that the government was actively engaged in preventing foreign reports from reaching the paper. According to Walter, 'the foreign captains were always asked by a government officer at Gravesend if they had papers for "The Times". These, when acknowledged, were as regularly stopped.' Yet despite such complaints, *The Times* of this period still managed to publish news of foreign events ahead of the rest of the London press.[135] Indeed, it is clear that government control of foreign news was never exercised in any systematic way, and throughout the period one can find instances of newspapers receiving news more speedily than officials, particularly where foreign information was concerned. Peel noted in the Commons in 1836 that he remembered many instances when the government received the first news of important events, especially during the Napoleonic Wars, from newspapers, often from those that opposed the government.[136]

Conclusion

Throughout the period 1695 to 1855, newspapers were subject to a variety of restrictions imposed by government. Taxation, first introduced in 1712, rose steadily until the end of the Napoleonic Wars, decreased in the 1830s and was finally abolished in 1855. More dramatic were the laws against sedition, which, coupled with the general warrant in the first half of the eighteenth century and the use of *ex officio* informations, gave the state powerful weapons

133. Ivon Asquith, 'Advertising and the press in the late eighteenth and early nineteenth centuries: James Perry and the *Morning Chronicle* 1790–1821', *Historical Journal*, **xviii**, 4 (1975), p. 716.
134. Aspinall, *Politics and the Press*, p. 184.
135. Bourne, *English Newspapers*, i. 281–2.
136. Aspinall, *Politics and the Press*, p. 187.

with which to keep the press in line. However, the impact of prosecutions could be very mixed. Although harassment and imprisonment could silence papers, they could also have the opposite effect and increase both their popularity and confidence. The publication of parliamentary proceedings provides a case in point. Parliament's attempts to protect its privileges in this matter ultimately failed, and produced a legal battle in which recalcitrant printers emerged as popular heroes.

For many historians, the heroic aspects of newspaper publishing were not apparent until the nineteenth century, when the press finally threw off its earlier, 'corrupt' incarnation. Before then, newspapers, and the political views which they promoted, were supposedly subject to the whim of politicians. However, it seems more likely that throughout our period, the relationship between newspapers and 'high' politics was more complex than that, and that political bribes had only a limited effect on the press. Political sponsorship was common, but without popular backing newspapers could not thrive and the propaganda contained within them was unlikely to win public approval. Moreover, most politicians were ambivalent in their relationship with the press, and few were willing or able to organise long-term campaigns (although many sought to improve their own standing by ensuring that their parliamentary speeches received favourable coverage). Finally, politicians could either help or hinder certain papers by offering free postal distribution, early intelligence and government advertising, or by withholding the latter and blocking newspapers at the post office. But once again, such actions were neither consistently nor always successfully carried out. Increasingly, newspapers were not dependent upon political patronage, but upon the support of their readers, the English public.

CHAPTER FIVE

Newspaper Management and Editorial Strategies

Throughout our period newspapers were becoming increasingly profitable. In London during the 1770s and 1780s annual profits were generally between £1,500 and £2,000, but by around 1820 Perry's *Morning Chronicle* was making £12,000 a year, whilst the *Morning Herald* and the *Star* brought in £6,000–8,000 each.[1] With rising profits, the value of newspapers also increased. In the 1780s, most London papers were valued at under £10,000.[2] In 1803, Daniel Stuart sold the *Morning Post* for £25,000, having turned the paper's fortunes around in the previous eight years.[3] The tremendous success of *The Times* meant that the paper was valued at almost £45,000 in 1819.[4] Its owner, John Walter II, retired from newspaper work in 1816 to live the life of a country squire and MP.[5] Similarly fortunate was James Harmer, who was said to have made over £300,000 by 1853, largely from his ownership of *Bell's Weekly Dispatch*.[6] As the scale of production increased and profits rose, the cost of launching a daily paper also increased. In the early

1. I.R. Christie, 'British newspapers in the later Georgian age', in I.R. Christie, *Myth and Reality in Late-Eighteenth-Century British Politics and Other Papers* (London, 1970), pp. 320–2.

2. Hannah Barker, *Newspapers, Politics, and Public Opinion in Late Eighteenth-Century England* (Oxford, 1998), p. 49.

3. Wilfrid Hindle, *The Morning Post 1772–1937: Portrait of a Newspaper* (London, 1937), p. 84.

4. *History of The Times*, vol. I: *'The Thunderer' in the Making, 1785–1841* (London, 1935), p. 174.

5. *'The Thunderer' in the Making*, ch. 11.

6. H.R. Fox Bourne, *English Newspapers: Chapters in the History of Journalism* (2 vols., London, 1887), ii. 101.

nineteenth century the sum involved could be as little as £2,000, but by the 1830s this figure had multiplied ten-fold.[7]

The provincial newspapers often appear as the poor relations of London papers, but this was not necessarily the case. Profit levels in the provinces could match some of those in the capital, and many provincial proprietors appear to have enriched themselves by their newspaper activities. According to Cranfield, an examination of wills and annuities reveals that the profits made by country printers rose steadily throughout the first half of the eighteenth century.[8] This picture was repeated during the rest of our period. Late eighteenth-century provincial newspaper owners such as Robert Goadby of the *Western Flying-Post*, William Jackson of *Jackson's Oxford Journal* and Robert Raikes of the *Gloucester Journal* all became wealthy men.[9] Christine Ferdinand's study of Benjamin Collins, one of the founders of the *Salisbury Journal* in 1736, who went on to assume sole ownership of the paper, provides a detailed study of another provincial newspaperman who prospered from his trade. Ferdinand suggests that his newspaper interests allowed him to diversify into various ventures associated with the print trade, most notably bookselling. When he died in 1785, he left an estimated £85,000–£100,000 and had assumed the status of a 'landed gentleman'.[10] As was the case in London, the profitability of provincial newspapers allowed proprietors to take a back seat and hire an editor to run papers on a day-to-day basis. In the late eighteenth century, Charles Pugh, who founded and owned the *Hereford Journal*, was able to live in London whilst he paid a man named Rathbone to act as editor, 'who wrote the paragraphs and in general superintended the publication'.[11] Ann Ward, who owned the *York Courant* during the same period, appears to have employed David Russell on a similar basis.[12]

7. Ivon Asquith, 'The structure, ownership and control of the press, 1780–1855', in George Boyce, James Curran and Pauline Wingate, eds., *Newspaper History From the Seventeenth Century to the Present Day* (London, 1978), p. 109.

8. G.A. Cranfield, *The Development of the Provincial Newspaper* (Oxford, 1962), pp. 254–5.

9. Barker, *Newspapers, Politics, and Public Opinion*, pp. 106–7.

10. C.Y. Ferdinand, *Benjamin Collins and the Provincial Newspaper Trade in the Eighteenth Century* (Oxford, 1997), ch. 1. Barker, *Newspapers, Politics, and Public Opinion*, ch. 4.

11. MS notes by John Allen, a Hereford printer and bookseller, which appear in the first bound volume of the *Hereford Journal* held at the Hereford Reference Library. His remarks are expanded by F.C. Morgan in 'Hereford Printers and Booksellers', *Transactions of the Woolhope Naturalists' Field Club, Herefordshire* (1941), 106–27.

12. York City Archives, Acc. 1663 M25 and M32 (Papers of the Yorkshire Association).

Advertising was an important source of newspaper profits. Looney has shown that the advertising revenue for papers in Leeds and York rose from a few pounds a year in 1720 to several hundred by the early nineteenth century.[13] As early as 1705, Defoe wrote that 'the principal support of all the public papers now on foot depends on advertisements',[14] and even early in the eighteenth century, profits of several hundred pounds a year were not unknown, with the *Gazetteer* reportedly making £1,400 between 1706 and 1707.[15] However, such figures were more common later.[16] By the nineteenth century, several thousand pounds' profit was typical, and Daniel Stuart recorded that £1,500 of the £8,000 profits made by the *Courier* in 1806 came from advertising relating to the general election alone.[17]

Advertisements could also attract readers as well as profit. The owner of the *Morning Post* claimed in 1806 that 'Numerous and various advertisements interest numerous and various readers.... They attract readers, promote circulation, and circulation attracts advertisements'.[18] From the eighteenth century onwards, certain newspapers concentrated on particular types of advertising, presumably in order to secure a niche market. Thus in the late eighteenth century, the *Public Ledger* had more shipping adverts, the *Morning Post* focused on auctioneers and the *Morning Chronicle* on books.[19] Yet it would be a mistake to view newspaper profits solely in terms of advertising revenue. Advertising did provide a vital source of income for newspapers, but sales were arguably of more importance. Not only did they produce a greater income for newspapers, but without high sales, advertisers would not place their advertisements in them.

13. J.J. Looney, 'Advertising and society in England, 1720–1820: a statistical analysis of Yorkshire newspaper advertisements' (Princeton University PhD thesis, 1983), p. 98.

14. J.A. Downie, *Robert Harley and the Press: Propaganda and Public Opinion in the Age of Swift and Defoe* (Cambridge, 1979), pp. 11–12.

15. Downie, *Robert Harley and the Press*, p. 12; Henry L. Snyder, 'The circulation of newspapers in the reign of Queen Anne', *Library*, 5th ser., **xxiii** (1969), p. 220.

16. Richmond P. Bond and Marjorie N. Bond, 'The minute book of the *St. James's Chronicle*', *Studies in Bibliography*, **28** (1975), p. 27.

17. Ivon Asquith, 'Advertising and the press in the late eighteenth and early nineteenth centuries: James Perry and the *Morning Chronicle* 1790–1821', *Historical Journal*, **xviii**, 4 (1975), p. 706.

18. Robert L. Haig, *The Gazetteer 1735–1797: A Study in the Eighteenth-Century English Newspaper* (Carbondale, Ill., 1960), p. 62.

19. Asquith, 'Advertising and the press in the late eighteenth and early nineteenth centuries', p. 709.

Given the potential for huge profits, it is not surprising that newspapers themselves paid great attention to advertising. Michael Harris has described the efforts made to publicise new papers early on in the eighteenth century. In the 1730s, the *Daily Advertiser* distributed large numbers of handbills, circulated the bulk of early editions free and advertised extensively in the press.[20] The proprietors of the *Salopian Journal* expended a considerable amount of time and money in publicising their new paper in 1793 and 1794. Advertisements were placed in the London daily papers, handbills and large bills were produced to be distributed and posted up 'throughout this and the neighbouring counties', and the first edition of the *Journal* (of 2,500 copies) was given away free, with some copies sent to London coffee-houses. As was common practice for other papers, the publishers of the *Salopian Journal* provided a uniform for the men employed to distribute the paper. Each newsman was to be 'furnished with a blue coloured upper coat with a red collar; a Hat edged with a lace band and a horn'. The costs totalled over £72.[21]

Costumes were also worn in London in 1776 to advertise the *Morning Post*. Horace Walpole wrote at the time, 'I heard drums and trumpets, in Piccadilly: I looked out of the window and saw a procession with streamers flying. At first I thought it was a press-gang, but seeing the Corps so well drest, like Hussars, in yellow with blue waistcoats and breeches, and high caps, I concluded it was some new body of our allies...'. To his disgust, he realised that it was a procession to advertise a newspaper: 'this mummery must have cost a great deal of money', he complained, 'what a country!'[22] John Bowles's complaint about the sale of newspapers on the Sabbath in 1807 reveals similar excesses:

> No pains are spared to make their distribution as general and as public as possible. Besides the gross indecency of announcing them by the blowing of horns, whenever they contain any extraordinary news, greengrocers, hairdressers and pastry-cooks throughout the metropolis and its vicinity, are furnished with signboards, intimating that particular papers are to be sold at their respective shops, and they are copiously supplied with copies, of which the number unsold are

20. M.R.A. Harris, 'Figures relating to the printing and distribution of the *Craftsman* 1726 to 1730', *Bulletin of the Institute of Historical Research*, **xliii** (1970), p. 236.

21. Shropshire Records and Research Unit, MS 1923 (papers of the *Salopian Journal*).

22. Hindle, *The Morning Post*, pp. 14–15.

returned on the Monday morning. These papers are also most diffusely circulated, by means of the stage coaches, throughout the country.[23]

Some newspaper historians have argued that patterns of newspaper ownership changed during the eighteenth and nineteenth centuries. Harris argues that newspapers were increasingly the property of consortia of booksellers from the 1730s,[24] whilst Christie claims that the 1790s witnessed the rise of 'newspaper tycoons', replacing syndicates as newspapers came under individual control.[25] These developments do not seem to have been as clear-cut as either Harris or Christie suggests. There were many single-proprietor newspapers in the mid-eighteenth century, whilst group ownership was still commonplace in the latter period. Even if these trends did hold broadly true in the capital, most provincial newspapers were owned by individuals or families for much of our period, and whilst the functions of ownership, editing, leader writing, management and reporting might have become progressively separated in late eighteenth-century London, this was not generally the case in the provinces. Ivon Asquith has calculated that of 125 provincial journalists and editors in the 1840s, sixty-nine owned the newspapers on which they were actively engaged as editors, whilst a further sixteen took some part in the production or management of their paper.[26]

As sales and profits rose during the eighteenth and nineteenth centuries, so the scale of newspaper production increased. Chapter 2 has described the ways in which new technology facilitated faster production methods, but it also showed that for much of the period, few such innovations were made. Steam printing presses were in common use only after the 1830s, and compositing work was still unmechanised and was highly labour-intensive, until the late nineteenth century. The more dramatic change in newspaper production to occur in our period was in the numbers of people employed in all aspects of reporting, printing, composing, financial management and editorial work. At the same time the newspaper trade, at least for those with higher status jobs, became increasingly

23. Arthur Aspinall, *Politics and the Press, c. 1780–1850* (London, 1949), p. 14.
24. M. Harris, *London Newspapers in the Age of Walpole: A Study in the Origins of the Modern English Press* (London, 1987), pp. 65–6.
25. Christie, 'British newspapers in the later Georgian age', p. 316.
26. Ivon Asquith, 'The structure, ownership and control of the press, 1780–1855', p. 114.

well paid and respectable.[27] This contrasts forcefully with the early eighteenth century, when Michael Harris argues that 'the status of these authors, whatever the glamour of their political or literary associates, was peculiarly low...'[28] In the early eighteenth century, Defoe was very secretive about his contributions to *Mist's Weekly Journal,* and apparently left his copy in a hole in Mist's 'back-shop'.[29] A hundred years later, men such as J.S. Mill and David Ricardo published material much less furtively.[30]

Throughout our period, women could also be found engaged in most aspects of newspaper work. As in many other sectors of the English economy during the eighteenth and nineteenth centuries, female workers played a significant part in newspaper production and distribution – often as part of family firms. In both London and the provinces, women could be found as owners of newspapers, working as printers, hawkers and agents. The position of Mary Say, a prominent London printer who published the *Gazetteer* from the 1770s until the 1790s, was in no way unusual. In the North-East of England, around 10 per cent of printing businesses were run by women between 1695 and 1855. This included the family printing firm which produced the *Newcastle Chronicle,* left by Thomas Slack in 1785 to his daughter Sarah, and her husband, Solomon Hodgson. When Solomon died in 1800, Sarah took over the business in an impressive manner, and remained in charge even when her two sons came of age in 1806 and 1814.[31]

Such women, like their male counterparts, had to adapt to the changing nature of newspaper production. A news compositors' report of 1820 described this as 'a complete revolution ... in the *nature* of newswork'.[32] In the early eighteenth century, newspapers

---

27. A. Aspinall, 'The social status of journalists at the beginning of the nineteenth century', *Review of English Studies,* **xxi**, 83 (1945).

28. Michael Harris, 'Journalism as a profession or trade in the eighteenth century', in Robin Myers and Michael Harris, eds., *Author/Publisher Relations During the Eighteenth and Nineteenth Centuries* (Oxford, 1983), p. 56.

29. James Sutherland, *The Restoration Newspaper and its Development* (Cambridge, 1986), pp. 217–18.

30. Ann P. Robson and John M. Robson, '"Impetuous eagerness": the young Mill's radical journalism', in Joanne Shattock and Michael Wolff, eds., *The Victorian Periodical Press: Samplings and Soundings* (Leicester, 1982); Ivon Asquith, 'James Perry and the *Morning Chronicle* 1790–1821' (London University PhD thesis, 1973), p. 258.

31. Hannah Barker, 'Women, work and the industrial revolution: female involvement in the English printing trades, c. 1700–1840', in Hannah Barker and Elaine Chalus, eds., *Gender in Eighteenth-Century England: Roles, Representations and Responsibilities* (Harlow, 1997).

32. *The London Compositor: Documents Relating to Wages, Working Conditions and Customs of the London Printing Trade 1785–1900,* ed. Ellic Howe (London, 1947), pp. 373–81.

were very small-scale affairs. The *London Journal*, for example, was produced by one publisher, a printer and three pressmen in 1721,[33] whilst Nathaniel Mist, the publisher of *Mist's Weekly Journal*, employed four journeymen and two apprentices in 1728, with the added labour of his wife and servant.[34] In the provinces, both printing and editing were often the job of one person. This was less likely to be the case in the capital, however, where such tasks were generally separated. As the century progressed, and newspaper staffs increased, greater use was made of additional writers, especially in London. Often termed 'newsgathers' rather than reporters, such individuals were unlikely to have been regularly employed by newspapers in the first half of the eighteenth century, but were paid on a casual, freelance basis. This meant that the same newsgatherers would work for several different papers.[35] In the second half of the eighteenth century the employment of writers became less flexible, with individuals increasingly drawing a salary from just one paper. Overall numbers also rose. By the 1770s, the *Gazetteer*'s editor listed fourteen separate correspondents who were paid for various contributions, including Guildhall and Bow Street intelligence, ship news, letters and paragraphs.[36] Most daily papers around this date also had one or two parliamentary reporters, but no regular foreign correspondents.

From the latter part of the eighteenth century, the writing and the production sides of the newspaper industry were increasingly unlikely to overlap as the rising scale of production led to increased specialisation and demarcation.[37] In 1797, *The Times* was produced with eleven men working as printers and compositors under the main printer, Charles Bell, who also had an assistant and a 'boy' working under him, as well as clerks, messengers and a bookkeeper. The writing staff of editors, reporters, translators and foreign correspondents increased the size of the staff even more.[38] When Charles Babbage visited *The Times* building thirty-four years later, he found nearly 100 people employed there, half of whom were

33. K.L. Joshi, 'The London Journal, 1719–1738', *Journal of the University of Bombay*, 9 (1940), p. 48.

34. R.L. Caparo, 'Typographic politics: the impact of printing on the political life of eighteenth-century England, 1714–1772' (Washington University PhD thesis, 1984), p. 159.

35. Harris, 'Journalism as a profession or trade in the eighteenth century', p. 43.

36. Haig, *The Gazetteer*, pp. 178–80.

37. Christie, 'British newspapers in the later Georgian age', p. 316.

38. *'The Thunderer' in the Making*, pp. 39–41.

compositors.[39] This was probably twice the size of other newspaper printing departments at the time.[40] In 1850, one commentator estimated that the average daily paper would have one editor, probably three sub-editors, sixteen parliamentary reporters, several foreign reporters and agents, about ten paid correspondents and a handful of other writers, plus provincial correspondents, and reporters who worked at the various law courts and in the City. On the production side, each paper would need about fifty men in the printing room, plus publishers and managers. The weekly payroll totalled £520, or about twenty times the costs of producing the *Public Advertiser* some eighty years earlier.[41]

In contrast to the situation in London, the average provincial printing office in the early nineteenth century was very small, and few employed more than three or four compositors and pressmen whilst the master printer himself generally worked at the trade (compared to the capital where he would have had a strictly supervisory role).[42] A large paper such as the *Manchester Guardian* probably employed about six journeymen in 1825. By 1838, fifteen men worked there under a head printer, with about four reporters. Payments were also made to freelance reporters in Manchester and south-east Lancashire.[43] However, the *Plymouth Times* had only one reporter in 1842, whose writing was supplemented by the editor's leaders and occasional pieces written by some of the proprietors.[44] The small staffs of provincial newspapers could greatly increase the production pressures on individuals. Richard Phillips recorded how an accident in the printing room, coupled with a short printing deadline, led to desperate space-filling methods in the *Leicester Herald* in the 1790s. Finding a column of 'pie' (a term used to describe a random collection of odd letters lying around the printing room), Phillips headed it 'Dutch news' and added a statement apologising for the lack of a translation which its late arrival had caused. His action reputedly

39. *'The Thunderer' in the Making*, p. 413.

40. *London Compositor*, pp. 407–12.

41. F. Knight Hunt, *The Fourth Estate: Contributions towards a History of Newspapers and of the Liberty of the Press* (2 vols., London, 1850), ii. 196–204; Asquith, 'The structure, ownership and control of the press, 1780–1855', p. 109.

42. A.E. Musson, 'Newspaper printing in the industrial revolution', *Economic History Review*, 2nd ser., **x**, 3 (1958), p. 413; Donald Read, *Press and People 1790–1850: Opinion in Three English Cities* (Aldershot, 1993), p. 64.

43. David Ayerst, *Guardian: Biography of a Newspaper* (London, 1971), pp. 81–2.

44. William Hunt, *Then and Now; Or, Fifty Years of Newspaper Work* (Hull, 1887), pp. 13–14.

led to much consternation amongst those readers who attempted to translate it.[45]

As newspaper profits rose in the late eighteenth and early nineteenth centuries, the salaries paid to editors and reporters increased too in real terms.[46] The wage bill for supporting a reporting and editorial staff rose accordingly: from around £20–30 per week in 1790, to over £300 in 1850. In 1781, James Stephen was paid 2 guineas a week as a parliamentary reporter, the same fee paid by James Perry when he hired Robert Spankie as a reporter on the *Morning Chronicle* in 1792.[47] This was probably double that paid to writers in major publications in the first half of the century.[48] Thomas Barnes's annual salary of £1,000 from 1817 was no doubt unusually high, but that was for editing *The Times*. It is over three times higher than Dennis O'Bryen claimed he was offered to edit 'the most fashionable paper in London' in 1779.[49]

Editors and reporters were responsible for filling their news-papers with up-to-date news. During our period the methods which they employed to do this became increasingly diverse. What was to prove one of the most long-standing practices attracted the complaints of one pamphlet-writer in 1728:

> Persons are employed (One or Two for each Paper) at so much a Week, to haunt Coffee-Houses, and thrust themselves into Companies where they are not known; or plant themselves at a convenient Distance, to overhear what is said, in order to pick up Matter for the Papers...

Other London newsgatherers were accused of befriending those in the service of the nobility and gentry in order to make 'matters sacred to Privacy and the fireside ... the talk of the World'.[50] In addition to gathering gossip from the city's coffee-houses and inns, London newspapers increasingly employed reporters to cover parliamentary debates, proceedings at various law courts, city and shipping news. Another source of domestic news for the London

45. Richard Phillips, *A Personal Tour Through the United Kingdom* (London, 1828), p. 4.

46. Christie, 'British newspapers in the later Georgian age', pp. 320–2.

47. *The Memoirs of James Stephen Written By Himself for the Use of His Children*, ed. Merle M. Bevington (London, 1954), p. 294; Ivon Asquith, 'Advertising and the press in the late eighteenth and early nineteenth centuries: James Perry and the *Morning Chronicle* 1790–1821', *Historical Journal*, **xviii**, 4 (1975), p. 101.

48. Harris, 'Journalism as a profession or trade in the eighteenth century', p. 52.

49. *'The Thunderer' in the Making*, p. 177; Dennis O'Bryen to Edmund Burke, March 1782, Woodhouse Wentworth Muniments, Sheffield City Archives, BK 1/1557.

50. Sutherland, *Restoration Newspaper*, p. 221.

press was provincial newspapers. This was a reciprocal arrangement, and indeed, the provincial press, with generally fewer resources for newsgathering, was the greater beneficiary in this process.

Yet material obtained was not used indiscriminately. Joseph Addison announced in *The Freeholder* in 1716 that '[T]he People of *Exeter, Salisbury*, and other large towns, are resolved to be as great Politicians as the Inhabitants of *London* and *Westminster*, and deal out such News of their own Printing, as is best suited to the Genius of the Market-Place, and the Taste of the Country.'[51] The *County Press for Northants, Beds, Bucks and Hunts* announced in January 1808 that 'The public are aware that a weekly provincial journal can have little original information. Its claim to notice must depend on the taste, the good sense, the discrimination of its selection from contemporary prints.'[52] The journalist James Amphlett recalled a newspaperman in Derby who 'was one of the best judges of a selection for a newspaper that I ever met with ... "What he thought the people would like to read" was his guiding star; and not what exactly suits the editor's taste and opinion of the selector.'[53] When employed by the *Plymouth Times* during the 1840s, William Hunt's job was to select 'from the London and other journals such items as were deemed suitable for our paper...'[54]

The eighteenth-century provincial press also largely relied on unpaid correspondents, but this had its drawbacks. The *Reading Mercury* announced in July 1742 that 'As the Proprietors of this Paper are desirous to have it very correct, and, as near as they can, to insert nothing but Facts, they hope their Correspondents in all parts will take care to transmit no Accounts but what they know to be true...' However, like other provincial papers, the *Mercury* was prone to practical jokes and mistakes and in 1799 it published a letter from J. Philpson, a surgeon from Henley, in which he stated: 'As you have consigned me to death in your last paper, you will please, in your next, to reanimate me, by contradicting that report.'[55] Larger staffs brought about improvements. The surviving

51. Kathleen Wilson, *The Sense of the People: Politics, Culture and Imperialism in England, 1715–1785* (Cambridge, 1995), p. 27.

52. Diana Dixon, 'Northamptonshire newspapers 1720–1900', in Peter Isaac and Barry McKay, eds., *Images and Texts: Their Production and Distribution in the Eighteenth and Nineteenth Centuries* (Winchester, 1997), p. 3.

53. James Amphlett, *The Newspaper Press, in Part of the Last Century, and up to the Present Period of 1860* (London, 1860), p. 37.

54. Hunt, *Then and Now*, p. 21.

55. K.G. Burton, *The Early Newspaper Press in Berkshire (1723–1855)* (Reading, 1954), pp. 15 and 19.

records of the *Manchester Guardian,* for example, show that between 1828 and 1831 two of the paper's journalists travelled to thirty-eight towns on 118 occasions to report on events outside the town.[56]

For both London and provincial newspapers the main source of foreign news for much of the eighteenth century was the official government paper, the *Gazette,* which reproduced reports made by British diplomats abroad, war despatches from military and naval officers and the details of treaties. This was supplemented by foreign newspapers, as well as by letters from merchants and travellers. Foreign news was important enough in the early eighteenth century to dictate the day on which papers were published. According to Sutherland, publication was timed to coincide with the mails from the continent.[57] As with domestic news, the veracity of foreign information was often open to doubt. In 1711, for example, the *British Mercury* reported a colossal defeat of the French which had not taken place. The paper was forced to publish a retraction when its error came to light.[58] In his *History of England,* published in 1735, John Oldmixon even accused ministers of sending misleading paragraphs to the Dutch press which would then be republished in Britain.[59] In 1750, the *Gazetteer* came under attack for publishing a false report that a plague ship had landed at Bristol from Smyrna with several deaths occurring as a result. Not only the Mayor of Bristol, but several Westminster politicians were involved in trying to dispel the rumour. Nevertheless, Bristol's trade was reputedly hurt.[60] Finally, Hester Thrale alleged that Samuel Johnson placed several fictitious stories about a battle between the Russians and the Turks in the London papers in 1770 as a ploy to teach Thrale's mother not to believe everything she read in the newspapers.[61]

The use of foreign newspaper reports – often translated verbatim – can appear striking to the modern reader, particularly in times of war when paragraphs produced by the enemy side, and thus highly critical of Britain, would nevertheless appear in the English press. During the Napoleonic Wars, for example, newspapers in Britain

56. Ayerst, *Guardian,* p. 35.
57. Sutherland, *Restoration Newspaper,* pp. 26–7.
58. Sutherland, *Restoration Newspaper,* pp.135–7.
59. Snyder, 'Circulation of newspapers', p. 211.
60. Haig, *The Gazetteer,* pp. 26–8.
61. Betty Rizzo, '"Innocent frauds": By Samuel Johnson', *The Library,* 6th ser., **8,** 3 (1986), pp. 249–50.

frequently carried tales of French bravery and military success. Such stories were almost always clearly marked as coming from a foreign source, but they suggest a level of discernment amongst the British reading public that many contemporaries refused to countenance, and which was explored more fully in chapter 1. In any case, by the late eighteenth century, English newspapers were becoming less reliant upon foreign sources of information. James Perry, editor of the *Morning Chronicle*, travelled to France in 1791 in order to send back reports to his paper.[62] As the nineteenth century progressed, it became more common for British newspapers to have their own correspondents posted abroad. Henry Crabbe Robinson, for example, travelled to Altona in Holstein as *The Times*'s correspondent in 1807, and in the following year, he went to Spain to cover the revolution,[63] whilst at various times in the 1840s, Engels acted as foreign correspondent for the *Northern Star*.[64] *The Times* was particularly keen to stress the pains which it took to ensure the speedy publication of foreign events. On 9 November 1840 it boasted that a courier carrying the King of France's speech had travelled from Paris to London in under twenty-two hours.[65] But other London papers were no less determined. As Plymouth correspondent for the *Daily News* in 1846, William Hunt once hired a special train to London in order to deliver particularly exciting news from South Africa and Australia.[66] With fewer resources than their London counterparts, provincial papers could not afford such heroic and expensive forms of obtaining information. But this did not mean that foreign news necessarily reached London first. News of the Swedish uprising in 1743, for example, was first published in an Edinburgh paper after a report came from a ship arriving at Leith. During the same period, Newcastle often received items of German or Baltic news, and Liverpool residents obtained reports from America.[67] During 1715, both *Farley's Bristol Post Man* and the Bristol *Weekly Mercury* took advantage of the city's direct trade route with Europe and America to get advance intelligence.[68] Over a

62. Asquith, 'James Perry and the *Morning Chronicle* 1790–1821', p. 17.

63. Henry Crabbe Robinson, *Diary, Reminiscences, and Correspondence* (3 vols., London, 1869), i. 231 and 269.

64. James Epstein, 'Feargus O'Connor and the *Northern Star*', *International Review of Social History*, **xxi** (1976), pp. 82–3.

65. 'The Thunderer' in the Making, p. 432.

66. Hunt, *Then and Now*, pp. 46–8.

67. Black, *English Press*, pp. 91–2.

68. Charles E. Clark, *The Public Prints: The Newspaper in Anglo-American Culture, 1665–1740* (Oxford, 1994), p. 65.

century later, in the 1840s, the *Manchester Guardian* paid £100 a year
to receive news from Liverpool about events in the United States.
However, with the exception of France and Germany, the *Guardian*
had no regular correspondents from abroad by the end of our
period and depended instead on news from other papers.[69]

The introduction of the telegraph from the late 1840s speeded
greatly the despatch of news for all papers. The first reports of the
1848 revolution in France, for example, reached Manchester by
telegraph from the special late editions of the London papers much
faster than by any other method.[70] However, whilst the telegraph
remained domestic rather than international – prior to the establishment of the London–Paris telegraph in 1851 – traditional methods
of bringing news to England were still used for most of our period.
In the 1840s, the *Hants Advertiser* described the activities of

> a few persons who, if it be a winter night, would scarcely be
> recognisable, disguised as they appear to be in greatcoats, comforters,
> and every kind of waterproof covering…. These persons are the
> outport Newspaper agents. They make for the head of the quay, and
> each jumps into a small yacht. … While making for the shore,
> sometimes in the most tempestuous weather … the foreign Journals
> are hastily examined by means of a lantern … the most important
> items of foreign News which they contain are immediately detected,
> and the form in which they must be transmitted to London arranged
> in the mind. The agents are landed as near as possible to the electric
> telegraph office, sometimes on the shoulders of their boatmen
> through the surf or mud.[71]

Such heroic efforts to obtain news were vital to a newspaper's
success, since their popularity was determined by their contents. In
chapter 4 it was argued that the importance of sales, rather than
political subsidy, to newspaper profits made the press freer of high
political influence and more sensitive to opinion amongst its
readership than has been presumed. This was certainly the view of
late eighteenth- and nineteenth-century politicians. In 1778,
Anthony Chamier, Under-Secretary in the Southern Department,
wrote to Sir Robert Murray Keith: 'As soon as Government has any
influence over a paper printed in this town, the sale of it decreases,
and an Englishman will like no newspaper that does not shew him
he is ill governed and on the brink of ruin.'[72] In 1800 Pitt informed

69. Ayerst, *Guardian*, pp. 104, 109–10.
70. Ayerst, *Guardian*, p. 106.
71. Hindle, *The Morning Post*, pp. 173–4.
72. Black, *English Press*, p. 135.

his brother that he was unable to stop many of the newspaper attacks against him, and commented: 'you really do not know how little means there are to keep printers in order.' George Rose, Secretary to the Treasury, described newspaper editors in 1802 as notoriously unmanageable, 'most of all, Mr. Walter', the editor of *The Times*.[73] This might have been a lesson which John Walter II, then in charge of the paper, learnt from his brother's unhappy editorship, which he gave up in 1802. According to Cobbett, *The Times* lost many of its readers through its defence of the Treaty of Amiens in 1801.[74] As William Wordsworth proclaimed in 1818, 'the people would only read that which flattered their passions'.[75] Such a pragmatic and commercial approach won newspapers few admirers amongst politicians. After *The Times* changed its political allegiance when the Tories lost popular support in 1823, William Hazlitt commented that the paper 'floats with the tide; it sails with the stream'.[76] Five years later, the Whig leader, Lord Grey, wrote to Princess Lieven that *The Times* was 'being conducted without the least regard to principles of any kind, and solely with the view of an extension of its sale', but that as a result, 'its frequent changes [may] be taken in general as no bad barometer of the general sentiment'.[77] According to Wellington, papers such as *The Times* and the *Morning Herald* were 'great mercantile concerns ... carried on upon principles of such a concern'. A paper's political stance on any matter was thus 'founded upon the views of advantage for the concern rather than upon any interest of a political or publick nature in favour of the movement'.[78]

Brian Harrison argues that press freedom and competitive proprietorship were not necessarily incompatible: 'The competitive pursuit of profit by newspaper proprietors requires them to engage in an energetic pursuit of readers and (through them) advertisers; this severely curtails their freedom to dissent from the existing views of their readership.'[79] But it would be a gross overstatement to say that all papers published in our period were produced for primarily commercial motives. For example, as we shall see in chapter 8,

73. Aspinall, *Politics and the Press*, p. 369.
74. 'The Thunderer' in the Making, pp. 120–1.
75. Aspinall, *Politics and the Press*, p. 356.
76. Stephen Koss, *The Rise and Fall of the Political Press in Britain* (London, 1981), p. 46.
77. 'The Thunderer' in the Making, p. 254.
78. Aspinall, *Politics and the Press*, pp. 469–70.
79. Brian Harrison, 'Press and pressure group in modern Britain', in *Victorian Periodical Press*, p. 261.

many radical and loyalist newspapers of the 1790s were controlled by men active in radical politics. The radical and useful knowledge papers of the early nineteenth century, discussed in chapter 9, were also very different in this respect (although amongst both can be found examples of flourishing businesses). Moreover, as we will see in the final section of this chapter, some newspaper editors held strong personal political views which imbued the papers which they ran. In contrast to Brian Harrison, Michael Harris has argued that in the earlier eighteenth century the commercial considerations of those who owned newspapers led them to place profit above politics and, as a result, to produce papers which avoided political controversy. Harris has asserted that booksellers established increasing control of the London press after the 1720s, and that their business and economic concerns led them to pursue political respectability.[80] There is no doubt that less overtly political newspapers were successful throughout the century; indeed, editors such as William Woodfall made it a selling point. But politically vocal papers appear to have been more prominent and to have captured an increasing proportion of the market as the period went on. Indeed, Harris also states that 'immediate commercial rivals ... tended to hold opposed political attitudes', since political neutrality was unusual 'and not apparently very successful'.[81]

It seems unlikely that individual newspapers were able to prosper without eliciting a favourable response from at least a section of newspaper readers. Moreover, newspapers could not have operated successfully if unaware of the tastes, preoccupations and concerns of the readers they hoped to appeal to. Even though the exact nature of readership response to newspapers is impossible to discern, it seems likely to have been connected in some way to political content. With so many titles being produced at one time, especially in the capital, and with competition intense, readers were faced with a choice that would probably have been made upon this basis, since it was politics which appear to have divided papers more than any other factor. Thus Matthew Flinders, a Lincolnshire surgeon, noted in his diary on 20 October 1775 that he would buy the Stamford paper rather than the *Cambridge Chronicle*, since the latter was 'very barren of entertainment, and partial on the furious and patriotic side'.[82] For this reason too, John

80. Harris, *London Newspapers in the Age of Walpole*; Black, *English Press*, pp. 118–19.
81. Harris, *London Newspapers in the Age of Walpole*, pp. 121–2.
82. Diary of Matthew Flinders, Lincolnshire Archive Office. I am grateful to Paul Langford for this reference.

Trusler, in his guide to London, described daily newspapers according to their political allegiances.[83] Likewise, a Stamp Office survey of 1811 divided the London press according to politics, with seventeen supporting the government, eighteen hostile to it, fifteen neutral and three wavering.[84]

Bob Harris has shown how two opposition journals were forced to alter their political stance in the 1740s due to changes in the popular mood. *The Craftsman* had attempted to defend the conduct of its former patron, William Pulteney, for a short time during the summer of 1742, but having underestimated 'the strength of popular revulsion created by Pulteney's alleged betrayal of the opposition cause' it swiftly adjusted its political line and deserted him. Similarly pragmatic in the face of popular opinion was the influential opposition journal *Old England*. Having been closely identified with the 'Broad-Bottom' opposition of 1742–5, the paper became the most outspoken critic of the group when it came to power in 1745 and failed to enact new measures. Harris concludes that 'the relationship between the political content of those newspapers which were predominantly concerned with politics, the "papers of faction" as pro-ministerial writers often called them, and the views of readers needed to be sufficiently close if a paper was to stand a reasonable chance of success or even survival'.[85] His views are supported by a 1744 pamphlet, which attacked the 'common writers', and asserted that they were 'guided by the common maxim of writing, what will most take and what will best sell'.[86]

The notion that a political stance could attract readers was certainly behind the *General Advertiser*'s belief that it could claim the *London Courant*'s old readership when it folded in 1783. The *Advertiser* tried to assume the role of the capital's leading radical paper, as a supporter of Whig administrations, the reform of parliamentary representation, the rights of the people and the 'glorious cause of liberty'.[87] Supporting unpopular causes was also blamed for many newspaper failures. On 13 February 1789, Peter Stuart, editor of the *Star*, claimed that he was leaving the paper since sales had fallen from over 2,000 a day to only 200–300. This

83. John Trusler, *The London Adviser and Guide* (London, 1786).
84. Christie, 'British newspapers in the later Georgian age', pp. 328–9.
85. Bob Harris, *A Patriot Press: National Politics and the London Press in the 1740s* (Oxford, 1993), pp. 15–18.
86. Harris, *A Patriot Press*, p. 18.
87. *General Advertiser*, 12 May 1783.

he blamed on the new political line required by the newspaper's partners.[88] The *Morning Chronicle*, which had been buoyant and confident in its espousal of radical politics in the early 1790s, suffered falling sales in the late 1790s in the face of a wave of popular loyalism.[89] Three decades later, *The Times*'s sales were boosted considerably because of its support of Queen Caroline, whilst papers such as the *Star*, *Globe* and *True Briton* trebled their sales by following suit.[90] Conversely, not supporting the Queen almost certainly lost the *Morning Chronicle* readers.[91] During the late 1820s and early 1830s, *The Times* once more adopted a popular line and became a vocal proponent of reform. When the official return of stamps was published in March 1822, the paper declared:

> It has been asserted again and again that our sale decreased in consequence of the part we have taken in that great Measure, and thence was inferred the indifference and indisposition of the people to Reform. We want no better criterion of the feelings of the people. Our sale for the year 1830 was 3,409,986. For the last year it was 4,328,025, so that the increase has been nearly 1,000,000. ... Such is the indifference to Reform! ... We observe that the great Conservative paper, the *Morning Post*, sells about 2,000 a day. So much for the popularity of Anti-Reform doctrines.[92]

Similar claims for the importance of maintaining a popular political line were made by the Chartist leader and journalist, Feargus O'Connor. In 1836 he stated that the unstamped press 'depended for support on the integrity of its principles – it could not live at variance with public opinion'.[93]

The success of provincial papers also depended upon their relationship to public opinion, albeit in a very localised form. This has not been apparent to those historians who have criticised the provincial press for its 'parasitic' relationship with its London counterpart, particularly in the eighteenth century. In *Politics and the Press*, Aspinall dismissed provincial newspapers for having low circulations and for filling their pages with advertising or with material copied from the London papers. He remarked that even at

88. Stanley Morison, *The English Newspaper: Some Account of the Physical Development of Journals Printed in London Between 1622 and the Present Day* (Cambridge, 1932), p. 191.

89. M.J. Smith, 'English radical newspapers in the French revolutionary era, 1790–1803' (London University PhD thesis, 1979), pp. 284–5.

90. J. Ann Hone, *For the Cause of Truth: Radicalism in London 1796–1821* (Oxford, 1982), p. 312.

91. Asquith, 'James Perry and the *Morning Chronicle* 1790–1821', p. 411.

92. *'The Thunderer' in the Making*, p. 245.

93. Epstein, 'Feargus O'Connor and the *Northern Star*', p. 53.

the end of the eighteenth century, very few provincial newspaper editors were capable of writing a leading article, since most were printers 'whose skill lay in a technical direction'; they therefore depended upon London newspapers to supply the contents of their own publications.[94]

Historians have largely accepted that provincial newspapers were small-scale, amateurish, 'scissors-and-paste' operations. For this reason they have generally struggled to explain their appeal. Their accounts stress the provision of local news of a non-political, uncontroversial nature, local advertising and the relative cheapness of a weekly provincial paper, as compared with those from the capital which appeared more frequently and may also have been less accessible. Yet the emphasis that most provincial papers put upon obtaining news from London 'by express', and the large sums expended in this endeavour, suggest that readers placed great importance upon the inclusion of very recent news. This might seem to give a competitive advantage to the more up-to-date newspapers of the capital, which appear to have been readily available in the provinces; however, the success of provincial papers in the face of opposition from the London press shows that this was not the case.

As we have seen, the provincial press was increasingly neither small-scale nor amateurish. Certainly, the way in which provincial newspapers were distributed and their publication timed appears to have been carefully calculated. It is also likely that what actually appeared in print was of great importance, not only in the more predictable coverage of local news, but also in the way national news was treated. Historians have not paid sufficient attention to the political character and content of the news carried in provincial newspapers prior to the 1790s, which did not follow blindly the political lead set by the capital's newspapers. It is true that provincial papers made extensive use of material from London. However, this appears to have been on a selective basis, so that the contents of the provincial publications often reveal identifiable and consistent political stances, distinct from those found in any of the capital's newspapers. Indeed, the material found in provincial newspapers suggests that by displaying a uniquely local set of political preoccupations and opinions, they could successfully ward off competition from papers produced elsewhere. Thus, the provincial press may have been localised not just in its production, but also in the views and opinions which it expressed.[95]

94. Aspinall, *Politics and the Press*, p. 350.
95. Barker, *Newspapers, Politics, and Public Opinion*, ch. 4.

An overriding concern of provincial editors appears to have been to aim newspapers at a local market. This preoccupation is most apparent in the 'mission statements' which many provincial papers carried in their first issues. These outlined the proprietor's or editor's vision of his or her new paper, and whilst usually full of self-congratulation for their owners and obsequious praise for potential readers, they are nevertheless of interest. Within these 'mission statements' the importance of representing a particular locality as distinct from other provincial regions was clear. The first copy of the *Shrewsbury Chronicle*, for example, stated that

> it has long been [a] just matter of admiration [*sic*], that there has never been a paper of this kind printed in the polite and opulent town of Shrewsbury; nor even in any part of the large, rich, and populous county of which this town is the chief; but the inhabitants have hitherto been beholden to the printers of other counties for their political information...[96]

The papers' pleas stressed the importance of a newspaper to a town or county of any prominence. The appeal of the new papers was supposedly based upon their local production. But in this respect, although some references were made to the greater accessibility of newspapers, there was rarely any mention of their relative cheapness. The case put to potential readers was based on the supposition that any place of importance ought to have its own newspaper: that, in effect, it should be properly represented. This, then, was an appeal to civic pride which attempted to exploit local inhabitants' sense of regional identity.

This suggests that those who ran provincial newspapers believed that they could exploit a unique local appeal. But in this context, the emphasis historians have tended to place upon the inclusion of local advertising and local news in provincial newspapers to explain their popularity may not tell the whole story. There were other, less obvious, editorial strategies to promote sales. One of these concerns the large coverage given to national and foreign news. Whereas the local news carried might appear uncontroversial and non-political in nature for most of the eighteenth century (although, as we shall see, its importance should not be discounted), the former, at least in so far as national affairs were concerned, was nearly always openly political and frequently partisan in tone. The lack of overt political bias evident in the local news published by many provincial papers may have stemmed from

96. Barker, *Newspapers, Politics, and Public Opinion*, p. 126.

a wariness on the part of eighteenth-century publishers not to offend people in local positions of influence coupled with more practical constraints upon newsgathering and writing imposed by a lack of staff. However, the situation may have been more complex than that. Jonathan Barry has argued that the apparent lack of discussion about local politics is illusory. In the case of Bristol he has argued that 'much of [the news] concerned with apparently remote matters of diplomacy or court intrigue, was intended to trigger responses which hardly required detailed comment'. Moreover, such techniques also allowed opposing groups to draw their own interpretations, and thus allow newspapers to appear unpartisan: often of great advantage to a printer.[97] By the late eighteenth and nineteenth centuries, provincial newspapers were generally more openly engaged in local politics and commonly criticised local government, promoted local concerns and commented on national issues from a local perspective. Thus in Oxford in the early nineteenth century, both *Jackson's Oxford Journal* and the *Oxford Herald* were frequent critics of the local corporation.[98]

As we have already seen, even if editorial control did not stretch as far as actually producing the coverage of national news in provincial newspapers independently for much of our period, it did seem to govern the choice of material. Like Jonathan Barry, John Money has taken issue with the idea that the provincial press was merely a register of local information and yesterday's events and that, in consequence, provincial opinion was no more than a delayed and passive replica of attitudes in the capital. He has argued that printers could play to a public already hostile to the ministry by extracting material from the most sensational productions of the London opposition press, and traces this tradition of opposition to government amongst the Midlands' papers to as early as the 1730s. In addition, he has outlined the particular political differences which existed between the various Coventry and Birmingham newspapers in the 1760s and 1770s, whilst his study of Birmingham and the West Midlands as a whole has shown that provincial opinion here had its own dynamic which did not necessarily follow that of London.

97. Jonathan Barry, 'The press and the politics of culture in Bristol, 1660–1775', in Jeremy Black and Jeremy Gregory, eds., *Culture, Politics and Society in Britain, 1660–1800* (Manchester, 1991), p. 70.

98. Rosemary Sweet, 'Reform and renewal in urban government: Oxford corporation before 1835', unpublished paper.

Other strategies which the producers of provincial newspapers appear to have used to increase their audience were more explicitly localised in their appeal. The local news columns of papers often carried regular reports of matters which would have been of particular interest to those in the area, such as crop prices or shipping and racing news. Moreover, although the 'news' itself in such local sections often (although by no means always) appeared uncontroversial, this was frequently not the case with the letters published by provincial newspapers. These could concern both local and national politics and might be highly partisan in tone. The letters were supposedly from local readers and often carried signatures and used modes of address which emphasised their local provenance and appeal. For example, 'A Man of Kent', who wrote frequently to the *Kentish Gazette*, addressed his letters 'to the freeholders of Kent' and 'the gentlemen of the county of Kent'. Readers of the *York Chronicle* read appeals to 'the independent gentlemen, clergy, and freeholders of the county of York ... ' from 'a fellow freeholder'. As is the case with such letters in the London press, whether or not they can be termed 'genuine' is perhaps not as important as the sense of immediacy between a paper and its readership which they would have enhanced. At no time would this have been more evident than during elections, when most provincial papers would be full of reports, letters and advertisements concerning local politics. In places where the election was contested, readers were also supplied with regular reports of the state of local polls and predictions of the results. Most of this material presumed to satisfy a very local appeal, and much of it addressed all or part of the local readership directly.

The importance of local news is clear in David Ayerst's examination of the *Manchester Guardian*. He notes that the editions which sold best between 1838 and 1840 were those concerning local politics, and especially the Anti-Corn Law League, when Manchester readers could see their names in print. Editions which covered Queen Victoria's wedding or the fall of the Melbourne government were certainly popular, but did not challenge reports of the League, or indeed of local disasters such as a hurricane in 1839 and a fire at the Macintosh factory in 1838.[99] According to William Hunt, a reporter for the *Plymouth Times* in the 1840s, the paper's sales could be dramatically increased by certain local events such as the building of a railway. The reports of one particularly

99. Ayerst, *Guardian*, p. 84.

stormy meeting in Bristol concerning a new railway was said to have led to a quadrupling of sales.[100]

Provincial newspapers produced in the same town were typically politically opposed, unless they somehow avoided direct competition, for example, by coming out on different days. According to Jonathan Barry, the political stance of Bristol printers was a 'crucial issue' in the eighteenth century, and the town's deep political and religious divisions were clearly represented in the newspapers it supported.[101] Similarly, the *York Gazetteer* declared in 1741 that it had been started 'to correct the weekly poison of the *York Courant*'.[102] The *Manchester Herald* was founded in 1792 by the Manchester Constitutional Society, because the town's other papers, the *Mercury* and the *Chronicle*, refused to publish any radical material,[103] whilst in Leicester, the *Leicester Journal* became more conservative in its politics in response to the formation of two new radical papers in the town, although the *Journal* still remained fiercely independent and very critical of the Tory corporation.[104]

According to Derek Fraser, 'the press of Leicester in the first half of the nineteenth century had one over-riding characteristic, it was fiercely partisan'.[105] Just as the *Leicester Journal* had insisted on its independence in the eighteenth century, so George Stretton, the editor of the *Nottingham Journal*, refused the advances of local Tories in 1812 to act as a vehicle for their propaganda, despite his sympathy for their cause. A new Tory paper, the *Gazette*, was launched as a result, but this failed within two years.[106] In Maurice Milne's examination of Sunderland newspapers in the early nineteenth century, he asserts that the success of individual papers was due in part to their politics, the nature of which would determine the number of readers they could attract. 'Political content was so integral to a Victorian newspaper', Milne argues, 'that absence of an editorial line was unlikely to command respect, allegiance, or assistance in time of trouble.'[107] Derek Fraser blames the worsening

100. Hunt, *Then and Now*, pp. 17–21.

101. Barry, 'The press and the politics of culture in Bristol', pp. 57–60.

102. Black, *English Press*, p. 22.

103. Archibald Prentice, *Historical Sketches and Personal Recollections of Manchester* (London, 1851), p. 5.

104. Derek Fraser, 'The press in Leicester c. 1790–1850s', *Transactions of the Leicestershire Archaeological and Historical Society*, **xlii** (1966–7), pp. 53–4.

105. Fraser, 'The press in Leicester', p. 68.

106. Derek Fraser, 'The Nottingham press 1800–1850', *Transactions of the Thoroton Society*, **lxvii** (1963), p. 48.

107. Maurice Milne, 'Survival of the fittest? Sunderland newspapers in the nineteenth century', in *Victorian Periodical Press*, p. 214.

fortunes of the *Nottinghamshire Mercury* in the late 1840s on the inconsistency of the paper's politics under a new editor, Thomas Bailey, who was described by a rival paper as 'everything by turns and nothing long'. Sales plummeted after Bailey took over, and the paper ceased publication in 1852.[108]

It was not only through their contents that a paper's politics could be proclaimed. Martin Smith has described how provincial newspaper offices in the 1790s were often used to deposit petitions. Thus Solomon Hodgson of the *Newcastle Chronicle* helped collect signatures for an anti-slavery petition in 1792, and for another against the Two Acts in 1795 (just as his predecessor, Thomas Slack, had collected money for the Bill of Rights Society's collection in aid of John Wilkes twenty years earlier).[109] Similar services were also carried out by the more radical papers in Sheffield, Chester and Manchester. The offices of radical papers were also used as centres for the collection of money for various political causes. In 1794, for example, newspapers in Cambridge, Newcastle and London were involved in a subscription fund to help defray the expenses of those prosecuted in the treason trials of that year, whilst others were designated agents in 1798 by a committee which aimed to raise money to relieve the families of those held in detention after the suspension of habeas corpus.[110]

However, despite the overriding importance of political stance, the use of such editorial strategies did not necessarily mean that newspapers were consciously targeted at particularly narrow groups. Provincial newspapers in particular were often keen to appeal to a broad spectrum of opinion. Besides, many newspaper readers would have looked at more than one paper. Thus Hogarth's 'Midnight Modern Conversation' from 1733 shows a coffee-house crowd reading both the pro-Walpole *London Journal* and the decidedly oppositional *Craftsman*, whilst a letter from 'Impartial' in the *St. James's Chronicle* in 1780 remarked: 'As I think it fair to hear both sides in every dispute, I take in a news-paper which professes to be an advocate of the Court, and one which stands up a Champion for the People.'[111] Charlotte Brontë noted that her family also bought newspapers with differing politics. In 1829 she wrote: 'We take two and see three newspapers a week. We take the *Leeds Intelligencer*, Tory, and the *Leeds Mercury*, Whig .... We see *John*

108. Fraser, 'The press in Leicester', p. 62.
109. Wilson, *Sense of the People*, p. 342.
110. Smith, 'English radical newspapers', pp. 115–16.
111. *St. James's Chronicle*, 17 August 1780.

Bull; it is a high Tory, very violent. Mr. Driver lends us it...'[112] But since political contents were clearly so crucial to securing readers, it was important that the press as a whole displayed a diversity of political stances and a varying intensity of party political loyalty in order to satisfy its entire audience.

The editor's role was crucial when it came to deciding a newspaper's politics. Michael Harris argues that different proprietors allowed editors differing degrees of independence in this matter. The *Grub Street Journal*'s editor, Richard Russel, for example, was apparently kept under close supervision in the early eighteenth century, with the proprietors organising weekly meetings to decide the paper's contents. The same was true of the *General Evening Post* in the later eighteenth century. According to Harris, such behaviour was motivated by the fear of prosecution.[113] Yet it was certainly not the norm. For most papers, the editor was largely responsible for what appeared in print. This is not to say that editorial control was foolproof. Occasionally references were made to material which was published without the editor's knowledge (although these are not always very convincing). In January 1724, for example, Nathaniel Mist claimed that an offensive letter had appeared in his paper when printers had searched a drawer in his office to find extra copy. Thomas Read denied any knowledge concerning a paragraph placed in the *St. James's Evening Post* in 1729, claiming that it had been inserted by a journeyman whose name he did not know.[114] At Henry Bate's trial for a libel on the Duke of Richmond in 1781, Robert Haswell, the paper's printer, claimed that paragraphs often appeared without Bate seeing them, since 'the Editor's office was a common room, dedicated to the business of the Morning Post' and, 'a great variety of persons came into it occasionally'.[115] John Almon maintained that one of 'Junius's' letters was placed in the *London Museum* in 1770 whilst he was out of town,[116] and that in 1788, a paragraph which attacked the King was inserted in the *General Advertiser* also without his knowledge.[117]

As we have seen, without a clear political line a paper could be in trouble. This was far more likely to happen without effective

---

112. Lucy Brown, *Victorian News and Newpapers* (Oxford, 1985), p. 27.
113. Michael Harris, 'The management of the London newspaper press in the eighteenth century', *Publishing History*, 4 (1978), pp. 104–5.
114. Sutherland, *Restoration Newspaper*, p. 215.
115. *Morning Post*, 24 June 1780.
116. John Almon, *The Memoirs of a Late Eminent Bookseller* (London, 1790), p. 62.
117. Almon, *Memoirs*, p. 136.

editorial control. William Jerdan worked on the short-lived daily newspaper the *Aurora*, which appeared for only a few months in 1781. He blamed its failure on management by committee, rather than by one editor, or as he put it a 'despotic power'.[118] The *Aurora* had been set up as a business venture by a group of hoteliers and inn landlords from the West End. Jerdan commented:

> ... our rulers of the hotel dynasties, though intelligent and sensible men, were neither literary not conversant with journalism; thus under any circumstances their interference would have been injurious, but it was rendered still more fatal by their differences in political opinion, and two or three of the number setting up to write 'Leaders' themselves. The clashing and want of *ensemble* was speedily obvious and detrimental; our readers became perfect weathercocks, and could not reconcile themselves to themselves from day to day. They wished, of course, to be led, as all well-informed citizens are, by their newspaper; and they would not blow hot and cold in the manner prescribed for all the coffee-room politicians in London.[119]

James Montgomery blamed his early lack of success with the *Sheffield Iris* in the 1790s on similar problems. Years later he commented that he had 'lost 1,000 subscribers in the first year, for I was too moderate for the Jacobins, and yet with the aristocratic party, I was reckoned a Jacobin...'[120] In 1830 the *Maidstone Gazette* proclaimed that 'The success which attends the course of the *Maidstone Gazette* we feel convinced is mainly attributable to the integrity and consistency of its principles.... Tory we are, Tory we still are, and Tory we shall remain...'[121]

Throughout our period there were newspaper editors whose personal political beliefs permeated the newspapers which they produced. In the case of eighteenth-century Bristol, Jonathan Barry has argued that many of the printers were committed partisans, or were sponsored to represent specific positions, whose rivalries were stimulated by competition, but cannot simply be explained in these terms.[122] Edward Baines, who ran the *Leeds Mercury* between 1801 and 1833, was a committed reformer who was active in Leeds

---

118. William Jerdan, *The Autobiography of William Jerdan* (4 vols. London, 1832), i. 89.

119. Jerdan, *Autobiography*, i. 89–90.

120. M.E. Happs, 'The Sheffield newspaper press and parliamentary reform, 1787–1831' (Oxford BLitt thesis, 1973), p. 96.

121. Kenneth J. Eaton, 'Newspapers and politics in Canterbury and Maidstone 1815–1850: opinion in two Kentish towns' (University of Kent MA thesis, 1972), p. 55.

122. Barry, 'The press and the politics of culture in Bristol, 1660–1775', p. 62.

politics and in campaigns against slavery and in favour of municipal reform. He was the principal speaker at parliamentary reform meetings in 1817, and became a Liberal MP for Leeds in 1833.[123] His views were clearly expressed through his paper. Similarly R.K. Douglas, who took over the *Birmingham Journal* in 1833, was first Chairman of the Chartist Convention and Secretary to the revived Political Union. Under his leadership, the paper was turned into a 'political clarion'.[124]

Yet so long as the views promoted secured a favourable public response, a politically committed editor could be a positive advantage to a paper. Being run by an individual with a powerful public political profile, such as John Almon, William Cobbett or Feargus O'Connor, served to reinforce the readers' response to a particular paper and to attract new readers. As Aled Jones has argued, the political identity of newspapers sprang not just from the beliefs of editors and proprietors, but also because 'editors calculated that a political "badge of belonging" might retain for their titles both a readership and an advertising base'.[125] Hence James Perry's constant advocacy of Whig principles kept the *Chronicle* in the public eye as the leading opposition paper in the 1790s and early eighteenth century. According to Asquith, Perry 'was as much an ardent Foxite as he was a businessman',[126] yet despite his allegiance, Perry still responded to his paper's decline in the later 1790s by moderating his paper's political opinions, 'doubtless partly to avoid alienating readers'.[127]

Conclusion

The increasing profitability of newspapers in the eighteenth and nineteenth centuries, driven largely by rising sales, led to a growth in the scale of newspaper production. For the most part, this did not stem from the introduction of new technology, but rather increases in newspaper personnel and with it greater job demarcation and specialisation. Provincial newspapers did not experience

123. Edward Baines, Jr., *The Life of Edward Baines* (London, 1851).

124. Asa Briggs, 'Press and public in early nineteenth-century Birmingham', *Dugdale Society Occasional Papers*, **8** (1949), p. 9.

125. Jones, *Powers of the Press*, p. 141.

126. Asquith, 'Advertising and the press in the late eighteenth and early nineteenth centuries', pp. 719 and 709.

127. Asquith, 'James Perry and the *Morning Chronicle* 1790–1821', p. 75.

the same degree of change as in the capital, but expansion did occur outside London. The way in which news was gathered also developed during our period, and greater use was made of paid reporters, both at home and abroad. However other sources, such as foreign newspapers, remained constant throughout the eighteenth and nineteenth centuries.

It has been argued that the importance of sales to newspaper profits forced papers to echo the political views of their readers in order to thrive. This was true not in London alone, but also in the provinces, where individual papers appealed to the uniquely localised nature of public opinion. A paper's political stance was thus crucial to its success, and the role of the editor was of vital importance in directing what that stance should be. In some cases, editors were politically active outside their involvement with their newspapers, but so long as such behaviour met with popular approval this could be a positive selling point for papers. Clearly the relationship between newspapers and public opinion was of great importance then, not just to newspapers, but to politicians and newspaper readers too.

PART TWO

Newspapers and Politics

Introduction

From the early eighteenth century, newspapers encouraged the wider population to take an interest in politics and even to play a part in it. The political information which the newspaper press imparted, coupled with the intense debate which it promoted, helped to bring politics out of the restricted arena of the political and social elite and into a much wider public sphere. Moreover, through the promotion of certain concepts of English liberty, in particular the belief that English men and women were free citizens living in a free state, newspapers encouraged the public to believe they had not just the opportunity, but the right, to involve themselves in the nation's political life and to protest when they disapproved of government action. Indeed, the press itself was to become the principal medium in which to articulate and disseminate protests against the government, and played a crucial role in the political education and politicisation of the English people.

As towns across the country witnessed a growth in population, newspapers helped promote a new political culture which encouraged individuals outside the political elite to form independent political organisations and to develop further notions of their own rights and liberties. This was particularly striking outside London, where increasingly during the eighteenth and nineteenth centuries both the performance and the identity of urban local authorities became the subject of intense scrutiny and fierce debate. Many towns witnessed growing demands to remove ruling oligarchies and to replace them with local government structures which were more representative of the local population. Over time, criticism of central government also developed into full-scale national movements which aimed to change the way in which society was run. As we shall see, newspapers both represented and helped to further such movements in crucial ways. However, it would be a mistake to assume that all newspapers were necessarily progressive and reforming. Although some historians in the past have depicted the press as part of an inevitable drive in British political life towards a more

democratic and free society, such a Whiggish teleology is misleading. Newspapers were not always radical or forward-looking in their
outlook. Throughout our period, the newspaper press could also be
a powerful force of conservatism. In common with the wider
popular political world of which they were part, newspaper politics
could be both complex and contradictory, as the following chapters
will show.

It is clear, then, that newspapers, and indeed print culture as a
whole, played an increasingly important role in English political life
as our period progressed. However, historians of the press must be
cautious not to ascribe to newspapers a degree of political power
they did not have. In contrast to the late twentieth century,
newspapers in the eighteenth and early nineteenth centuries did
not – as a rule – dictate to individual politicians or governments, nor
could they effect policy changes on a day-to-day basis. The power of
the press, and of public opinion itself, was still relatively weak,
but this does not mean that the press did not influence politics at
all. A fundamental acknowledgement that government was based
on consent meant that sucessive administrations were neither
unaffected by newspapers, nor were they unbending in the face of
popular protest. As we shall see, the political elite became increasingly sensitive to the tenor of extra-parliamentary politics and, on
certain occasions, particularly during periods of political crisis, the
press played a decisive role in altering or promoting existing
governmental policy. Moreover, as speeches made in parliament,
at election hustings and in public meetings became more
commonly reported, speakers at such events were increasingly aware
that their message would be conveyed to a much wider audience,
and, as a result, often modified what was said. As our period
progressed, the frequency with which newspapers influenced political decision-making, and the degree of impact which the press had
on the general political climate, became more and more marked.

In part, this development was related to the increased prominence of print culture as a whole in English political life. However,
the place of newspapers in the hierarchy of political print also
changed significantly during our period. In the early part of the
eighteenth century, newspapers carried little comment on political
events, but were preoccupied with conveying the most basic information on domestic occurrences and news of foreign affairs. Their
value to readers lay in the contemporaneity of their reporting,
rather than their interpretation of events. This latter function of
providing a commentary on current affairs and actively contributing

to public debate was a task fulfilled by pamphlets, alongside other forms of print such as handbills, song-sheets and satirical prints or cartoons. Of course newspapers did not necessarily need to make explicit political remarks to influence public opinion: their very choice of news could be comment enough. But as the political content of newspapers both grew and changed over time, so the prominence and influence of the newspaper press increased in relation to other forms of political print. This was not a swift process. By the mid-eighteenth century, newspapers were still not the most important forum for public debate. Pamphlets were still prominent, and would continue to be so, but the weekly essay paper was arguably more influential: so much so that newspapers began to copy from these sources and to paraphrase their contents.

But by the 1770s another shift was occurring. The essay paper was on the decline after the 1760s, and although pamphlets were still hugely important during the American war, they were being slowly eclipsed by newspapers, which were now not only providing their readers with the most up-to-date news, but were also publishing their own commentary on events. Moreover, the extensive publication of letters meant that the relationship between readers and the political opinions espoused by newspapers appeared to be particularly close, a fact which made them more attractive to their audience. By the 1780s, newspapers had emerged as a force to rival all other forms of political print. Their dominance of the popular political sphere was reinforced by the part they played in several nationally-based extra-parliamentary campaigns in the 1780s and 1790s, in particular the parliamentary reform and anti-slavery movements, and in the role of the press in the fierce political debate surrounding the French Revolution. From this point on, newspapers increasingly dominated public debate: a situation which was not to change until the late twentieth century.

CHAPTER SIX

1695–1759

In the late Stuart period, public opinion emerged as a powerful and unpredictable force. At moments such as the Exclusion crisis, the Glorious Revolution and after the Triennial Act of 1694, politicians had to cope with mass demonstrations and expressions of popular political sentiment.[1] Even with its dramatic appearance, it is arguable, especially in comparison with later periods, that popular sentiment had only a limited impact on the way in which the country was run. For much of the period, government was decided by a tight circle dominated by the court and the aristocracy. Indeed, many of the public outcries which did take place were constructed and encouraged by members of the social and political elite, rather than stemming spontaneously from those out-of-doors. However, despite the political dominance of a small class, the secretive and traditional form of politics which they practised was increasingly under attack from a popular print culture which espoused openness, was often critical of government and during periods of acute political crisis was able to influence the way politicians chose to act. Thus on a few notable occasions in the first half of the eighteenth century, popular protests – and newspapers – made a decisive impact on government policy. Moreover, even if popular opinion was sometimes orchestrated or influenced by an elite, the fact that it was useful, appropriate or necessary for them to do so was arguably more significant. Whether 'genuinely' extra-parliamentary in origin or sponsored by the political elite, popular opinion

1. T. Harris, *London Crowds in the Reign of Charles II: Propaganda and Politics from the Restoration to the Exclusion Crisis* (Cambridge, 1987); William Speck, 'The electorate in the first age of party', in C. Jones, ed., *Britain in the First Age of Party 1680–1750* (London, 1987); Mark Knights, *Politics and Opinion in Crisis, 1678–81* (Cambridge, 1994).

emerged as an important factor in the nation's political life and the newspaper press was increasingly associated with the formation and articulation of such sentiment.

From the late seventeenth century, several of the capital's newspapers were overtly political. The first London daily, the *Daily Courant*, was Whig in its politics, as was George Ridpath's *Flying Post* and John Tutchin's *Observator*, whilst Abel Roper's *Post Boy* was a Tory paper, and so too were William Pittis's *Heraclitus Ridens* and Charles Leslie's *Rehearsal*.[2] As we shall see, the partisan nature of the majority of London newspapers never really changed. Throughout the eighteenth and nineteenth centuries, newspapers in the capital were vocal in their political allegiances and proved themselves to be fierce critics of those of whom they disapproved. The same was increasingly true outside London, where provincial newspaper readers were accustomed to such divisions from an early date. Thus in 1710, Sir John Verney was persuaded to continue sending copies of London newspapers to a poor woman running a coffee-house in Stony Stratford in Buckinghamshire because a neighbouring coffee-house was supplied by Verney's political rival.[3]

Indeed, 1710 witnessed one of the earliest instances in which popular politics and political print had a significant impact on eighteenth-century political life. A year earlier, the Reverend Henry Sacheverell was impeached by the Whig government for preaching a sermon in which he denied the right of resistance to a legitimate monarch and so, ministers thought, questioned the legitimacy of the Glorious Revolution of 1688. The government's action against Sacheverell provoked much public hostility. When the impeachment proceedings took place at Westminster in 1710, they were accompanied by great public disorder. Sacheverell was found guilty, but was only banned from preaching for three years. Alarmed by the popular criticism which it had attracted, the government feared that anything more severe might have provoked even more serious disturbances. Instead, the country witnessed widespread celebrations as a result of Sacheverell's 'victory'. In such circumstances, Defoe's advice in the *Review* to 'laugh at him, let him alone', predicting that by these means Sacheverell would 'vent his

2. William Speck, 'Politics and the press', in Michael Harris and Alan Lee, eds., *The Press and English Society from the Seventeenth to Nineteenth Centuries* (London, 1986), p. 47.

3. H.T. Dickinson, *The Politics of the People in Eighteenth-Century Britain* (Basingstoke, 1995), p. 23.

gall, and then he'll be quiet'[4] seemed unconvincing (though had that been his advice before impeachment it might have made sense).

Perhaps as many as 100,000 copies of the printed version of Sacheverell's sermon were circulated,[5] and these were soon joined by several hundred pamphlets, sermons and books concerning the controversy. Although they contributed to the debate in a limited way, in relation to other forms of print newspapers did not give the Sacheverell controversy a great deal of coverage and indeed paid far more attention to foreign news. However, the trial did not pass unnoticed by the newspaper press: its dates were published and on 6 March the *Daily Courant* noted that a clergyman had been sacked by the Bishop of London for praying for Dr Sacheverell 'as a person under persecution'. The *Evening Post* further reported Sacheverell's guilty verdict, as well as the riots that ensued.[6] Newspapers therefore did not keep the public abreast of the debates surrounding the Sacheverell controversy, but they did inform it on a daily basis of basic developments in a way that less frequently published printed matter could not.

The Sacheverell trial greatly influenced the general election which followed a few months later, in which many Whigs lost their seats. In the City of London, the Tory candidates advertised in the newspapers for support. They denied Whig accusations that they were either Jacobites or Papists, and accused the existing government of risking both Church and state in their pursuit of power.[7] The *Norwich Gazette* reported that the triumphant Tory candidates were chaired around the town with pictures of Charles I, Queen Anne and Sacheverell carried on poles in front of them.[8] The Whig/Tory divisions concerning Sacheverell which were evident in the press at the time of the trial were still clear three years later when his suspension from preaching was lifted. The *Post Boy* reported a 'joyful celebration' on a national scale, and noted that 'the prodigious Multitude of his Congregation is inconceivable to those who did not see it'. The *Worcester Post-Man* also remarked on the nationwide rejoicing. Three years later, the same paper

4. G. Holmes, *The Trial of Doctor Sacheverell* (London, 1973), p. 76.

5. Holmes, *Trial of Doctor Sacheverell*, p. 75.

6. *Evening Post*, 21 March 1710.

7. Mary Ransome, 'The press in the general election of 1710', *Cambridge Historical Journal*, **6**, 2 (1939), p. 219.

8. Nicholas Rogers, *Whigs and Cities: Popular Politics in the Age of Walpole and Pitt* (Oxford, 1989), p. 311.

reported that the government was still trying to smear the doctor.[9] The *Flying Post*, on the other hand, described disparagingly 'a very great Mob' who had come to hear him.[10]

However, the continuing debates over the rebel cleric were soon overshadowed by the much greater spectre of Jacobite rebellion. During the first half of the eighteenth century the Hanoverian succession was seriously threatened by the ousted Stuarts and their supporters, the Jacobites. James II had fled to the continent in 1688 rather than face William of Orange's invasion forces, yet he and his followers did not relinquish his claim to the throne. In 1715, and again in 1745, serious attempts were made to topple the Hanoverian monarchy by force. In both cases, the majority of domestic support came from Scotland, with most English men and women apparently less than eager for a restoration of the Stuart line. Supporters of the Pretender were further hampered by a lack of unity and the failure of adequate assistance from abroad, yet Jacobite sentiments continued to pervade British society for many years. The culture of Jacobitism could be found equally in polite society and amongst the lower orders, in part because it was an extremely flexible creed, which could be taken up by those with a variety of grievances against the Hanoverians. However, amongst the lower orders in particular, the use of Jacobite slogans and songs during times of riot and popular unrest should be seen as a means of protesting against the iniquity of the social and legal system, as much as a sign of a genuine wish to restore the Stuarts to the throne.[11]

During the early eighteenth century, Tory newspapers were credited with 'keep[ing] up the spirit of Jacobites and ... inflam[ing] the Mob against the Governement and all good Subjects'. Yet As Kathleen Wilson points out, papers such as the London *Post-Boy*, the *Bristol Postman*, *Worcester Postman*, *Newcastle Courant* and the *Norwich Gazette* all published details of the Whig offensive against Jacobitism and the ineffectual nature of the Tory response, as much as they sympathised with the Jacobite cause.[12] Indeed, most English newspapers were supportive of the Hanoverian

9. G.A. Cranfield, *The Development of the Provincial Newspaper* (Oxford, 1962), pp. 118–19.

10. William Bragg Ewald, *The Newsmen of Queen Anne* (Oxford, 1956), pp. 77–8.

11. Nicholas Rogers, 'Popular disaffection in London during the forty-five', *London Journal* (1975) and 'Popular disturbances in early Hanoverian London', *Past and Present* (1978).

12. Kathleen Wilson, *The Sense of the People: Politics, Culture and Imperialism in England, 1715–1785* (Cambridge, 1995), pp. 112–13.

regime. In Norfolk, William Chase, printer of the *Weekly Mercury or Protestant Packet*, used his paper to disseminate Whig propaganda and attack Tory-Jacobite plots to subvert the constitution.[13] The Exeter paper, the *Protestant Mercury*, warned the 'good people of England against the abominations of Popery, wooden shoes [a reference to the French] and the Pretender'.[14] In London, the *Daily Courant* published a loyal address to the King from Hastings which expressed the freeholders' 'utmost indignation' that the Pretender 'should entertain Thoughts of invading your Dominions'.[15] It was soon followed by addresses from Northampton, Lincoln, Bedford and Kent,[16] and helped to present a picture of national unity against the Jacobite threat.

In 1745, during the second serious Jacobite rebellion, the English press was even more emphatic in its rejection of Jacobitism, particularly after the defeat of Hanoverian forces at Prestonpans on 21 September shocked and alarmed the whole country. All the capital's newspapers were firmly behind the Hanoverian regime. The *General Advertiser* and the *Penny London Post* even printed the slogans 'No Popery', 'No Pretender', 'No Arbitrary Power', 'No Slavery' and 'No Wooden Shoes' in the margins of their front pages.[17] Anti-Jacobite sentiment was often fused with English bigotry: hence the *General Evening Post* described the rebel army on 26 October 1745 as 'a bloody Host of Robbers from the woods and Bogs of *Ireland*, Droves of Savages from the Rocks and caverns of the *Highlands*, void of letters, and, even of Humanity, armed with Ignorance, Brutality, and barbarous zeal...'[18]

To reinforce anti-Jacobite sentiment in both London and provincial papers, various items of loyalist propaganda were printed, including anti-popery essays, espiscopal letters to clergy, extracts from anti-Jacobite pamphlets, broadsides, speeches and letters. *Felix Farley's Bristol Journal* of 7 September 1745, published a letter which proclaimed:

> Let every true *Briton* put his Hand on his own Breast and ask himself, whether he thinks he should enjoy the like [liberty and property], under an arbitrary tyrannical Power? And such a one as undoubtedly

13. Wilson, *Sense of the People*, p. 381.
14. Cranfield, *Development of the Provincial Newspaper*, p. 119.
15. *Daily Courant*, 10 August 1715.
16. *Daily Courant*, 22 and 23 August 1715.
17. Bob Harris, *A Patriot Press: National Politics and the London Press in the 1740s* (Oxford, 1993), pp. 193–4.
18. Harris, *A Patriot Press*, p. 214.

we must be under, if ever the present *Pretender* to the throne should ever sit thereon. But GOD forbid that ever any *Popish* Arbitrary Prince should rule over us![19]

In addition, provincial papers published reports of local loyalist associations, loyal demonstrations and addresses. The Bristol *County Advertiser*, for example, described celebrations in the city on 5 November when effigies of the Pope, the Pretender and the Devil were paraded through the town followed by standard-bearers carrying banners with the mottoes 'No Slavery', 'No Pretender' and 'No Arbitrary Power'. At the end of the procession, said to be attended by 'many thousands of the Populace', the effigies were burnt.[20]

With the fortunes of both sides constantly changing during the 1745 rebellion, newspapers became a particularly valuable source of up-to-date information, and their popularity and influence grew as a result. Bob Harris has shown how provincial newspapers in the North and Midlands were often better placed than their London counterparts to exploit private or semi-official sources of information about the '45. Newcastle newspapers in particular had the advantages of proximity to Scotland and the fact that the city was a major mobilisation point for the military forces under General Wade. The three Newcastle papers thus became important sources of information for the London press and for other provincial newspapers.[21]

The London press printed a number of letters from inhabitants of Edinburgh, Carlisle and Derby, all towns whose loyalty had been called into question by their capitulation to, or supposed support of, the Pretender on his march southwards. Such pieces were sent to declare the anti-Jacobite sentiments of the towns involved.[22] According to Harris, whilst there were divisions at local levels, provincial papers 'may well have contributed to the creation of something of an illusion in late 1745: the illusion that most Britons were able to sink their differences in an apparently spontaneous outpouring of public support for the Hanoverian and Protestant succession'.[23] The *Westminster Journal* described the role of the

19. Harris, 'England's provincial newspapers and the Jacobite rebellion of 1745–1746', *History*, **80** (1995), pp. 12–13.
20. Harris, 'England's provincial newspapers and the Jacobite rebellion', pp. 13–14.
21. Harris, 'England's provincial newspapers and the Jacobite rebellion', p. 8.
22. Harris, *A Patriot Press*, p. 203.
23. Harris, 'England's provincial newspapers and the Jacobite rebellion', p. 16.

press at the height of the Jacobite rebellion more favourably on
12 July 1746:

> It was at this Time, if ever, that the Liberty of the Press was the great
> Palladium of our other Liberties. All who made use of it, except those
> who had engag'd to be the Engines of Destruction, turn'd it to awaken
> a too secure and drowsy People. They accomplished their Design, as
> soon appear'd in the spirit of zeal and loyalty that was every where
> diffused.[24]

Between the first and second Jacobite rebellions, the newspaper
press had clearly assumed a higher profile in England and was
taking a more active role in opinion-forming. Moreover, it was able
to present a picture of national unity to its readers which would also
have to have been self-fulfilling and thus a significant boost to the
anti-Jacobite cause.

Yet despite the frequency with which anti-Jacobitism was
expressed by newspapers during the attempted invasions of 1715
and 1745, and the undoubted importance of such coverage in
promoting public hostility towards the Stuarts and their supporters,
some Jacobite sentiments were still evident in certain sections of the
press throughout the first half of the eighteenth century. Nathaniel
Mist's *Weekly Journal*, for example, ran for twenty years, first as *Mist's
Weekly Journal* and then as *Fog's Weekly Journal*. During its boldest
stage between 1720 and 1723, the paper's title illustration included
a figure surrounded by rays of light – a representation of James III
as a sun-god – with the caption 'Advenit Ille Dies' [that day is
coming]. In the provinces, Henry Crossgrove's *Norwich Gazette*
(1715–43) and Elizabeth Adam's *Weekly Courant* in Chester were
also known for their Jacobite sympathies. In addition, periodicals
such as the *Freeholder's Journal* (1722–3), *Common Sense* (1737–9),
the *National Journal* (1746), the *Mitre and Crown* (1748–50) and the
True Briton (1751–3) were associated with Jacobitism.[25] For much of
the early eighteenth century it is also true that newspaper hostility
towards the Hanoverian monarchs was common, even in papers
not associated with Jacobitism. British public opinion was not
impressed by George II's conscientiousness as a monarch or bravery
as a soldier. As Paul Langford has noted, 'In the gutter press he was
treated with open contempt. His sexual habits were mocked, his

24. Harris, *A Patriot Press*, p. 215.
25. Paul Monod, *Jacobitism and the English People 1688–1788* (Cambridge, 1989),
pp. 29–30, 78.

personal foibles, especially his irascibility, derided.'[26] As we shall see, it was not until the later part of his successor, George III's reign that significant sections of the English press began to champion the King. An examination of newspapers and Jacobitism thus reveals the contradictory and complex nature of public opinion, as well as providing some evidence of the role that newspapers played in influencing it.

The potential of the newspaper press to shape opinion was not lost on the most prominent politician of the early eighteenth century, Sir Robert Walpole, who attempted to use it to consolidate his power. However, despite his best efforts to tar all his opponents with a Jacobite brush, a lively opposition press still emerged from the later 1720s which was not generally Jacobite, but which challenged his rule as one of corruption and undue influence. Two of Walpole's greatest and most famous critics were William Pulteney and Lord Bolingbroke, who joined forces in the essay paper, *The Craftsman.* They espoused 'country' politics, as opposed to those of the court, and campaigned for shorter parliaments and against both a standing army and Walpole's corrupt use of the Crown's influence. As H.T. Dickinson has shown, they were not alone in their attacks on Walpole, and the majority of the provincial press was largely hostile towards the Prime Minister, often reprinting material from journals such as *The Craftsman* to prove it. The assault on Walpole involved many of the most prominent provincial papers, including the *York Courant, Newcastle Journal, Exeter Journal, Chester Courant, Norwich Gazette, Farley's Bristol Newspaper, Worcester Journal* and *Jopson's Coventry Mercury.* The *York Courant* was perhaps the most openly opposed to Walpole, and from 1729 on it reprinted the leading article from *The Craftsman* each week.[27]

For the most part, the constant tirade of press criticism which Walpole encountered did not seem to affect his rule. Thus Walpole's premiership outlived papers such as *The Craftsman,* which folded in 1736, and he survived general elections, the accession of a new king and scandals such as the South Sea Bubble crisis. But Walpole was profoundly affected when press criticism coincided with particularly powerful bursts of public sentiment, most notably in 1733 and between 1739 and 1740. The first of these accompanied the Excise crisis of 1733–4. Walpole had hoped to abolish

---

26. Paul Langford, *A Polite and Commercial People: England 1727–1783* (Oxford, 1989), p. 35.
27. Dickinson, *Politics of the People in Eighteenth-Century Britain,* pp. 206–7.

Land Tax by increasing the excise on tobacco and wine, yet the uproar which this action caused took the government by surprise. Fifty-four counties and boroughs sent formal constituency instructions against the measure to MPs and the country was flooded with pamphlets, broadsides and newspapers condemning Walpole's actions. As the *London Evening Post* noted, 'the *Sense of the People* in general is against the Promoters of the Excise and other pernicious Projects'.[28] The *Weekly Worcester Journal* asserted that there was no other cry heard 'than what is the *universal Voice of the People* throughout the kingdom, *No Excise, Liberty and Property*'.[29] Horror stories exploited fears that the extensive powers of search given to revenue officers would put traditional privacy over property at risk and that the right to trial by jury was also under threat.

One of the causes of both the wave of alarm which swept the country and Walpole's ultimate and humiliating defeat was the advance news of the scheme disseminated by the press, and by *The Craftsman* in particular, during the winter of 1732. Rumours spread like wildfire in the newspapers, where they were copied assiduously. According to the government paper, the *London Journal*, 'had not some Gentlemen, *out of Power*, set up *Incendiary Journals* to *deceive* and *inflame*, not one Man in a thousand would have said a Word against the Administration'.[30] As in London, provincial papers such as the *Gloucester Journal*, published reports of meetings held by merchants and traders across the country and warned readers of the dangers of the Excise Bill. According to one report of a meeting in Southwark, the measure would prove 'highly prejudicial to the Trade, Manufactures, and Navigation, as well as dangerous to the Liberties of the whole Kingdom'.[31] In Norwich, the Tory printer Henry Crossgrove kept the readers of the *Norwich Gazette* informed of anti-excise developments across the country as well as local initiatives to contest the next election on an anti-excise ticket.[32]

Once the constituency instructions to MPs began to appear, these too were published by opposition newspapers, as were lists showing how individual MPs voted when the measure was presented in parliament.[33] An address from the inhabitants of Rye in Sussex to

28. Wilson, *Sense of the People*, p. 128.
29. *Weekly Worcester Journal*, 12 October 1733.
30. Paul Langford, *The Excise Crisis: Society and Politics in the Age of Walpole* (Oxford, 1975), p. 48.
31. *Gloucester Journal*, 16 January 1733.
32. Rogers, *Whigs and Cities*, p. 326.
33. Speck, 'Politics and the press', p. 57.

their MPs which appeared in the *Gloucester Journal* warned that such a measure would 'create a Murmering and Dissatisfaction amongst many Wellwishers to the present happy Establishment'.[34] The *Newcastle Courant* reported that a meeting of the principal merchants and traders in the town culminated in the lighting of 204 candles [the number who had voted against the Excise Bill in parliament] in honour of the 'WORTHY PATRIOTS, who for the LIBERTY of their COUNTRY, and for the GOOD of TRADE, made so glorious a STAND against the Increase of Excise Laws'.[35] In response to newspaper attacks on one ministerial candidate, an electoral agent of the Duke of Dorset wrote in 1733 to complain: 'The enclosed Canterbury newspaper (which is dispersed over the county) will do us a great deal of mischief unless the edge of it be taken off by something handsomely written on the other side.'[36] In the same year another government supporter in Sussex bemoaned the lack of supportive newspapers there: 'I wish we had some proper news Papers etc: to disperse here ... We have no news Papers here except the London Journal on our side tho' the Craftsman is very industriously sent down to the Tory Coffeehouse every weeke.'[37]

Most contemporary accounts would seem to back the *London Evening Post*'s claim that 'no other Cry is heard than what is the universal Voice of the People throughout the Country, No Excise, Liberty, and Property'.[38] Indeed, when the London *Daily Courant* made disparaging remarks about the merchants who opposed the bill, it was burnt in the city by the common hangman.[39] The withdrawal of the scheme prompted widespread public celebration, confirming, Paul Langford asserts, 'that perseverance would have been dangerous indeed'.[40] In the aftermath of the agitation, *The Craftsman* claimed that 'The *Spirit of Liberty* is not yet extinct in this Kingdom ... the original Power of the People, in their collective Body, is still of some Weight, when vigorously exerted and united'.[41] Although Walpole survived, he lost the clear support of

34. *Gloucester Journal*, 6 March 1733.
35. Rogers, *Whigs and Cities*, p. 374.
36. Jeremy Black, *The English Press in the Eighteenth Century* (Beckenham, 1987), p. 136.
37. Cranfield, *Development of the Provincial Newspaper* p. 21.
38. G.A. Cranfield, 'The "London Evening Post", 1727–1744', *Historical Journal*, 6 (1963), p. 24.
39. Rogers, *Whigs and Cities*, p. 53.
40. Langford, *Polite and Commercial People*, pp. 30–1.
41. Wilson, *Sense of the People*, p. 134.

the electorate and the propertied public to which he could lay claim before. During the 1734 general election, the Excise Bill was still an important issue and greatly affected the government's electoral standing. This, the Duke of Dorset did not hesitate to blame on the popular resentment created by the bill.[42] In the most populous constituencies, those MPs who had voted for the excise found themselves in serious trouble.[43] According to the *London Evening Post*:

> despite the vain Boastings of the Friends of the Excise Scheme ... For tho' your little Boroughs are venal and corrupt, almost all the Counties in England are sound and untainted, as may be seen by those Counties which have already elected the Representatives; which plainly shows that the Sense of the People in general is against the Promoters of the Excise and other pernicious Projects.[44]

Although Walpole remained in power, his majority in parliament was much reduced and he was left with very little room for manoeuvre.

Between 1738 and 1742, Walpole was again subjected to a popular and broad-based anti-ministerial coalition, this time deeply critical of his conduct regarding Spain. Whilst Walpole favoured a peaceful policy, much of the rest of the country was more bellicose, with attacks on British trade being held up as a just cause for war. In 1738, petitions from London, Bristol, Glasgow and Liverpool were accompanied by well-orchestrated press campaigns. Against the backcloth of further public hostility in 1739, Walpole narrowly secured a majority in the Commons to ratify a treaty with Spain. This prompted another round of protests, and by the end of the year war was formally declared. Walpole was deeply unhappy, but was powerless in the face of both a parliamentary opposition and a public clamouring for war and whose mood had infected some of his colleagues in government. According to *The Craftsman*:

> The general Cry is *War, Revenge on the Spaniards, Restitution for past Losses, Satisfaction to our National Honour*, and above all, *ample Security to our future Trade and Navigation* – The *Country Gentlemen* and *Farmers* who are distress'd with *peaceable* Taxes, pray for an *honourable* and *vigorous* War. The *Merchant*, who is always the greatest Sufferer upon such Occasions, is in the same Disposition, and ready to sacrifice his present Profit to the future Interest of his Country. The poor *Tradesman*,

---

42. Dickinson, *Politics of the People in Eighteenth-Century Britain*, p. 52.
43. Langford, *The Excise Crisis*, p. 139.
44. Cranfield, 'The "London Evening Post", 1727–1744', p. 27.

Mechanick, and *Husbandman,* who can hardly supply their Families with the Necessaries of Life, seem willing to part with their last Mite in this glorious Cause. Our *Sailors,* both *Officers* and *private Men,* are alert, and want nothing so much as an Opportunity of revenging themselves on their *cruel Enemies.* – What can any *Minister* desire more in his Favour? [45]

Provincial papers such as the *York Courant* joined the cries of the London newspapers for war with Spain and the end of corruption at home. [46] In 1740, the Bishop of Chester complained to the Duke of Newcastle of 'the unwearied industry of some to poison the common people with ill thoughts of the Administration'. 'This poison is', he claimed, 'chiefly conveyed by a course of newspapers dispers'd all over these and neighbouring parts. We have a printing press here at Chester, another at Manchester, another at Leeds, and other places, all under the direction of seditious and disloyal men, scattering their papers all over the country at low prices ... The authors pick their news out of the London prints, and take care to publish everything that is against the government, but give by half, or with some sneer, whatever is favourable to it.' [47]

Much of the popular opposition to Walpole focused on the figure of Admiral Vernon, the hero of the naval success against the Spanish at Porto Bello in 1739. When news of his victory reached England in March 1740, public celebrations were held in his honour. Vernon was fêted by merchants in particular, but he was popular amongst a much wider section of society since, like Drake and Raleigh before him, he represented 'the intrepid naval commander of a Protestant island battling the Catholic foe'. [48] Moreover, as a former MP and vocal critic of the government, he was a powerful focal point for opposition to Walpole's ministry: a patriotic antidote to Walpolean corruption. As the *London Evening Post* argued in April 1740, 'a certain great Man should interpret all the *Applauses* heap'd upon Admiral Vernon as so many *Satires* upon himself'. [49]

Newspapers played a key role in championing Vernon's cause. In 1741, for example, the *Norwich Gazette* recorded a procession in Wymondham in Norfolk to celebrate another of Vernon's victories at Cartagena. The *Gazette* asserted that 'the whole was the general sense and free Act of the People, being in no way promoted by any

45. Cranfield, 'The "London Evening Post", 1727–1744', p. 29.
46. Cranfield, *Development of the Provincial Newspaper,* pp. 132–3.
47. Dickinson, *Politics of the People in Eighteenth-Century Britain,* pp. 206–7.
48. Gerald Jordan and Nicholas Rogers, 'Admirals as heroes: patriotism and liberty in Hanoverian England', *Journal of British Studies,* **28** (1989), pp. 205–6.
49. Cranfield, 'The "London Evening Post", 1727–1744', p. 29.

leading Gentleman'.[50] The paper also published a poem dedicated
to Vernon, which exhorted Britons to view with awe 'this Son of
Freedom ... Who Midst Corruption uncorrupted stood/His Heart
and Hand devoted to your Good'.[51] The press as a whole was full of
reports of Vernon's successes, and newspaper reports were accompanied by pamphlets, prints, poems and ballads. Vernon was exalted
as 'the incarnation of British liberty and patriotic virtue ... who
dared to stand up to the Catholic powers of Europe'.[52] Huge
celebrations were organised in 1741 to mark his birthday, and as
with John Wilkes some twenty years later, his image was commemor-
ated on plates, bowls, teapots and other pottery objects – all part,
claims Wilson, of 'a vigorous national political culture focused on
Admiral Vernon'.[53] 'The geography of support for Vernon', she
argues, 'clearly evinces the tentacular reach of the press, provincial
and London, and the widespread audience for news in urban centres
in the "pre-radical" period of British politics.' Indeed, the newspaper press not only acted to disseminate news of Vernon's exploits,
but also endowed them with specific political significance.[54]

Walpole's standing did not improve once war was declared.
Indeed, his position became increasingly untenable as his conduct
of the war came under attack. Again, part of the pressure on him
came from newspapers. The *London Evening Post* claimed that 'it is
as common for them [the Spaniards], notwithstanding the War, to
drink *Don Roberto's* Health, as it is his Catholick Majesty's; tho'
some Wags have upon this jocularity replied, *They have good Reason
for that: they know their Friends.*'[55] In March 1741, the *Weekly Worcester
Journal* published a poem 'proper enough for this tempestuous
season' in which Britain was compared to a ship, and Walpole to its
incompetent pilot:

> See how BRITANNIA labours in the storm
> Tho' greatly shock'd, still of Majestick form
> Collected in her Strength, Still lives her CREW
> Tho' sorely troubl'd, yet of courage true
> Not so the Pilot, by whose blunders she
> Thus drives, all trembling, all counfounded he

50. Wilson, *Sense of the People*, p. 143.
51. Rogers, *Whigs and Cities*, p. 337.
52. Wilson, *Sense of the People*, p. 143.
53. Wilson, *Sense of the People*, pp. 145–52.
54. Kathleen Wilson, 'Empire, trade and popular politics in mid-Hanoverian
Britain: the case of Admiral Vernon', *Past and Present*, **121** (1988), p. 92.
55. Cranfield, 'The "London Evening Post", 1727–1744', p. 30.

The poem predicted that once the pilot was thrown overboard by the crew, the storm would cease.[56] Such was the weight of public opinion against Walpole that the Duke of Newcastle predicted that 'If we go on despising what people think and say, we shall not have it long in our power to direct what measures shall be taken'.[57]

Walpole's fall from office in February 1742 was due in part to the abortive attack on Cuba in late 1741, which was blamed on the government's failure to send Vernon sufficient support. The *Daily Post* reported on 17 December that letters from Vernon declared that 'he has zealously labour'd for the Glory and the Good of the Nation, as long as he thought himself in a Condition to do so', but having sailed to Cuba he had found himself 'destitute of Necessaries to finish his Expedition with Glory'. Nothing in defence of the government appeared in the paper to counter Vernon's claims. Celebrating Walpole's political demise, the *Worcester Journal* observed: 'we may affirm there never was a more general Joy than that which appear'd even upon the Rumour of a late resignation.' According to Wilson, 'it was one of the many occasions in the eighteenth century when the "sense of the people" had direct and material results, despite the structural odds against its doing so.'[58] Walpole's downfall was as much the result of popular hostility outside parliament as it was a more powerful opposition within it. As we have seen, much of this popular hostility was directly related to newspaper coverage.

Nor did press attacks against Walpole end at this point. The *London Evening Post* expressed typical fury and demanded an inquiry into Walpole's rule: 'Should any Great M–n–st–r, after a blundering Administration of twenty Years', the paper asked, 'be permitted at last to retire with the Spoils of his Country; and without mentioning the immense Sums he has in that Time squander'd, enjoy at Ease the vast Fortunes he has rais'd, the stately Palaces he has built ... and for his glorious Services created a [Peer] of the Realm...?'[59] The *Champion* noted:

Since the late change in our councils, the Cry of Vengeance against those who have so long and so notoriously abused the K–––, and oppress'd his people, has seem'd to prevail above every other

56. *Weekly Worcester Journal*, 26 March 1742.
57. Nicholas Rogers, 'Resistance to oligarchy: the city opposition to Walpole and his successors, 1725–47', in John Stevenson, ed., *London in the Age of Reform* (Oxford, 1977), p. 9.
58. Wilson, *Sense of the People*, p. 163.
59. Cranfield, 'The "London Evening Post", 1727–1744', p. 35.

consideration; not only public papers, instruction, etc., being full of it, but almost every mouth in every company.[60]

In the provinces, the *Norwich Gazette, York Courant* and the *Stamford Mercury* all reacted angrily to the creeping realisation that Walpole would not be punished. The *Stamford Mercury* noted bitterly: 'we have seen the P[rerogative] R[oya]l brought into Play to force the only Means out of our Hands which could have thrown the necessary Light upon these dark and iniquitous Transactions.'[61]

The degree of popular unrest provoked by Walpole's government was not repeated for many years. Indeed, Nicholas Rogers has argued that following the '45, urban radicalism outside London was dampened for a time by the growth of oligarchy in some provincial towns. Thus one finds the last two episodes to be examined in this chapter – popular clamour over the Jew Bill in 1753, and attacks on the administration for the loss of Minorca in 1756 – were more London-focused that had been the anti-Walpole sentiment in the 1730s and 1740s.[62]

The Jewish Naturalisation Bill was introduced in 1753 with a general election due the following year. Although it was relatively modest in its scope and passed easily through parliament and onto the statute book, the measure provoked a flood of anti-Semitic feeling: in the press, in petitions and in popular demonstrations and riots. Much of this was whipped up by newspapers. The *London Evening Post*, for example, ran a major campaign against the bill, described it as a fillip to Jewish financiers expert in 'the Mysteries and Iniquities of Stock-Jobbing', and to those who had acquired 'Vast Estates by plundering the public'. Another writer in the paper predicted that 'When the M[iniste]r has the riches of the Jews always at hand, he is deliver'd from all dependence on the Commons, and can, as he likes, either buy a Majority of the House, or send them to their homes, and order Jewish Centinels to keep Watch over them.'[63] Yet another correspondent warned of Britain being swamped by Jews: 'their numbers shall pour in upon us, from all Parts of Europe, to be naturalis'd, and those Numbers daily

60. Bob Harris, 'The London press, popular power and the fall of Sir Robert Walpole (1741–1742)', in Karl Schweizer and Jeremy Black, eds., *Politics and the Press in Hanoverian Britain* (Lewiston, NY, 1989), p. 63.

61. Cranfield, *The Development of the Provincial Newspaper*, p. 134.

62. Nicholas Rogers, 'The urban opposition to Whig oligarchy, 1720–1760', in M. Jacob and J. Jacob, eds., *The Origins of Anglo-American Radicalism* (London, 1984), pp. 141–6.

63. Rogers, *Whigs and Cities*, p. 90.

acquire more Wealth and Strength, more Influence and Interest and Power.'[64]

The *Post* produced the most hostile accounts of Jews and Judaism in the capital, and its extensive use by the provincial press meant that its stories were spread across the whole country.[65] Philip Yorke wrote from Wrest in Bedfordshire:

> We do not talk quite so much about the Jew Bill as you do in Town and yet I find upon enquiry that People have received the same bad impression of it. How should it be otherwise? The *London Evening Post* is retailed in the *Northampton Mercury* and the riders who are employed by the dealers in town to transact with the county shopkeepers, bring down with them specimens of their politics as well as their goods.[66]

Like most other provincial newspapers, the *Cambridge Journal* also campaigned against Jewish naturalisation. It proclaimed the Jews to be 'alone of all Animals, when harbour'd and well treated, grow more venomous and cruel'.[67] *Jackson's Oxford Post* had a similar approach. Throughout 1753 it printed letters opposing the legislation and published many reports critical of Jews and accusing them of crimes such as theft, fraud, usury and violence against Christians. On one occasion the paper carried a report of the traffic in stolen goods in the capital, and commented that 'Numbers of Jews are employed in this vile traffick – pretty fellows indeed, and very proper for naturalization!'[68]

Newspapers which opposed the Act encouraged candidates for the forthcoming general election to speak out against it and voters to back those who had not supported its passage in parliament.[69] Numerous candidates placed advertisements in the newspapers avowing their consistent opposition to the measure or recanting their earlier allegiance.[70] Faced with widespread disapproval, compounded by several instructions to MPs and violent rioting, Pelham's government felt its parliamentary position weakened and was forced to repeal the Act. As Paul Langford notes: 'If Pelhamite government was an oligarchy, it was evidently one which

64. G.A. Cranfield, 'The "London Evening-Post" and the Jew Bill of 1753', *Historical Journal*, **viii**, 1 (1965), p. 21.

65. Cranfield, 'The "London Evening Post", 1727–1744', p. 20.

66. Karl Schweizer and Jeremy Black, eds., *Politics and the Press in Hanoverian Britain* (Lewiston, NY, 1989), p. viii.

67. Cranfield, *Development of the Provincial Newspaper*, p. 138.

68. Thomas W. Perry, *Public Opinion, Propaganda, and Politics in Eighteenth-Century England: A Study of the Jew Bill of 1753* (Cambridge, Mass., 1962), pp. 95–100.

69. Perry, *Public Opinion, Propaganda, and Politics*, p. 136.

70. Perry, *Public Opinion, Propaganda, and Politics*, p. 137.

was remarkably sensitive to the opinions of those whom it governed.'[71] In parliament Earl Hardwicke, the Lord Chancellor, admitted that 'however much the people may be misled, yet in a free country I do not think an unpopular measure ought to be obstinately persisted in'.[72] Indeed, well in advance of the 1754 general election, the Duke of Newcastle warned that the furore over the measure would affect constituencies in the West Riding of Yorkshire. The Bishop of Oxford predicted in June 1753 that 'the Bill for permitting Jews to be naturalized hath not only raised very great clamours amongst the ignorant and disaffected, but hath offended great numbers of better understandings and dispositions, and is likely to have an unhappy influence on the elections of the next year'.[73] In the event, it was an issue at several election contests across the country.[74]

Whilst the government survived the 1754 election, it was brought down two years later when public opinion was aroused by the loss of Minorca. Initially, the government was able to blame Admiral Byng for the defeat, and carefully edited extracts of Byng's correspondence were published in the *Gazette* which suggested that he bore sole responsibility. According to Nicholas Rogers, such misinformation had the desired effect initially, but the opposition press soon began to blame the ministry as well as Byng for the island's fall.[75] Alongside pamphlets, a prominent section of the capital's newspapers fully exploited the government's embarrassment and demanded an inquiry into the alleged mishandling of the situation. Marie Peters describes how using 'a variety of devices – letters, paragraphs of comment, full reporting of all moves to instruct or address and constant assertions of the right of the people to speak out – the *London Evening Post* kept up its campaign, with warm support from the *Gazetteer* and *Monitor*'.[76] 'Britannicus', writing in the *London Evening Post*, was keen to link Byng's failure with that of the ministry, and spoke of the loss of Minorca as 'a certain Event of the Treachery, Negligence, or Incapacity of those who were entrusted with Power'.[77]

71. Langford, *Polite and Commercial People*, p. 225.
72. Dickinson, *Politics of the People in Eighteenth-Century Britain*, p. 212.
73. Perry, *Public Opinion, Propaganda, and Politics*, p. 135.
74. Dickinson, *Politics of the People in Eighteenth-Century Britain*, pp. 52–3.
75. Rogers, *Whigs and Cities*, pp. 95–6.
76. Marie Peters, *Pitt and Popularity: The Patriotic Minister and Public Opinion during the Seven Years War* (Oxford, 1980), pp. 48–52.
77. Wilson, *Sense of the People*, p. 183.

Opposition papers in the capital were joined in their effort to vilify the government and implicate it in the naval failure by newspapers across the country, which described how effigies of Admiral Byng and government ministers were burnt in public displays of resentment. The *Salisbury Journal* noted how in Devizes, 'an Effigy most finically dress'd, and emblematically ornamented, to shew the reverse of a Hero ... was advanc'd to Haman's Height on a Gibbet ... and then cut down and burnt amidst a vast concourse of People, loudly exclaiming against Treachery and Cowardice, the Bane of our Liberties'.[78] Petitions and instructions to MPs began to flood in from across the country, and these too were given full coverage by the newspaper press. Admiral Byng was eventually executed and, despite his parliamentary backing and royal support, Newcastle was forced to resign.

The King then had to accept William Pitt as leader of the government since he was able to command popular support. Indeed, Pitt's claim to 'popularity' was a substantial element of his political strength[79] and clinched his reinstatement in 1757 after he was temporarily replaced. According to Paul Langford, the importance of 'opinion out of doors' should not be underrated when considering the actions of the politicians involved. 'There is no denying the essential fact', he argues, 'the he [Pitt] owed his victory in 1757 first and foremost to his credit outside the restricted world of Whitehall and Westminster'.[80] In part, such credit stemmed from the support which he received from the newspaper press, who chose to champion the 'Great Commonor'. As we will see in the next chapter, when Pitt lost this support, his reputation and political power were seriously affected.

Conclusion

This chapter has shown that popular clamour had a limited effect on government prior to 1760, but that it could make a difference at times of political crisis. During such periods, newspapers gained increasing prominence, although they were still not as important as pamphlets or essay papers in influencing the nature of public debate. The newspaper press was involved in the Sacheverell

78. Wilson, *Sense of the People*, p. 180.
79. Peters, *Pitt and Popularity*, p. 1.
80. Paul Langford, 'William Pitt and public opinion, 1757', *English Historical Review*, **88** (1973), p. 54.

agitation at the start of the century, and played an important part in publicising and promoting anti-Jacobite sentiment in the face of the 1715 and 1745 rebellions (although it is also true that a small section of the press helped keep loyalty to the 'king across the water' alive). Newspaper involvement in the anti-excise agitation of 1733–4 was more emphatic and contributed to the government's abandonment of its new taxation plans, as well as seriously weakening Walpole's grip on power.

Walpole came under attack again between 1738 and 1742 over his Spanish policy when the newspaper press championed Admiral Vernon as the antithesis of Walpolean corruption and narrow self-interest. The failed attack on Cuba proved to be the final straw for many and helped to topple Walpole's government. Finally, the 1750s witnessed a campaign against the Jewish Naturalisation Act in which newspapers encouraged a wave of anti-Semitic sentiment, and in 1756, the administration's unpopularity over the loss of Minorca meant that the war with Spain had cost Britain another government. William Pitt was the beneficiary, since his popular support ensured him a place in government.

CHAPTER SEVEN

1760–1786

The accession of George III in October 1760 is often presented as heralding a new phase in British history. In particular, his reign has been linked to a growth in radical dissent and the increasing involvement of 'the people' in the nation's political life. In both cases, the newspaper press is seen to have played an important role. However, not every historian is convinced of the novelty of politics under George III. Linda Colley, for example, has argued that the 1760s did not witness the beginning of focused radicalism in Britain, and that parliamentary reform arguments were being rehearsed long before that.[1] Indeed, as we saw in the last chapter, the popular voice was active in English political life from the early part of the eighteenth century. There are good grounds to see some of what happened in the later part of the eighteenth century as a continuation of earlier developments. However, there are also convincing arguments to differentiate the later period, particularly in terms of the increased coherence and prominence of extra-parliamentary movements after 1760. Moreover, such differences may well have been more marked in the provinces, where Nicholas Rogers has suggested that local oligarchies which had pre-dominated during the previous two decades were increasingly challenged by a more independent and egalitarian form of politics.[2] What is not in doubt is that the short-term aims of various reform movements between 1760 and 1789 ultimately failed, but that by the end of the period, there had emerged a more politically

1. Linda Colley, 'Eighteenth-century English radicalism before Wilkes', *Transactions of the Royal Historical Society* 5th ser., **31** (1981).
2. Nicholas Rogers, 'The urban opposition to Whig oligarchy, 1720–1760', in M. Jacob and J. Jacob, eds., *The Origins of Anglo-American Radicalism* (London, 1984), pp. 141–6.

informed public with a wider social base. This was a transformation in which newspapers played an important part.

We have already seen how the newspaper press of the earlier part of the century could, at certain times, prove both very hostile or extremely supportive of particular politicians. This would result either in great discomfort or increased confidence for the individual involved, and also allowed the press to exert a degree of political influence. As we saw in the last chapter, William Pitt was one politician who benefited from his treatment prior to 1760. However, during the second year of George III's rule, Pitt lost this traditional source of support and fell foul of both the press and public opinion. The cause of this abrupt turnaround was Pitt's acceptance of a peerage for his wife and a £3,000 annuity for himself upon his resignation from the government in October 1761. As a result, the 'Great Commoner' became the Earl of Chatham. Rumours concerning Pitt's honours circulated on the day before they were officially announced, but were widely contradicted by the capital's papers as 'a design to tarnish the lustre of a certain great character'. When the *Gazette* published the true story an observer in Dick's coffee-house noted that 'it was really diverting to see the effect it had upon most people's countenances ... it occasioned a dead silence, and I think every body went away without giving their opinions of the matter.'

The official announcement was met with a flurry of newspaper paragraphs and pamphlets attacking Pitt's decision. The *London Evening Post* predicted that the 'idol of the People' would become 'the Object of their Execration'.[3] Some commentators at the time, and a few historians since, have blamed the King's favourite, the Earl of Bute, for these attacks. However, it seems unlikely that Bute was wholly responsible.[4] It is far more probable that Pitt fell victim to an outpouring of genuine popular outrage. As the *Monitor* later admitted, 'a general stagnation of sentiment' towards Pitt took place.[5] Eventually, Pitt was able to rescue the situation by publishing a letter in his defence in the *Public Ledger*. All 3,000 copies of the paper were sold before noon and it was quickly reprinted by the

3. Nicholas Rogers, *Whigs and Cities: Popular Politics in the Age of Wapole and Pitt* (Oxford, 1989), p. 120.

4. Karl W. Schweizer, 'Lord Bute and the press: the origins of the Press War of 1762 reconsidered', in Karl W. Schwiezer, *Lord Bute: Essays in Re-interpretation* (Leicester, 1988).

5. Marie Peters, *Pitt and Popularity: The Patriotic Minister and Public Opinion during the Seven Years War* (Oxford, 1980), p. 208.

Gazetteer and other papers.[6] His popularity in the City was thus restored, though it remained shaky elsewhere, and his reputation and political strength were adversely affected.[7] The incident served as a warning to others of the fragility of public support and the speed with which the press could turn on a former champion.

Perhaps no one individual became more aware of the potential fury of press attacks in the second half of the eighteenth century than the Earl of Bute. When George III came to the throne he appointed Bute, his former tutor and trusted adviser, to the cabinet. In 1762 Bute became First Lord of the Treasury following the resignations of William Pitt and the Duke of Newcastle. As a political leader, he was outstanding only in terms of his unpopularity. At least in part, this was his own fault: not only did Bute broker a widely criticised peace with France, but as a promoter of royal prerogative and independence he became a symbol of the King's supposed attempts to subvert the constitution by increasing the influence of the Crown. But Bute was also attacked in ways which seem less fair: he was a Scot, which brought out the worst in English bigotry, and the Earl, having the unfortunate surname of Stuart, was linked to both Catholicism and Jacobitism. On top of that, rumours abounded of his supposed affair with the King's mother.

In June 1762, the first appearance of the essay paper, the *North Briton*, marked the beginning of a flood of anti-Bute propaganda. Within weeks, the London newspaper press was filled with attacks on Bute and numerous pamphlets appeared whose authors were eager to pour scorn on the King's favourite. According to John Brewer, 'nearly every paper – with the exception of the *London Chronicle* – was dominated by correspondence that was overwhelmingly anitpathetic to the favourite and predisposed to Wilkes and the opposition'.[8] Indeed, there was much in the newspapers that was hostile to Bute, although a lot of this material was taken from journals such as the *North Briton* and the *Monitor*. Anti-Bute propaganda also spread to the provinces. According to one writer in *Boddely's Bath Journal*, Bute's nationality was enough to damn him, since 'Scotchman . . . is a Term which implies every Thing that

6. Robert R. Rea, *The English Press in Politics 1760–1774* (Lincoln, Nebr., 1963), pp. 20–1.

7. Peters, *Pitt and Popularity*, pp. 211–39.

8. John Brewer, 'The misfortunes of Lord Bute: a case-study in eighteenth-century political argument and public opinion', *Historical Journal*, **xvi**, 1 (1973), p. 16.

is vile and detestable'.[9] In addition to his vilification in newspapers and pamphlets, Bute was also famously attacked in caricatures and cartoons. At least 400 prints hostile to Bute appeared in a matter of months. One of these, Benjamin Wilson's 'The Repeal or the Funeral Procession of Miss Americ-Stamp', sold approximately 16,000 copies.[10] In the summer of 1762, Horace Walpole claimed that his father, Sir Robert, 'was not more abused after twenty years than Lord Bute is in twenty days. Weekly papers swarm, and like other swarms of insects, sting.'[11]

In the face of such full-scale abuse, Bute sought to fight back. In the summer of 1762, two new essay papers were brought out in his defence and with his backing. The *Briton* and the *Auditor* were run by hired hacks, and although concerted attempts were made to appeal to the public, neither was a great success (although material taken from them was reprinted by some daily papers). One of Bute's writers, John Campbell, also wrote letters to other London papers, particularly the *London Chronicle*, whilst Ralph Courteville wrote pieces defending Bute for the *Gazetteer*.[12] However, such efforts were generally lost in a welter of negative publicity. A braver and more robust politician than Bute might have put up with the attacks made on him, but he proved unable to stand the strain and resigned in 1763. Bute hoped to carry on influencing government from a less conspicuous position, and indeed rumours that he operated a sinister 'secret influence' circulated for the next twenty years. However, very soon any influence he had over the King had all but disappeared. It seems no overstatement to say that Bute had been hounded out of power by the combined efforts of the press. Although previous politicians had suffered in similar ways, this was the first time that print had played so prominent a role in effecting a change in government. The newspaper press was not the most prominent element in this process, but it played an important supporting role and its influence was clearly on the increase.

Whilst the press war of the early 1760s forced the Earl of Bute into the political wilderness, it helped secure one of his main critics, John Wilkes, the MP for Aylesbury, both fame and influence. Despite his personal failings and dubious commitment to the cause, Wilkes quickly became a champion of English radicalism. He did

9. *Boddely's Bath Journal*, 28 June 1762.
10. Brewer, 'The misfortunes of Lord Bute', p. 16.
11. Peters, *Pitt and Popularity*, p. 242.
12. John Brewer, *Party Ideology and Popular Politics at the Accession of George III* (Cambridge, 1976), pp. 222–6.

not have a radical programme as such, but was able to persuade the English people that his personal cause and that of English liberty were one and the same. By making appeals to the mass of the people, and not just the political nation in its narrower sense, Wilkes was able to create a popular movement on a national scale. Although based in the capital, the Wilkesite movement received strong support in industrial areas such as the West Midlands and the West Riding of Yorkshire, as well as in seaport towns which were traditionally politically active, including Liverpool, Newcastle upon Tyne and Bristol, and a number of market towns and cathedral cities, notably Worcester and King's Lynn. Wilkes's support came predominantly from the middling ranks of urban society: small merchants and manufacturers, shopkeepers, craftsmen and innkeepers, although those involved in Wilkesite crowds could come from much lower down the social scale. As we shall see, his success in capturing much of public opinion outside the ruling elite was given clear expression in the country's press.

Support for the Wilkesite cause was mobilised and demonstrated in a variety of ways. One of the most striking was the deployment of Wilkesite consumables, mostly decorated with the symbolic 'No. 45' (representative of the infamous issue 45 of Wilkes's *North Briton*, discussed below). Pictures, badges, cartoons, porcelain, buttons, rings and glassware were all circulated to generate excitement and demonstrate loyalty to Wilkes's cause, in a process which Brewer has described as the 'commercialization of politics',[13] and which bore striking similarities to the celebration of Admiral Vernon some twenty years earlier. But of arguably greater importance than such consumer items was the distribution of the printed word: pamphlets, squibs, songs, broadsides and, of course, newspapers. It was in these formats that descriptions of events and Wilkesite arguments spread throughout the country: a process which was promoted yet further by the adherence of many printers to the Wilkesite cause. Wilkes himself was on friendly terms with many of London's leading newspapermen, including John Almon, of the *London Courant*, Roger Thompson of the *Gazetteer*, Cuthbert Shaw of the *Middlesex Journal* and Henry Sampson Woodfall of the *Public Advertiser*.[14] Wilkes and his supporters were thus not only familiar with the way in which the press operated, but they also had many

13. John Brewer, 'Commercialization of politics', in Neil McKendrick, John Brewer and J.H. Plumb, eds., *The Birth of a Consumer Society: The Commercialization of Eighteenth-Century England* (London, 1982).
14. Brewer, *Party Ideology and Popular Politics*, p. 174.

contacts through whom they could ensure that material was published. This was something which Wilkes actively promoted; he even wrote material for publication whilst in prison.[15]

Very soon after he founded the *North Briton* in June 1762, both Wilkes and his paper had become notorious. The reputation of both was based on the *North Briton*'s scurrilous attacks on Bute and the royal family. Indeed, Horace Walpole claimed that 'The *North Briton* proceeded with an acrimony, a spirit, and a licentiousness unheard of before even in this country.'[16] The most famous edition was published on 23 April 1763. Issue number 45 of the *North Briton* attacked both the King and the handling of the Peace of Paris. 'Every friend of his country', the paper remarked sarcastically, 'must lament that a prince of so many great and amiable qualities, whom England truly reveres, can be brought to give the sanction of his sacred name to the most odious measures, and to the most unjustifiable, public declarations, from a throne ever renowned for truth, honour, and unsullied virtue.' Such comments infuriated the King and were deemed to be seditious. The Prime Minister, George Grenville, accordingly issued a general warrant for the arrest of those responsible. Although Wilkes was imprisoned, he was soon freed again on the grounds that his arrest violated his privileges as a Member of Parliament. The newspaper press fêted Wilkes as a hero. 'Truth and justice' in *Berrow's Worcester Journal* described Wilkes as attempting to 'break the Iron rod of Ministerial power', and called his cause 'the cause of Every English Subject; the Security of the whole Person, and House, is to be determined by it'.[17] The *London Evening Post* published copies of Wilkes's speeches to the court in detail, and one of its correspondents described Wilkes as 'the bold assertor of the genuine freedom of this country'.[18]

Always the self-publicist, Wilkes was determined not to let the matter rest and sued the government for trespass. His subsequent legal victory led to the ending of general warrants (see chapter 4). However, Wilkes was soon forced on to the defensive after another of his publications, the *Essay on Woman*, was deemed obscene, and he fled to Paris to escape further prosecution. In his absence, the Commons voted for his expulsion. Public sympathy for Wilkes declined during his exile, but it quickly resurged when he returned to England for the 1768 general election. Wilkes hoped that he

15. Rea, *English Press in Politics*, pp. 164–5.
16. P.D.G. Thomas, *John Wilkes: A Friend to Liberty* (Oxford, 1996), p. 21.
17. *Berrow's Worcester Journal*, 2 June 1763.
18. *London Evening-Post*, 7, 10 and 14 May 1763.

could escape the sentence of outlawry that had been passed against him if he could secure re-election. He was duly elected as MP for the populous borough of Middlesex, but immediately imprisoned on the outstanding charges of blasphemy and libel. His treatment provoked serious rioting in the capital, and in May, seven died at the 'Massacre of St. George's Field'. 'An Englishman' in the *Gazetteer* was clearly critical of the government, and described the deaths of 'English subjects, lovers of King George, unarmed, and assembled ... either in favour of liberty, or out of mere curiosity'.[19]

Wilkes's attack on the administration over the massacre provoked his expulsion from the House of Commons. A new election was called at Middlesex and Wilkes was returned once more, only to be expelled by the Commons. A bye-election was held for a third time, with the same result, only on this occasion the defeated opponent, Colonel Luttrell, was declared elected in Wilkes's place. For many this was the action of an autocratic government riding roughshod over the legitimate wishes of the people. This was certainly the view encouraged by newspaper writers. 'Decens' wrote in the *Public Advertiser.* 'When the great Pillar of public Liberty is shaken from it's [*sic*] Foundation; when the Bill of Rights is violated, and the Freedom of public Elections notoriously broke through by an Handful of corrupt Men, we may then be assured the Consummation of Despotism is at hand, and that nothing remains but to fit our Necks to the Yoke...'[20] Wilkes's struggle clearly represented wider political issues for English men and women, and even in the far North, newspaper readers were kept apprised of events in Middlesex. Indeed, the *Newcastle Chronicle* provided every purchaser of its issue of 10 June 1769 with a copy of the Middlesex petition.[21] The *Newcastle Courant* commented: 'As Mr Luttrell did not take his seat by virtue of the FREE choice of the majority of the Middlesex electors, many of the said Middlesex electors would be glad to know, whether the *elect,* or the *electors* are his constituents?'[22]

Like their London counterparts, provincial newspapers were crammed with information and debate concerning Wilkes. Of course, much of this was due to the manipulation of the press by small, dedicated groups of Wilkesite supporters such as the Bill of

19. *Gazetteer,* 21 May 1768.
20. *Public Advertiser,* 27 April 1769.
21. H.T. Dickinson, *Radical Politics in the North-east of England in the Later Eighteenth Century* (Durham, 1979), p. 5.
22. *Newcastle Courant,* 29 April 1769.

Rights Society, but there can be no doubt that this was also a sign of genuine popular support. Material taken from the London papers was supplemented by the opinions of the editor and of local correspondents, so that 'the issues of parliamentary representation, political corruption, and even that of the ballot were all rehearsed in considerable detail'.[23] Provincial newspapers published reports of radical demonstrations, as well as Wilkesite propaganda and even the Bill of Rights.[24] In the West Midlands, for example, the *Coventry Mercury* proved itself increasingly supportive of the Wilkesite cause throughout the 1760s. In May 1763, the paper reprinted Wilkes's attack on the King's speech from number 45 of the *North Briton*. Over the next eighteen months this was followed by a steady stream of pieces on the liberty of the press, general warrants and the future of English liberties. In 1768 the *Mercury* showed concern for the massacre in St. George's Field, and printed Wilkes's addresses to the Middlesex freeholders.[25] Wilkesite ideas seem to have received popular backing from newspaper readers. In July 1763, a Sussex shopkeeper and local official, Thomas Turner, recorded in his diary: 'In the even read several political papers called *The North Briton*, which are wrote by John Wilkes ... I really think they breathe forth such a spirit of liberty that it is an extreme good paper.'[26]

Although Horace Walpole claimed in 1763 that 'no citadel was ever taken by popguns', he had, as he later admitted himself, underestimated the long-term influence of Wilkesite propaganda.[27] Such propaganda was boosted from 1769 by the writings of another famous government critic, the anonymous 'Junius'. Letters from Junius first appeared in the *Public Advertiser* in January 1769, with a vigorous attack on the Grafton ministry on behalf of 'a nation overwhelmed with debt; her revenues wasted; her trade declining ... the whole administration of justice become odious and suspected to the whole body of the people'. Junius proved to be an immediate sensation and his success was further heightened at the end of the year by a letter addressed to the King, in which Junius advised him to dismiss the current administration, pardon Wilkes and 'come forward to your people. ... Tell them you are

23. Brewer, *Party Ideology and Popular Politics*, p. 176.
24. Kathleen Wilson, *The Sense of the People: Politics, Culture and Imperialism in England, 1715–1785* (Cambridge, 1995), p. 232.
25. John Money, *Experience and Identity: Birmingham and the West Midlands 1760–1800* (Manchester, 1977), pp. 64–6.
26. *The Diary of Thomas Turner 1754–1765*, ed. David Vaisey (Oxford, 1985), p. 275.
27. Rea, *English Press in Politics*, p. 37.

determined to remove every cause of complaint against your government; that you will give your confidence to no man who does not possess the confidence of your subjects.' As a result of such letters, sales of the *Public Advertiser* almost doubled.[28]

In such a climate, Wilkes's release from prison in 1770 prompted celebrations across the country. Newspapers in Newcastle and Salisbury reported local demonstrations of support for Wilkes, and the papers themselves delighted openly in his freedom. The *Leeds Mercury* reported that in Bradford a bonfire was erected with the motto: 'The scum of the earth let courtiers despise/But the scum to the top for ever will rise.'[29] The *Norwich Mercury* recorded a celebratory procession through Norwich by forty-five textile workers and a band. The *York Courant* noted that windows in the city were illuminated by forty-five candles bearing the words 'no. 45, *Magna Charta* and *Bill of Rights*'.[30]

Although the Wilkesite movement has been described traditionally by historians as pioneeringly radical, there is much that was 'patriotic, loyalist, even conservative in its ideological stance'.[31] The country platform from the earlier eighteenth century provided the basis for many Wilkesite ideas, along with a powerful dose of English nationalism – seen most clearly in the attacks made upon the Earl of Bute and the Scots, and in Wilkes's posturing as the guardian of English liberties. Yet, there were also important aspects of the movement which were truly innovative and rightly described as radical. We can see this most clearly in the popular nature of the movement, and specifically in its appeals to the wider political nation, based upon the belief in popular sovereignty. Wilkes was conscious to lay particular stress in his writings on the liberties of 'ordinary people': to confer that his was the struggle of 'the ordinary, honest citizen struggling with the ever-increasing powers of the Crown and its servants', and he thus encouraged his supporters 'to think of themselves not only as the defenders of liberty and the persecuted, but as participating vicariously in his well-publicised nose-thumbing antics against the government and civil authority'.[32] Not surprisingly, such arguments won particular favour from a newspaper press whose readership spanned a broad

28. Rea, *English Press in Politics*, pp. 174–6.
29. Wilson, *Sense of the People*, pp. 232–3.
30. Brewer, *Party Ideology and Popular Politics*, p. 179.
31. Frank O'Gorman, *The Long Eighteenth Century: British Political and Social History 1688–1832* (London, 1997), p. 226.
32. Brewer, *Party Ideology and Popular Politics*, pp. 168–70.

social spectrum. Moreover, the Wilkesite campaign, and the newspapers which helped to publicise it, served to politicise a significant proportion of the population. People were drawn into both local and national politics by a cause which raised issues about the way in which the country was governed at the peripheries, as well as at the centre. In several places, a permanent opposition emerged to challenge local elites, whilst in the capital the government of the City of London became the focus of anti-ministerial agitation. It is for these reasons that Wilkesite activity has been linked to later developments, such as movements for the abolition of the slave trade and for religious toleration for Protestant Dissenters, which will be explored in the next chapter.

From the mid-1760s onwards, Wilkesite politics became bound up with the looming crisis in America. Disquiet with British rule had been smouldering in the American colonies since the 1760s. It was evident in the débâcle over the Stamp Act in 1765, when the British government tried to make the colonists pay for the protection which British rule afforded them, further exacerbated by the attempt to raise revenue duties after 1767, and came to a climax with the Boston Tea Party of 1773 and the ensuing Coercive Acts. Armed resistance to British rule began in 1775, after which British forces and American colonists became engaged in a full-scale war. As the American crisis intensified, it was greeted with a flood of pamphlets, satirical prints and newspaper commentary. From the initial stirrings of American unrest, newspapers were full of reports of colonial developments, and later on, with the most important documents from the American Congress. Indeed, Congress explicitly planned a public relations campaign in England in an attempt to sway public opinion, and its agents in London were ordered to distribute important material to the newspapers.[33] Thus in 1775, the petition of Congress to the King, the 'Declaration of the Causes and the Necessity of Taking up Arms', the colonial appeal to the English public, 'The Twelve United Colonies to the Inhabitants of Great Britain', and most importantly, the Olive Branch petition, all received widespread coverage in the English metropolitan and provincial press.[34]

Yet such American propaganda did not go unanswered. Similarly wide coverage was given to the royal proclamation of 23 August

33. Brewer, *Party Ideology and Popular Politics*, pp. 203–4.
34. James E. Bradley, *Popular Politics and the American Revolution in England: Petitions, the Crown and Public Opinion* (Macon, Ga., 1986), pp. 91–7.

which supported the suppression of both the rebellion in America and sedition at home. The proclamation prompted numerous loyal addresses, which some newspapers had openly predicted and arguably encouraged. These addresses also received widespread coverage and in turn promoted the presentation of petitions for peace, many of which explicitly stated that the loyal addresses should not be taken as representative of public opinion.[35] Once military action commenced, most newspapers celebrated British victories. The capture of New York in 1776, for example, was greeted with delight in Bristol. *Bonner and Middleton's Bristol Journal* reported 'great rejoicings in this city and its neighbourhood. ... "God Save the King" was vociferated from all quarters, and the zeal of the populace was greater than we have remembered on any former occasion.'[36] However, defeats were also used as an excuse for the opposition to attack the administration.

H.T. Dickinson has argued that in the case of the American war, 'there are good grounds for thinking that the array of printed propaganda and other expressions of public opinion indicated majority support for the government's policies'.[37] However, it is also clear that a significant minority of the public supported the American cause, and this led to important political divisions. Certainly William Cobbett remembered the period as one of sharply divided opinions, even in rural Surrey. In his autobiography, written in 1834, Cobbett recalled his father taking him to a hop fair at Weyhill as a boy:

> a great company of hop-merchants and farmers were just sitting down to supper as the post arrived, bringing in the extraordinary Gazette which announced the victory [of Britain over the colonists at Long Island]. A hop-factor from London took the paper, placed his chair upon the table, and began to read in an audible voice. He was opposed, a dispute ensued, and my father retired taking me by the hand, to another apartment where we supped with about a dozen others of the same sentiments.[38]

A correspondent in the *Salisbury Journal* shared Cobbett's view, and wrote in March 1776: 'I Believe there is not a person in this kingdom but is more or less interested in the present struggle between us and our American Colonists, and not many so totally

35. Bradley, *Popular Politics and the American Revolution in England*, pp. 98–100.
36. Peter Marshall, *Bristol and the American War of Independence* (Bristol, 1977), p. 5.
37. H.T. Dickinson, *Politics of the People in Eighteenth-Century Britain* (Basingstoke, 1995), p. 271.
38. Wilson, *Sense of the People*, p. 237.

divested of all concern for the event, as to take no side in it; but every one seems to have attached himself to one or the other.'[39]

Newspapers from across the country both represented and helped promote very different reactions to events in America. In London the *Gazetteer* reflected the wave of indignation amongst the English propertied classes prompted by the Boston Tea Party and compared the Americans to Jacobites: 'Instead of Charles Stuart at the head of the Highland Clans, Sam Adams now led a banditti of hypocrites against Great Britain.'[40] But many others, merchants in particular, were alarmed at the prospect of war, particularly if France and Spain were involved, not least because of fears of high taxation. Complaints about the costs of war were exacerbated in the late 1770s by North's use of favoured contractors to supply materials and goods needed for the war effort, giving rise to accusations of corruption. Some argued that the war was started and sustained by greedy contractors, keen to reap the benefits of wartime spending. Many of the beneficiaries were supposed to be Scottish, hence the *Public Advertiser*'s reference to the war in February 1776 as 'this ruinous Scotch contest with the *Anglo-Americans*'.[41] A paragraph in the *London Evening Post* in March 1779 concluded that taxes were so high 'To support a most contemptible ministry in their places, and to carry on the most bloody, expensive, and impracticable war, that the nation ever was involved in'.[42]

The American crisis also generated fierce discussion about the very nature of the British constitution. Many critics of the government outside parliament supported the American challenge to parliamentary sovereignty and the principle of 'no taxation without representation'. Some were convinced of the claim made by one colonial agent, Arthur Lee, that 'the cause of *America* is the common cause of the realm ... both countries have the same complaint, and therefore claim the same friends'. Lee publicised his views by writing a series of newspaper letters under the pseudonym 'Junius Americanus'. He was joined in his endeavours by English radicals such as Thomas Hollis.[43] Others maintained – in what was a more commonly held position – that the colonists were

39. C.Y. Ferdinand, *Benjamin Collins and the Provincial Newspaper Trade in the Eighteenth Century* (Oxford, 1997), p. 167.

40. Solomon Lutnick, *The American Revolution and the British Press 1775–1783* (Columbia, Mo., 1967), p. 38.

41. John Sainsbury, *Disaffected Patriots: London Supporters of Revolutionary America 1769–1782* (Kingston, Ont., and Montreal, 1987), p. 120.

42. Sainsbury, *Disaffected Patriots*, p. 152.

43. Bradley, *Popular Politics and the American Revolution in England*, pp. 203–5.

dangerous and unjustified insurgents. It was argued that they should pay taxes to fund their own protection, and that they were represented as well as most inhabitants of Britain, who likewise did not elect their representatives directly, but were 'virtually represented' by parliament as a whole. The *Morning Post* spoke of the 'pride, hypocricy and dishonesty', which 'in the course of human events' led 'a subordinate community to shake off the duty and allegiance which in honour and in necessity they owe'.[44] One writer in the *London Chronicle*, calling himself 'Hermes', predicted that 'Unanimity among ourselves, the combined voice of the sensible and virtuous in addresses to a justly-beloved Sovereign will effectually strengthen the nerves of Government, restore order and obedience to the laws in our Colonies, and the triple-headed hydra [of opposition in England] will shrink into its original obscurity and nothingness'.[45]

Variations of opinion were evident outside the capital as well. Provincial papers such as the *Kentish Gazette, Salisbury and Winchester Journal, Norfolk Chronicle* and *Leeds Mercury* were vociferous in their support for the colonists. The *Norfolk Chronicle* of 7 September 1776 blamed the North administration for the current situation: 'Our empire is split asunder! The ties which united us are dissolved in brother's blood – and we can never again be the same people! ... Are we so destitute of all public spirit, that the authors of our calamity sleep fearless of our justice?'[46] But papers which supported government action were also published widely, such as the *Manchester Mercury, Hampshire Chronicle* and *Creswell's Nottingham, Newark and Worksop Journal*.[47] A writer to the Nottingham paper described the conduct of the American colonialists as 'insolent and dangerous', and continued: 'the late coercive laws [are] necessary; the opposition to these laws [is] rebellion; the enforcing [is] now a point of necessity.'[48] Pronounced splits were apparent in the South-West and the West Midlands, and in towns such as Leeds, Halifax and Newcastle upon Tyne.[49] The fierce animosities which existed over the American crisis, and the rival efforts which took place to mobilise public opinion, led to furious debates in the local press between rival papers. In the West Midlands, the *Birmingham Gazette*

---

44. Lutnick, *American Revolution and the British Press*, p. 75.
45. Bradley, *Popular Politics and the American Revolution in England*, p. 100.
46. Wilson, *Sense of the People*, p. 237.
47. Bradley, *Popular Politics and the American Revolution in England*, p. 91.
48. *Creswell's Nottingham, Newark and Worksop Journal*, 10 December 1774.
49. Bradley, *Popular Politics and the American Revolution in England*.

and the *Birmingham and Stafford Chronicle* were, for a period, involved in direct confrontation. Whilst the *Gazette* supported the loyalist petition sent in 1775, for example, the *Chronicle* presented the opposition case, greatly affected by mercantile interests, and linked the petition to narrow interests.[50] The Midlands readership was a knowledgeable one. From the stirrings of American resistance in the 1760s, those living in the Midlands had been kept closely informed of events by the local press. Much of the debate concerning America in the Birmingham and Coventry papers centred on the question of trade and more specifically the loss of trade for local merchants and manufacturers which a prolonged dispute would produce.[51] Newspapers in Hampshire and Wiltshire were also divided over their attitude to the war. The *Hampshire Chronicle* supported the government, whilst the *Salisbury and Winchester Journal* backed the opposition. In both counties there was much debate about the proper course of action at a local level, and public meetings to discuss possible petitions appear to have been stormy affairs, particularly in Southampton.[52]

Despite the significant numbers of English people who opposed the war, the numerous voices in favour of punitive action meant that the government could claim that the country was genuinely supportive of its measures. Yet American ideas and their resistance to 'unfair' rule did have important implications for English popular politics. In particular, arguments about representation were to be reiterated for the rest of our period. For increasing numbers of English people, virtual representation in Britain was seen to be as meaningless as it had been in colonial America. In addition, the idea that paying taxes gave one a right to direct political participation was an important development in English radical thought, and encouraged those urban and mercantile interests who began to resent the difference between their financial power and lack of political clout to demand changes in the representative system. As with Wilkesite agitation, the newspaper press served not only to disseminate such ideas, but also to encourage readers' sense of involvement in the political process.

This development was apparent again in the formation of a national reform movement in the early 1780s. The high costs of the war with America, coupled with fears that taxes were being pushed

---

50. Money, *Experience and Identity*, pp. 59–61.
51. Money, *Experience and Identity*, pp. 162–3.
52. Bradley, *Popular Politics and the American Revolution in England*, pp. 104–5.

up even further by corrupt government practices, prompted the rise of a new national extra-parliamentary campaign. The first reform agitation began in Yorkshire in December 1779, when several members of the local gentry, led by Christopher Wyvill, called a county meeting to discuss 'economical reform'. The resulting parliamentary petition, signed by over 8,000 freeholders, alleged that government squandering of public money had allowed the Crown to gain undue political influence over the House of Commons, and that traditional liberties were being threatened as a result. Such moderate proposals were soon overtaken by the more ambitious plans for parliamentary reform put forward by more radical groups in London and by the Yorkshire reformers themselves. In 1780, Wyvill and his followers began to campaign for triennial parliaments and additional seats in the Commons for one hundred 'knights of the shire' – county MPs who were believed to be particularly immune to Crown-inspired corruption. However, despite some politicians proclaiming their support for a change in the representative system, most MPs lacked the political will to produce modifications of any substance. Even Charles James Fox and William Pitt – two professed supporters of reform – seem to have lacked a real conviction to carry through reform, sufficient to survive once they achieved office.

Radical reformers, most influential in the capital, dismissed the piecemeal alterations proposed by those in Yorkshire in favour of far more sweeping plans for changes in parliamentary representation, such as annual parliaments, universal male suffrage and a more 'equal representation' of the people (to be achieved by redistributing parliamentary seats according to the size of the electorate and abolishing the notorious rotten boroughs). John Jebb, a leading light in the radical London reform movement, argued that a popular association could dictate to parliament and even supersede it if the Commons failed to represent the people.[53] Wyvill's failure to unite the movement did not augur well for its prospects of success. Despite meetings of representatives from various county associations being held in 1780 and 1781, and a renewed petitioning campaign in 1783, only minor reforms were enacted by parliament in 1782, whilst there were just fleeting prospects of legislative change in 1780, 1783 and 1785, when Burke and then Pitt introduced half-hearted and inadequately supported Reform Bills.

53. *The Works ... of John Jebb*, ed. John Disney (3 vols., London, 1787), ii. 475–81.

As with the American crisis of the 1770s, newspapers from the 1780s reflect great variations in provincial political opinion, whilst in the capital public debate was even more prone to rifts.[54] Across the country, the discussion of reform appears to have had profound implications for the way English men and women thought about the constitution, about individual rights and liberties, and about their representation in government. Between 1779 and 1785, a significant proportion of the capital's press produced a powerful and coherent argument in favour of parliamentary reform by fusing elements of an older country ideology with newer radical theories which challenged the adequacy of the Revolution Settlement. Reformist newspapers such as the *London Courant* were eager to promote the radical platform of parliamentary reform and made frequent references to the importance of restoring the ancient constitution. The call for annual parliaments was to become one of the *Courant*'s most consistent political themes. Letters from 'Alfred', 'Drusus' and 'Buckingham' not only conjured up historical ideals of freedom with their signatures, but also repeatedly demanded that elections be held every year. This, 'Drusus' claimed on 10 May 1780, in a letter to 'the People of England', was an historically-based right.[55] A writer in the *General Advertiser* stressed the need, 'at this alarming juncture', to 'stop the progress of corruption and venality, to restore the freedom of election, and the liberties of the people to their ancient purity'.[56]

The radical reforming ideas of certain prominent writers in the capital were highly influential in public debate. In April 1780, John Cartwright, John Jebb, Capel Lofft, Granville Sharp and Thomas Day formed the Society for Constitutional Information (SCI) specifically to spread propaganda in favour of a radical reform of parliament. Their aims were explicitly set out in one of the SCI tracts:

> ... the design of this Society is to diffuse throughout the kingdom, as universally as possible, a knowledge of the great principles of Constitutional Freedom, particularly such as respect the election and duration of the representative body. With this view, Constitutional tracts, intended for the extension of this knowledge, and to communicate it to persons of all ranks, are printed and distributed GRATIS, at the expense of the Society. Essays, and extracts from

54. Hannah Barker, *Newspapers, Politics and Public Opinion in Late Eighteenth-Century Britain* (Oxford, 1998).
55. See also *London Courant*, 22 March 1780.
56. *General Advertiser*, 4 January 1780.

various authors, calculated to promote the same design, are also published under the direction of the society, in several of the news-papers...[57]

For the SCI, newspapers were essential organs for the expression and dissemination of radical ideology. Jebb's letters in favour of annual parliaments and other reforms appeared in the *London Courant* and the *St. James's Chronicle* under the pseudonym 'Alfred',[58] whilst he wrote on other political issues as 'Mentor' and 'Lælius'. The SCI also used the *General Advertiser* as a vehicle for propaganda. This included placing in it extracts from Cartwright's pamphlet *Give Us Our Rights*[59] and Burgh's *Political Disquisitions*.[60] Between 1780 and 1783, the group also sent out at least 88,000 copies of some thirty-three different publications.[61]

One of the most significant developments in the radical ideology put forward by London newspapers occurred when the impetus for reform was removed from parliament and placed with the public. Although it was still largely accepted that any restructuring of the constitution would have to be a parliamentary procedure, parlia-mentary politicians were increasingly held to be too corrupt to enact such change unless powerful extra-parliamentary force was bought into play. This major shift followed the failure of the first round of petitions in 1780. Prior to this, a newspaper correspondent calling himself 'Metellus' had claimed: 'If our constitution has any chance, it is by the people resolving to demand of Parliament, a strict examination into the expenditure of public money, and a reduction in all exorbitant salaries and useless places. Then, and only then, can we hope for the Crown to be kept within its proper limits.'[62] After North had made clear his intention to resist the petitioners' calls for reform, the *London Courant* despaired at the level of parliamentary corruption, but stated that 'what the people at large will do, is not so certain. The matter now lies upon them.'[63] Similar beliefs were also

57. *Tracts Published and Distributed Gratis by the Society for Constitutional Information, with a Design to Convey to the Minds of the People a Knowledge of Their Rights; Principally Those of Representation* (London, 1783), p. i. Also cited in *Works ... of John Jebb*, i. 156.

58. See examples of letters signed 'Alfred', in *Works ... of John Jebb*, iii. 285–333, and in the following: *London Courant*, 29 January 1780, 8 February, 9 March, 24 September 1781; *General Advertiser*, 26 March 1783.

59. *General Advertiser*, 2 September 1782.

60. *General Advertiser*, 23 September 1782.

61. Edward Royle and James Walvin, *English Radicals and Reformers, 1760–1848* (Brighton, 1982), p. 30.

62. *London Courant*, 1 January 1780.

63. *London Courant*, 16 February 1780.

expressed in the provincial press. According to the *Gloucester Journal*, 'nothing but the determined resolutions of the people, the temperate and firm decisions of Englishmen, united in one plan, and pressing to one point, can save them. Thus united, thus exerting themselves, no Prince however obstinate, no Parliament however venal, can oppose or resist them.'[64] With parliamentary corruption so rife, the *Bath Chronicle* was incredulous that 'the nation should have been *deceived* by the *arts* and *interests*' of MPs for so long, and noted: 'it is hoped the people at large will now begin to think, and judge, and act for themselves.'[65] The *York Courant* acknowledged the battles waged in Parliament concerning reform, but concluded: 'it is now in the power of the People to defeat the purposes of their Constitutional Enemies, if they will stand up firm in this hour of which they may truely [*sic*] call their own.'[66]

But despite such appeals to popular sovereignty, reformist newspapers in the provinces did not display the same radical commitment of those in London. Radical arguments did appear: in the *Cambridge Chronicle* on 15 April 1780 for example, 'Alfred' described the rights of Englishmen's Anglo-Saxon ancestors and posed a series of rhetorical questions to readers, including asking whether all taxpayers should not be able to vote and if annual parliaments were not preferable to septennial. However, such ideas were expressed infrequently in provincial newspapers. In keeping with the more moderate ideas of Wyvill and his followers, the *Kentish Gazette* concluded in March 1780 that Wyvill's proposals for more equal representation, abolishing rotten boroughs and adding one hundred knights of the shires to parliament would 'fully secure the independence of parliament, and strike at the very root of corruption'.[67] Wyvill himself worked hard to try to influence the contents of the newspapers. His correspondence with the York committee's clerk, William Gray, attests to his efforts to shape the contents of northern provincial newspapers, and those of Yorkshire in particular.[68] Yet even Wyvill's Herculean endeavours could not guarantee that the York press depicted the reform movement in the manner he wished. This was especially marked when local opinion began to turn away from the movement in the mid-1780s.[69]

64. *Gloucester Journal*, 7 February 1780.
65. *Bath Chronicle*, 6 January 1780.
66. *York Courant*, 12 September 1780.
67. *Kentish Gazette*, 22 March 1780.
68. York City Archives, Acc. 1663.
69. Barker, *Newspapers, Politics and Public Opinion*, ch. 5.

In comparison to the provinces, the Wyvillite stance was rare in London papers and was certainly overshadowed not just by radical claims, but also by the weight of material published which was hostile to reform *per se*. Those papers which were opposed to parliamentary reform espoused a coherent set of arguments to defend the constitutional status quo. Newspapers such as the *Morning Post* and the *Morning Herald* maintained that prescription and practicality were much better guarantors of political stability than theoretical propositions. For all its faults or imperfections, the British constitution, as it stood, provided the best form of government possible: as the *Post* termed it, 'the best modelled constitution in the world'.[70] 'An Englishman' wrote in May 1780: 'What can be more absurd than to suppose that the resolutions of inexperience, and often of intemperance, can bear any competition with those which are debated with so much solemnity, and resolved upon with so much consideration as in the parliament of a nation?' The *Public Advertiser* claimed that 'the rage of patriotism' had deluded 'many well-meaning people' to support the petitions, with committees and associations which had brought the country 'to the very verge of a civil war...'.[71] Another recurrent theme in the conservative press was that the reform movement was the work of disappointed opposition MPs, and lacked real or valid popular support. The traditional 'high' political focus of newspapers opposed to reform placed them in stark contrast to the reformist press which concentrated so strongly on extra-parliamentary activity. On 14 December 1779, the *Morning Post* asserted that 'A flaming petition is now on the anvil, at which a certain Marquis [Rockingham] is and, the never-to-be forgotten Charley Turner [*sic*] are working day and night; it is to contain a variety of national grievances the unsuspecting freeholders of Yorkshire never even dreamt of...' It was argued that the people would not have imagined 'any public evil' if the libels circulated by the opposition had not 'set their imaginations at work, and made them dream and talk of evils which they never felt'.[72] As the *Newcastle Courant* put it, the reform movement was the result of 'dangerous and selfish views'.[73]

70. *Morning Post*, 4 April 1780.
71. *Public Advertiser*, 22 April 1780. See also 29 June 1780; *St. James's Chronicle*, 22 August 1780; *Morning Post*, 8 December 1780; *Morning Herald*, 3 and 23 January 1781.
72. *Morning Post*, 28 December 1779.
73. *Newcastle Courant*, 29 January 1780.

As was the case with the American war, fierce divisions over the issue of reform were apparent not just in the capital, but also in many provincial towns. The *Leeds Intelligencer* and the *Leeds Mercury*, for example, were deeply divided. The *Intelligencer* was staunchly opposed to the reform movement, whose ideas it claimed were 'entirely subversive of the principles of the constitution; and would, if well founded, be productive of the greatest confusion and mischief...'.[74] The *Intelligencer*'s rival, the *Mercury*, took an entirely different line. It was a staunch advocate of those involved in the reform movement, of whom it claimed 'a dignified moderation has marked their proceedings, and a steady perseverance in their original demands of redress promises a happy effect to their measures'. The paper also noted that 'it is yet some comfort that history affords no example in which the people, when under oppression, did not at length stand forth in their own cause, and in which the cause of the people did not therefore ultimately triumph'.[75] A similar situation existed in Newcastle. The *Newcastle Courant* attacked the opposition and the reformers, and on 24 March 1781 one of its correspondents commented: 'that there are at present in this country, associations of men combined for the horrid purpose of creating a civil war amongst us, is most notorious'. The *Newcastle Chronicle*, on the other hand, was highly supportive of the 'public-spirited' reformers who set 'so virtuous and patriotic an example',[76] whilst it remained critical of 'our squandering Ministry'.[77] Newspapers produced in these towns reflected bitter local political divisions in the late eighteenth century, which local historians have already noted. In Newcastle, a strong radical and Dissenting interest has been identified amongst Newcastle freemen who sought to challenge the power of the city's corporation.[78] The corporation's merchant oligarchy was also the

---

74. *Leeds Intelligencer*, 1 February 1780.
75. *Leeds Mercury*, 13 March 1781.
76. *Newcastle Courant*, 8 January 1780.
77. *Newcastle Courant*, 29 January 1780.
78. Dickinson, *Radical Politics in the North-East of England*; T.R. Knox, 'Popular politics and provincial radicalism: Newcastle upon Tyne, 1769–1785', *Albion*, **xi**, 3 (1979) and '"Peace for Ages to Come": the Newcastle elections of 1780 and 1784', *Durham University Journal*, **lxxxiv**, 1 (1992); J.E. Bradley, *Religion, Revolution and English Radicalism* (Cambridge, 1990); Wilson, *Sense of the People*, ch. 7; F. O'Gorman, *Voters, Patrons, and Parties: The Unreformed Electorate of Hanoverian England 1734–1832* (Oxford, 1989), pp. 302–4; see also [J. Murray], *The Contest* (Newcastle upon Tyne, 1774).

subject of criticism in Leeds, where a rich Dissenting elite was excluded from political power.[79]

Politicians were quick to blame newspapers for the tenor of local politics. In May 1780, Rockingham wrote to a York correspondent, John Carr, complaining of the 'radical' direction which the Yorkshire reformers were taking. Part of the cause of this he attributed to newspapers, which had helped to propagate the 'speculative propositions' of more frequent elections and the need for extra county MPs. Rockingham argued that as 'the calamities and distresses which this country now feels agitates men's minds exceedingly – reforms in the constitution are advertised in the papers either in letters or pamphlets – like quack medicines and the poor suffering patient rapidly catches at whatever is held out as a radical cure'.[80] Four years later, Rockingham's successor, Lord Fitzwilliam, received similar accounts of the undesirable influence of the press in the provinces. Richard Fenton informed him that: 'the minds of the people are so poisoned by virulent letters & paragraphs in the news papers &c &c – that it seems to be apprehended the most serious consideration will be required – whether any effectual opposition can be made at present to this much to be lamented delusion...'[81] Fitzwilliam had allied himself to a parliamentary group which was proving very unpopular. In March 1783, a political coalition was negotiated between the followers of Charles James Fox and those of Lord North. Previously enemies, the two agreed to co-operate in a bid for power. The coalition's weight of support in the Commons allowed it to form a government in spite of the King's disapproval, yet it could not win over the country at large. Given the animosity that had existed between Fox and North in the past, particularly over North's handling of the American war, the coalition was seen by many as 'unnatural'. Outside parliament there was deep shock at the apparently unabashed and unprincipled ambition which drove the formation of the new administration.

79. R.G. Wilson, *Gentlemen Merchants: the Merchant Community in Leeds, 1700–1830* (Manchester, 1971); R.G. Wilson, 'Georgian Leeds', and R.J. Morris, 'Middle-class culture, 1700–1914', both in D. Fraser, ed., *A History of Modern Leeds* (Manchester, 1980); R. Sweet, *The Writing of Urban History in Eighteenth-Century England* (Oxford, 1997).

80. Copy of Rockingham to Carr, Grosvenor Square, 22 May 1780, Wentworth Woodhouse Muniments (WWM), Sheffield City Archives, R1/1897.

81. Fenton to Fitzwilliam [Bank Top, Barnsley?], 14 March 1784, WWM F34/82.

The King admitted the coalition to office with great reluctance in April 1783, then waited for a chance to dismiss it. The defeat of the Foxite India Bill in December provided an ideal opportunity, and William Pitt was appointed as First Lord of the Treasury at only 24 years of age. His government was termed the 'mince pie administration' by its critics, because it was not thought that it could last past Christmas without a majority in the Commons. In March 1784 the King dissolved parliament and the two sides fought an historic general election campaign. Fox's supporters claimed that they fought for parliament (and by implication, the people) against an unduly powerful king who was corrupting the constitution. But this was not how it was seen by many contemporaries, who described instead a battle between a selfish aristocracy and an embattled king and his people. Although Pitt made use of Crown and government influence in the elections, there is no doubt that he had popular opinion on his side, and he won seats in some of the larger boroughs and counties. With the son of the Great Commoner on his side, rather than an unpopular Scottish aristocrat as had been the case twenty years earlier, the King won considerable public support, which the press both represented and helped to promote. The newspapers were full of loyal addresses to the Crown applauding the King's actions, and during the first three months of 1784, over 200 addresses were published in the *London Gazette*,[82] whilst petitions against the Fox–North coalition were signed by 53,500 people.[83] The *London Post* claimed that 'the political struggle in this country has hitherto been the king and mock representatives, called the House of Commons against the people: witness the Middlesex election, American war, and every other business in the present reign. The case is now altered; the king and people are united against the mock representation, who speak the voice of the people as much as a Polish Diet does the sense of the people of America.'[84] The *Public Advertiser* claimed that 'A majority in favour of the Ex-Ministry is certainly to be found nowhere but in the House of Commons. In all the great cities, and the principal manufacturing towns, the same sentiments are breathed as in the great metropolis; notwithstanding all the *expensive arts* of Opposition.'[85]

82. Dickinson, *Politics of the People in Eighteenth-Century Britain*, p. 276.
83. John Cannon, *The Fox–North Coalition* (Cambridge, 1969), p. 188.
84. *Morning Post*, 27 February 1784.
85. *Public Advertiser*, 3 March 1784.

From his York home, Stephen Croft warned Lord Fitzwilliam that 'the cry against Mr Fox is most astonishing, I see it strong in the light you state that *the people* are really against themselves ... [*sic*]'.[86] Peregrine Wentworth wrote of a visit to York that:

> The York paper which I got yesterday morning informed me of the nonsense, and mischief that was carryed forward in this town, which induced me to order my horses and to set [out] immediately to be satisfied. I am sorry to acquaint your Lordship, that I am far from being satisfied in the matter I could wish, as I see such I may almost say an universal propensity in the People to be very awkward and untoward. ... I see such a determined set of people in the towns, in favor of Mr Pitt, that I cannot help being very much alarmed....[87]

Newspapers across the country published letters in support of Pitt and the King, whilst pouring scorn on the coalition.[88] The *Kentish Gazette* described a 'daring faction' who had 'attempted to render the king a nullity, and to subvert our glorious constitution; but thanks to the active exertions of our *real* patriots, their detestable machinations were discomfited; and every Englishman has now the satisfaction to find, that *Pitt* and *Liberty* are synonimous [*sic*] terms.'[89] John Cannon has questioned the extent to which public opinion could make itself felt 'through the hardened arteries of the unreformed representative system', even though 'the rout of the coalition was so devastating and the hostility of the people so manifest that the victims themselves tended to subscribe to the view that the result was due to popular frenzy'.[90] However, given what we have already seen of the increasing influence of the newspaper press during the century, claims for at least a partial role in the defeat of the coalition do not seem to be unreasonable.

Conclusion

The newspaper press became increasingly prominent in English political life after 1760, due largely to the part it played in various extra-parliamentary campaigns. Newspapers were also influential in

---

86. Croft to Fitzwilliam, York, 6 March 1784, WWM F34/53.
87. Wentworth to Fitzwilliam,Wakefield, 11 February 1784, WWM F34/34.
88. *Jackson's Oxford Journal,* 13 March 1784; *Reading Mercury,* 5 April 1784; *Western-Flying Post,* 15 March 1784; *York Chronicle,* 12 March 1784; *Cambridge Chronicle,* 10 April 1784; *Kentish Gazette,* 13 March 1784; *Leeds Mercury,* 23 March 1784.
89. *Kentish Gazette,* 6 March 1784.
90. Cannon, *Fox–North Coalition 1782–4,* pp. 225–6.

deciding the fate of individual politicians. The popularity of Pitt the Elder was seriously threatened towards the end of his career by a well-publicised scandal, and the Earl of Bute was effectively driven out of office by the combined efforts of a hostile press. For John Wilkes, on the other hand, the press proved to be a positive boon. Wilkes was a skilled propagandist who managed to transform himself into a popular hero with the help of the press. By linking his personal cause with that of English liberties and individual rights, he was able to secure a broad popular appeal, whilst the dissemination of Wilkesite ideas throughout the country by newspapers played an important part in the continuing politicisation of the wider English public.

Wilkesite ideology was also bound up with debates concerning the American crisis in the 1770s. Here newspapers both reflected and promoted significant splits in public opinion, with some of the population supporting the cause of the American colonists, whilst others condemned the rebellion. The same type of divisions existed in relation to the reform movement of the 1780s, where it was also evident that newspapers were attempting to appeal to a divided readership. In this case debates within the press served to broaden popular conceptions of the public and its role in political life. By the time the Fox–North coalition was formed in 1783, the press was more than confident of its right to comment on public affairs. Newspapers were important in bolstering the position of Pitt the Younger, and in decreasing any popular support there was for the coalition. By presenting the struggle as one of the King and his people against a selfish aristocracy, newspapers helped to ally further their cause with that of their readers.

CHAPTER EIGHT

1787–1814

The failure of the parliamentary reform movement in the mid-1780s did not deter non-elite English men and women from continuing to involve themselves in the nation's political life. The following decades witnessed a huge extra-parliamentary campaign to abolish the slave trade, whilst the French Revolution and its aftermath had a major impact on British politics and prompted a variety of popular responses and activity out-of-doors. As a result of the turmoil in France, Britain was engaged in almost continuous warfare between 1793 and 1815, and this too contributed to the increasing polarisation and intensity of popular politics. In the midst of such upheaval newspapers played an increasingly prominent part in political life. They kept the public minutely (although not always accurately) informed of all-important events across the Channel; they were instrumental in facilitating and furthering a variety of political campaigns, both radical and conservative; they helped promulgate and promote new ideas about the ways in which society should operate and the country should be run; and they ensured that popular political debate was both dynamic and heated, whilst seemingly open to all. In so doing, the newspaper press – alongside other types of print culture and various forms of popular association – played a vital role in one of the most vigorous episodes of English history. As a result of such involvement, newspapers were themselves transformed, becoming increasingly politicised and politically polarised. This was most striking in the provinces, where the war promoted a new level and permanence of political vocalness and articulateness amongst newspapers.

From the 1780s, England witnessed large-scale efforts to mobilise public opinion in the campaign for the abolition of the slave trade. The campaign was eventually successful and the British slave trade ended in 1806–7, whilst British Caribbean slavery ceased in 1833. Although historians continue to place great emphasis on the role of economics in determining British involvement in the slave trade, the importance of politics is still clear and is indeed given pride of place in many works tracing the build-up to abolition and emancipation. Moreover, it is evident that whilst parliamentary politics were central to bringing about a change in policy, what happened outside parliament was also crucial. In particular, the increasingly vocal public condemnation of the slave trade had a major impact on the way politicians behaved, as they reacted to large-scale petitioning campaigns, the prominence of anti-slavery issues during local elections and the way in which print represented popular sentiment.

The London Abolition Society was founded in 1787 and local committees soon sprang up in towns across the country, including Bristol, Birmingham, Manchester, Sheffield, Coventry, Norwich, Hull, York, Leicester, Nottingham and Newcastle upon Tyne. The anti-slavery movement was dominated by Quakers and Evangelicals, but its appeal was far broader and the campaign arguably attracted the widest support of any extra-parliamentary movement in the eighteenth century, with followers from amongst Anglicanism and the Dissenting Churches alike, and from both the middle classes and those lower down the social scale. Abolitionists publicised their cause with lecture tours, printed propaganda, West Indian sugar boycotts and Wedgewood's famous cameo of a slave bearing the motto 'Am I not a man and a brother?'. The popular assault on parliament was organised largely in the form of petitions, which secured the signatures of many thousands of supporters and culminated in a huge round of national petitioning in 1792.

Such activity was dependent upon propaganda and a positive press. From the 1780s onwards, concerned clerics denounced slavery from their pulpits and political writers began to attract public attention through pamphlets and letters to the papers. Magazines and newspapers also began to give the issue serious consideration.[1] As James Walvin notes, 'for the next half-century, slavery and all its ramifications, were to generate an unprecedented volume of printed materials; of books, tracts, verses, cartoons, periodicals and newspaper space'.[2] Following in the footsteps of

---

1. James Walvin, *England, Slaves and Freedom, 1776–1838* (Basingstoke, 1986), pp. 104–5.
2. Walvin, *England, Slaves and Freedom*, p. 109.

parliamentary reformers a decade earlier, anti-slavery campaigners made extensive use of newspapers. In the capital, the London Anti-Slavery Committee organised the publication of abolitionist propaganda in sympathetic papers including the *Diary*, the *General Evening Post* and *Lloyd's Evening Post*, as well as in several provincial newspapers.[3]

In the provinces, the anti-slavery campaigners Thomas Clarkson and Joseph Plymley made plans in October 1791 to place extracts of Wilberforce's evidence against the trade to the Commons in the Shrewsbury paper, and 'in as many county Papers as cou'd be'.[4] In Bristol, an active anti-slavery lobby also kept the local papers supplied with material. In July 1787, both *Felix Farley's Bristol Journal* and *Bonner and Middleton's Bristol Journal* published 'A summary View of the Slave Trade...'. The following month both papers published letters supporting abolition.[5] Five days after Wilberforce gave his major Commons speech on abolition in April 1792, it was reproduced at length in *Felix Farley's Bristol Journal*, taking up the whole of the front and back pages.[6] Across the country, local abolition committees followed suit and used the local press to publicise their meetings and petition campaigns. According to J.R. Oldfield, 'publicity of this kind helped to create a "competitive humanitarian market" in which abolition became inextricably linked with matters of civic pride'. Thus a writer to the *Leeds Intelligencer* in 1788 urged readers not to be 'backward in so laudable a business', since 'This borough hath not been the last in other generous and humane designs. Let it not on this occasion be said, that we want either religion or humanity.'[7] No such coaxing was needed in Manchester, where the abolitionist cause had been popular from an early date. The *Manchester Mercury* was firmly behind the campaign, whilst the paper's publisher, Thomas Cooper, kept in close contact with the London Committee.[8] Other newspaper editors also actively supported the abolitionist cause, including William Woodfall, of the London *Diary*, Daniel Holt of

3. J.R. Oldfield, *Popular Politics and British Anti-Slavery: The Mobilisation of Public Opinion Against the Slave Trade 1787–1807* (Manchester, 1995), p. 59; Roger Anstey, *The Atlantic Slave Trade and British Abolition 1760–1810* (London, 1975), p. 257.

4. Oldfield, *Popular Politics and British Anti-Slavery*, pp. 58–9.

5. Peter Marshall, 'The anti-slave trade movement in Bristol', in Patrick McGrath, ed., *Bristol in the Eighteenth Century* (Bristol, 1972), p. 194.

6. Marshall, 'The anti-slave trade movement in Bristol', pp. 206–7.

7. Oldfield, *Popular Politics and British Anti-Slavery*, p. 104.

8. J.R. Oldfield, 'The London committee and mobilization of public opinion against the slave trade', *Historical Journal*, **35**, 2 (1992), p. 336.

the *Newark Herald*, Robert Trewman of the *Exeter Flying Post* and George Burbage, printer of the *Nottingham Journal*.[9]

Not surprisingly, those with interests in the slave trade sought to combat these efforts with local committees of their own, as well as with counter-petitions and propaganda which defended the slave trade on the grounds of economic and imperial benefits. The pro-slavery lobby was particularly powerful in Liverpool, and in 1788 the *Liverpool General Advertiser* published a letter from 'R. O.' which claimed that a petition raised in Manchester

> does not contain the real sentiments of the inhabitants, but ... it contains the names of people who never existed and ignorant boys, not able to sign their names, who, misguided by the enthusiasm of those they thought their superiors and by whose opinion they were entirely led.[10]

In Bristol, pro-slave trade letters began to appear in the local press soon after the abolitionists launched their campaign.[11] In the capital, pro-slavery propaganda was more organised, and from 1792 members of a sub-committee of the London Society of Planters and Merchants began to meet daily at Ibbotson's Hotel to peruse the newspapers so that 'what may be therein inserted by the Favourers of the abolition of the slave trade' could be picked out and controverted. London papers such as the *Public Ledger*, *Star*, *Whitehall Evening Post* and the *Argus* were noted to be particularly 'open to the directions of the committee'.[12] Yet such propaganda never matched the abolitionist material either in quantity or quality. In May 1792, Sir Samuel Romilly concluded that 'the cause of the negro slaves is at present taken up with much warmth in almost every part of the kingdom as could be found in any matter in which the people were personally and immediately interested ... All persons, and even the West India planters and merchants, seem to agree that it is impossible the trade should last many years longer.'[13]

However, despite winning the battle for popular opinion, the anti-slavery campaigners did not manage to convince most parliamentarians for several years and bills introduced in 1789, 1792 and

9. Oldfield, *Popular Politics and British Anti-Slavery*, pp. 131–2.

10. E.M. Hunt, 'The anti-slave trade agitation in Manchester', *Transactions of the Lancashire and Cheshire Antiquarian Society*, **79** (1977), pp. 55–6.

11. Marshall, 'The anti-slave trade movement in Bristol', p. 195.

12. Anstey, *The Atlantic Slave Trade and British Abolition*, p. 292.

13. James Walvin, 'The public campaign in England against slavery, 1787–1834', in David Eltis and James Walvin, eds., *The Abolition of the Atlantic Slave Trade: Origins and Effects in Europe, Africa, and the Americas* (Madison, Wis., 1981), pp. 63–4.

1796 failed to become law. Abolition remained an important subject however, and was prominent during the 1806 general election, when once again newspapers helped to bring the issue to the forefront of political discussion. Indeed, General Gascoyne, the Liverpool MP and anti-abolitionist, was later to complain to parliament that 'The attempts to make a popular clamour against the trade were never so conspicuous as during the last election, when the public newspapers had teemed with abuse of this trade ... '[14] One such newspaper was *Felix Farley's Bristol Journal*, which reported in November 1806 that

> the friends of the oppressed African race will be pleased to learn that during the course of the election in various parts of the kingdom the popular sentiment has been very strongly expressed against the continuance of that traffick in human flesh, which to the disgrace of this enlightened country, is still permitted, if not encouraged, by our laws.[15]

In Leeds, the two local papers, the *Leeds Intelligencer* and the *Leeds Mercury*, publicised the three-way Yorkshire election battle between the abolitionist William Wilberforce; the other incumbent, a Pittite and inheritor of a Barbadian slave plantation, Henry Lascelles; and a hopeful Whig contender, Walter Ramsden Fawkes. Much of the debate concerned the candidates' stance regarding abolition, which both Wilberforce and Fawkes promised to promote and even printed songs in the newspapers to emphasise their position. Despite publishing vague denials that he 'uniformly supports the slave trade', Lascelles was forced onto the defensive and eventually withdrew from the contest.[16] When a bill was finally carried in 1807, the *Manchester Mercury* was in no doubt that this was directly attributable to public pressure, and wrote to 'heartily congratulate our fellow subjects'.[17]

There was a lull in anti-slavery activity in the decade after 1794 which can be attributed largely to events in France and their impact on English politics. In July 1789, the storming of the Bastille in Paris gave the world a dramatic demonstration of the chaotic state of French affairs, yet few in Britain at that time could have foreseen the profound affects which the French Revolution was to have on

14. Seymour Drescher, 'Whose abolition? Popular pressure and the ending of the British slave trade', *Past and Present*, **143** (1994), p. 148.

15. Drescher, 'Whose abolition?', p. 145.

16. Drescher, 'Whose abolition?, pp. 145–6; Edward Baines [Jr.], *The Life of Edward Baines* (London, 1851), pp. 64–7.

17. Hunt, 'The anti-slave trade agitation in Manchester', p. 70.

their own domestic politics. Most Britons welcomed the early events of the Revolution. It appeared not only as a blow to a traditional enemy, but also the start of a process whereby a tyrannical government was replaced by a constitutional monarchy together with a parliamentary system on the British model. Newspapers served both to publicise the events of the revolution, and, in these early years at least, to present them in a favourable light. Faced with a public eager to find out all they could about events across the Channel, and as quickly as possible, the newspaper press was in an enviable position compared with other forms of print. As a result, its version of events was extremely influential. Like many other English newspapers in the summer of 1789, the *World* was in celebratory mood, and claimed that 'They propose our constitution to be a model of theirs ... the name of ENGLAND is RESPECTED'.[18] For its part, the *Morning Post* asserted that 'An Englishman not filled with esteem and admiration at the *sublime* manner in which one of the most IMPORTANT REVOLUTIONS the world has ever seen is now effecting, must be dead to every sense of virtue and of freedom'.[19]

The press reflected a unanimity amongst the English public which did not last long. Largely as a result of the French Revolution, English popular politics became increasingly polarised during the 1790s. The revival of popular support for parliamentary reform was evident in many towns and cities across Britain. However, loyalist and conservative sentiment, which challenged the impetus for reform, was to become even more widespread and influential. For both sides of this ideological divide, print in general and newspapers in particular proved a vital source of information and propaganda, and for the newspaper press, the hotly debated politics of the period provided a political focus, exciting copy and an increased readership. Moreover, the popular political arena which newspapers increasingly dominated became an important site of political contestation as both radical and conservative propagandists sought to appeal to an explicitly lower class of readers. This was an extremely important development, and heralded the start of a new type of print culture which was both democratic and demotic.[20] Conservative propagandists such as Hannah More, William Jones, John Bowles and, for a time, William

18. *World*, 20 July 1789.
19. *Morning Post*, 21 July 1789.
20. Iain McCalman, *Radical Underworld: Prophets, Revolutionaries, and Pornographers in London, 1795–1840* (Cambridge, 1988).

Cobbett specifically aimed their writing at a popular audience, using simple and impassioned tones which consciously adopted the form and writing style of other types of popular literature.[21] Radical writers did the same. Thus in the early 1790s the radical Daniel Isaac Eaton produced the cheap weekly periodical, *Politics for the People*, Thomas Spence's *Pig Meat* sold for only one penny per issue, whilst Paine's *Rights of Man* was published in a variety of cheap editions, and sold between 100,000 and 200,000 copies in the first three years after its publication.

Given the widespread circulation of the *Rights of Man*, the high incidence of multiple readership and the prevalence of other methods whereby the text was brought to illiterate sections of the population (see chapter 3), Mark Philp has suggested that it is likely 'that a substantial proportion of all classes would have had some acquaintance with Paine'. Thus he argues that the literary discussion of the French Revolution was turned into a truly mass debate[22] – a debate in which the newspaper press played an active part. Although both conservative and radical writers who sought to appeal to the 'common man' used a variety of types of printed matter to do so, not the least of which was the pamphlet, newspapers also proved to be an important medium for ideas and arguments from both sides. Not only did newspapers reprint material and allow it to reach a much wider audience than was possible in its original form, but they provided commentary on it and added original contributions of their own, whilst the frequent publication of newspapers helped promote a sense of immediacy and urgency in the discussions taking place.

For reformers in Britain the revolution in France was particularly exciting since they believed that the French were about to inaugurate a new era of enlightenment and reform which others (including, it was hoped, the British) could copy. This was a view which many newspapers were eager to promote. The *Sheffield Register* spoke of 'twenty six millions of our fellow creatures bursting their chains and throwing off, almost in an instant, the degrading yoke of slavery', and predicted that governments would henceforth cease to be conspiracies of the few against the many, but would now

21. Susan Pedersen, 'Hannah More meets Simple Simon: tracts, chapbooks, and popular culture in late eighteenth-century England', *Journal of British Studies*, **25**, 1 (1986), p. 88.

22. Mark Philp, *The French Revolution and British Popular Politics* (Cambridge, 1991), p. 5.

strive to promote the common good.[23] In October 1789, the *Kentish Gazette* carried an address 'To the Freeholders of Great Britain' which hoped that the example set by the revolution in France would promote reform at home:

> At a time when a nation on the Continent, formerly despised by us on account of its abject slavery, is asserting the indefeasible rights of mankind, and about to establish liberty on the broadest basis, it is too dreadful to consider that in this land of hereditary freedom there should still exist laws as repugnant to common sense and common right...[24]

It was in towns where a tradition of Whig opposition or Protestant Dissent was strong that reform was particularly popular and the French Revolution was greeted with most enthusiasm. Sheffield, Norwich, Newcastle upon Tyne, Manchester, Birmingham and London were particularly active and supported a politically vocal press. Here reform societies and clubs were started, or, like the Society for Constitutional Information, were rejuvenated, and all made much use of both London and provincial newspapers to spread their message. According to Goodwin, the existence of a local radical newspaper often provided the impetus with which radical societies were formed. This may well have been the case in Sheffield, where Joseph Gale's *Sheffield Register* promoted radical views and provided a focus for local radical groups, whilst an associated radical journal, *The Patriot*, proved both original and influential, and was closely linked with newspaper editors on the *Doncaster Journal*, *Manchester Herald*, *Chester Chronicle* and *Leicester Chronicle*. In Manchester, the situation was reversed. Local radicals, frustrated at the hostility of the town's existing papers, produced the *Manchester Herald* between 1792 and 1793, which soon became the organ of the radical movement throughout the industrial North-West. The paper proudly declared itself '*decidedly* the PAPER OF THE PEOPLE' and preached distinctly Paineite ideas.[25] Some radical provincial papers such as the *Cambridge Intelligencer* even had a national circulation. A correspondent of the *Anti-Jacobin* predicted that the *Intelligencer* 'for its rancour and scurrility might

23. M.J. Smith, 'English radical newspapers in the French revolutionary era, 1790–1803' (London University PhD thesis, 1979), p. 22.
24. Peter L. Humphries, 'Kentish politics and public opinion 1768–1832' (Oxford DPhil thesis, 1981), pp. 158–9.
25. Albert Goodwin, *The Friends of Liberty: The English Democratic Movement in the Age of the French Revolution* (London, 1979), pp. 177, 224, 228–31.

do much mischief among the Yeomanry and Peasantry of the Northern Counties'.[26]

By 1792, the general euphoria which had greeted the revolution was giving way in many quarters to intense trepidation. France had declared war on its neighbours and, in September, a series of massacres revealed how violent the revolution had become. The September massacres were followed by a tirade of anti-French sentiment in the press, and newspapers proved themselves to be important vehicles for a sensational type of 'atrocity' literature feeding the public mood. The *Kentish Gazette* showed a very different attitude now towards events in France. One of its correspondents, 'Philo Britannicus', was typically critical of the tyrannical French regime which oppressed religion, ill-treated the King and indulged in execution without trial. 'If this is a fair statement of the affairs in France', he declared, 'if such are the effects of *Jacobin* Societies and Republican schemes ... may God in his mercy deliver every nation ... from such ideas, such principles, and such men.'[27] In January 1793 Louis XVI was executed and, in the following month, France declared war on Britain. Despite Pitt's efforts to remain detached from events on the continent, Britain was drawn into a vast and expensive war which was to last, in effect, for the next twenty years.

Although English radical newspapers, like English radical politics, had never shown an entirely united front, they appeared increasingly divided after the events of 1792–3. The trial and execution of Louis XVI was one of the episodes which brought these divisions to the fore. The *Newcastle Chronicle*, which, like the *Kentish Gazette*, had formerly welcomed events in France, now spoke of the revolutionaries as 'those inhuman butchers'. The *Sheffield Register*, on the other hand, ranked the King's death as no more shocking than the abuses of the British constitution.[28] The *Register*, like the town it served, was famously radical in its politics, and the previous year had applauded a series of demonstrations to celebrate the French victories at Valmy. At one such event, 5,000 or 6,000 were reported to have followed 'a caricature painting representing Britannia – Burke riding on a swine – and a figure, the upper part of which was the likeness of the Scotch Secretary [Henry Dundas, the Home Secretary], and the lower part that of an ass ...'[29]

26. Michael Murphy, *Cambridge Newspapers and Opinion 1780–1850* (Cambridge, 1977), p. 32.
27. Humphries, 'Kentish politics and public opinion 1768–1832', p. 163.
28. Smith, 'English radical newspapers', pp. 24–5.
29. E.P. Thompson, *The Making of the English Working Class* (London, 1963), p. 113.

The eclipse of the Jacobin regime which followed two years later in 1794 was generally welcomed by radical English papers, many of whom saw a return to the genuine principles of 1789. According to the *Derby Mercury* the French were 'abandoning those shocking principles which every lover of genuine liberty has so long reprobated', and were instead embracing those ideals 'which are an honour to themselves and their country. Justice tempered with mercy, now rules in the seat of judgement.' Only the *Courier* was critical of the moderation of the new government.[30] Radical newspapers were also largely united in their belief that Britain was to blame for the outbreak of hostilities and many suggested that Pitt had begun the war in order to divert popular attention from parliamentary reform: hence the *Morning Post*'s assertion in 1795 that the war was 'commenced for the protection of Rotten Boroughs and Corruption'.[31]

But it was the ruinous expense of the war which was the most constant complaint of the radical press. The result, according to the *Newark Herald*, was that 'Battles are fought – blood is spilt – money is exhausted – taxes are multiplied – debt is doubled – trade at a stand – bankrupts increase – the *poor* cannot maintain the *poor*.'[32] Benjamin Flower's *Cambridge Intelligencer* was also highly critical of the war with France and of its cost. In 1797 he attacked the huge sums spent 'in the unsuccessful prosecution of this war of frenzy and wickedness', whilst he accused ministers of wounding the constitution 'in its most precious vitals' and having robbed the people 'of some of our best birth-right privileges'.[33] In London, the *Morning Chronicle* also questioned British involvement in the war from the start. According to the paper, each section of English society was hostile to, or fearful of, the war, and thus 'the great mass of the people' opposed war, recognising that in spite of the execution of Louis XVI, the French were trying to follow the lines of the British constitution.[34] The paper subsequently blamed the war for the distress of industrial workers caused by the interruption of trade and the massive increase in taxes. In 1798, the *Chronicle* published the satirical 'Loyal Song':

30. Smith, 'English radical newspapers', p. 28.
31. Smith, 'English radical newspapers', p. 39.
32. Smith, 'English radical newspapers', p. 48.
33. Murphy, *Cambridge Newspapers and Opinion*, p. 30.
34. Clive Emsley, *British Society and the French Wars 1793–1815* (London, 1979), pp. 17–18.

If your Money he take – why your Breeches remain;
And the flaps of your Shirts, if your Breeches he gain;
And your Skin, if your Shirts; and if Shoes, your bare feet;
Then, never mind TAXES – *We've beat the Dutch fleet!*[35]

Despite the popularity of reform and the growing appetite for radical print, there were opposing voices from the early 1790s: Edmund Burke's *Reflections on the Revolution in France*, published in November 1790, being perhaps the most famous example. Although Burke's *Reflections* met with rather a muted response when it first appeared, his conservative ideas gained increasing prominence as the decade progressed and events in France revealed the anarchy and violence into which the Revolution had descended and the threat which this posed to Britain. Moreover, even before the intellectual riposte to the Revolution was being worked out, there were indications that popular conservative forces were already at work, often in the very towns where radicalism had gained a foothold. In 1791, it appeared that Anglican concerns over the Dissenters' campaign to repeal the Test and Corporation Acts were at the root of the 'Priestley riots' in Birmingham, where the home of the eminent Dissenting minister, Joseph Priestley, was attacked along with those of other prominent Dissenters. Although the radical press was a great proponent of religious toleration, on this occasion it seemed that local newspapers had promoted the very opposite. The *Morning Chronicle* blamed the Birmingham press for the formation of the unrest and commented that 'certain it is that those who filled the newspapers with inflammatory letters and paragraphs previous to the 14th, and those who countenanced the practice, may be justly charged with pre-disposing the minds of the People to whatever mischievous impulse they might on that day receive'.[36]

In Manchester, a conservative Church and King Club was formed in 1790 and 'Church and King' became an increasingly common cry amongst crowds from 1792 onwards. This was also the year that John Reeves founded the Association for Preserving Liberty and Property against Republicans and Levellers. He publicised the Association in every metropolitan newspaper and distributed its resolutions to the provincial press, promoting a torrent of

35. Emsley, *British Society and the French Wars*, pp. 31 and 64.
36. Karl Schweizer and Jeremy Black, 'The eighteenth century British press: problems and perspectives', in *Politics and the Press in Hanoverian Britain* (Lewiston, NY, 1989), p. xi.

correspondence from people offering support and requesting more details.[37] Within a few months of its foundation, Reeves's association had spawned over 2,000 local patriotic clubs. According to H.T. Dickinson, in most places where such associations were formed loyalists easily outnumbered radicals, and indeed only in Sheffield were loyalists forced on the defensive.[38] The members of loyalist associations adopted various measures to oppose and intimidate their radical opponents. As we saw in chapter 4, two royal proclamations against the spread of seditious writings and radical activities in May and December 1792 not only produced almost 500 loyal addresses from across the country, but encouraged local prosecutions against printers and booksellers and persuaded magistrates to refuse licences to innkeepers who allowed radical meetings and newspapers on their premises. Effigies of Tom Paine were burnt in their hundreds and local populations were bullied into signing loyalist addresses. Even more insidiously, assaults were made by loyalist mobs on the persons and property of prominent radicals. The *Evening Mail* was fulsome in its praise of such initiatives:

> The great, the good, the wise, the honest, the industrious subjects have but one mind in respect to the welfare of their Country; and it must afford general satisfaction to find that they are uniting to preserve public and private property from the plundering system on which the Republican banditti have built their hopes of success. Supported by the strength of such association – by the Civil, the Military, and the Naval force of this Country, our Constitution may then look with the most sovereign contempt on all those dark assassins, who have for some time past been lurking in holes and corners in order to find a favourable opportunity to stab our national peace to the heart.[39]

Yet such loyalist actions did not go unchallenged. The *Morning Chronicle* was damning of the combined efforts by the government and loyalist associations. In December 1792 it complained of the attempt 'openly made to deter the People of Great Britain from publishing their thoughts on subjects most interesting to their happiness, not merely by men invested with high trusts, but a

37. E.C. Black, *The Association: British Extra-parliamentary Political Organization 1769–1793* (Cambridge, Mass., 1963), pp. 238–9.
38. H.T. Dickinson, *The Politics of the People in Eighteenth-Century Britain* (Basingstoke, 1995), p. 281.
39. Black, *The Association*, p. 271.

combination of individuals, in a manner hitherto unknown in this country...'[40]

Yet the *Morning Chronicle* was swimming against the tide. In places such as Kent, local newspapers were full of patriotic addresses, resolutions and advertisements for forthcoming loyalist meetings and worked hard to cultivate local hatred of Tom Paine, 'the great demagogue of licentiousness', as he was called by the *Kentish Chronicle*.[41] In December 1792, when the *Manchester Herald* organised a subscription to aid the widows and orphans of 'those Brave French Patriots who have nobly fallen in defence of the LIBERTIES OF MANKIND',[42] the conservative *Newcastle Advertiser* promptly attacked the paper along with all English radicals:

> To the astonishment of all who think, the partisans of the Jacobins in Manchester have published a justification of the murders committed in France during the late tumults, and an invitation to support the authors of them by a subscription! – A vindication of murder the mind naturally revolts at – what then can be expected from such principles – such actions – and such an overthrow of justice, humanity and order? The most depraved mind could scarcely dare to wish this or any other kingdom under the influence which now actuates the inhabitants of France.[43]

The conservative press depicted British radicals as traitors infected with the dangerous French disease of revolutionary fervour. The aims of such individuals were deliberately misrepresented and readers were warned that they threatened to destroy both the monarchy and the Church and inspire social and economic chaos by seizing the property of their social superiors. The *Sheffield Courant*, for example, spoke of reformers as 'vermin ... diabolical monsters in human form' whose 'seditious affiliating societies ... and correspondence with their friends the jacobins' had 'raised the French to such a pitch of presumption as to declare war against Britain'.[44] In September 1793, the *Manchester Mercury* criticised 'The wickedness of [Paine's] attempt to sow the seeds of sedition

---

40. Black, *The Association*, p. 254.
41. Humphries, 'Kentish politics and public opinion 1768–1832', pp. 165–6.
42. Nicola Courtenay, 'Representations of radicalism and loyalism in Manchester newspapers 1792–1793' (Keele University BA thesis, 1998), p. 23.
43. H.T. Dickinson, *Radical Politics in the North-East of England in the Later Eighteenth Century* (Durham, 1979), p. 18.
44. M.E. Happs, 'The Sheffield newspaper press and parliamentary reform, 1787–1831' (Oxford BLitt thesis, 1973), p. 42.

amongst the working people of this country...'[45] In the same
year, the *Cambridge Chronicle* applauded local proceedings when an
effigy of Tom Paine was paraded through the streets and cere-
monially burnt on Market Hill 'amidst the loyal acclamations of
surrounding hundreds'.[46] The threat posed by 'English Jacobins'
was presented as very real, and was designed to provoke a strong
reaction amongst readers. In December 1792 the *World* reflected
the common fear that the country was facing possible domestic
insurrection:

> Not withstanding the activity of Government, exertions of Adminis-
> tration, and the associations of the Loyalists, rebellion lurks in the
> many parts of this great city; and in a well frequented coffee-house,
> yesternight the dethronement of all kings, and their final extirpation
> from the earth, was maintained as necessary to the welfare of all ranks
> in society.[47]

Clive Emsley has termed this widespread belief that domestic
revolution was afoot 'the great fear' of 1792–3. He notes that other
papers, such as the *London Chronicle*, gave detailed reports of the
'revolution plans' of English Jacobins, which included the destruction of the House of Lords, the Horse Guards, St. James's Palace
and the law courts.[48]

Events in France were described by loyalist newspapers as
anarchic, violent and immoral: lurching from mob rule to military
dictatorship. Moreover, readers were told that it was not just the
upper classes who would suffer if Britain experienced revolution,
even the most humble citizens would be adversely affected by the
political upheaval and social chaos which would follow. Readers
were asked to compare social conditions in Britain and France by
way of proof. In January 1793, *The Times* presented a sorry picture of
the French, as 'a wretched, misguided, miserable people, without a
ray of moral virtue or a spark of revealed religion'. By contrast, the
English were 'rich, flourishing, happy and contented ... and
living under a constitution which long has been the admiration
and the envy of surrounding empires. Their unanimity to support it
sets intrigue at defiance, and laughs sedition to scorn.'[49] The

45. Courtenay, 'Representations of radicalism and loyalism in Manchester newspapers 1792–1793', p. 41.
46. Murphy, *Cambridge Newspapers and Opinion*, p. 24.
47. *World*, 13 December 1792.
48. Clive Emsley, 'The London "Insurrection" of December 1792: fact, fiction or
fantasy?', *Journal of British Studies*, **xvii**, 2 (1978), p. 66.
49. *The Times*, 9 January 1793.

Manchester Herald thought 'Englishmen ought to glory in the extreme tranquillity of their country, the equity of their laws, and the mildness of their constitution'.[50] The *Morning Chronicle* suggested that 'If any English Gentlemen, Ladies or others, are unfortunately afflicted with the rage of Revolution, let them repair to Paris, and drink moderately of the waters of the Seine for a fortnight; they may depend, under the blessing of God, on a perfect cure.'[51]

H.T. Dickinson has claimed that radicals were defeated in the 1790s, at least in part 'by the force of their opponents' arguments',[52] and that, in effect, the bulk of the British people were won over by the persuasiveness of the conservative cause. Moreover, Dickinson claims that conservative propaganda during the 1790s – in the shape of newspapers, journals, verse, popular ballads, novels, broadsheets and caricatures – was probably more substantial than that disseminated by radicals. Dickinson further points out that radical newspapers were never in a majority, and in towns where conservative and radical newspapers coexisted, as was the case in Manchester, Leicester and Newcastle, it was the conservative paper which survived the political contest.[53] This was generally true, yet in Sheffield at least it appears that the radical Joseph Gale's *Register* was the town's most successful paper, and its rival, the *Courant*, accused it of being 'more formidable to England than all the arms of France, since a great proportion of those who read them [its articles], take every suggestion for authentic doctrine'.[54] When loyalists tried to attack Gale's office in 1793, Gales reported that he was defended by 'a hundred stout democrats [who] stood before us singing "God Save Great Thomas Paine!" to the loyal tune'.[55] When a similar assault took place on the offices of the *Manchester Herald*, no such help was given.[56]

Yet even the radical *Sheffield Iris* acknowledged as the war commenced that 'a spirit of unanimity and patriotism, unexampled

---

50. Courtenay, 'Representations of radicalism and loyalism in Manchester newspapers 1792–1793', p. 43.

51. *Morning Chronicle*, 12 January 1793.

52. H.T. Dickinson, *Liberty and Property: Political Ideology in Eighteenth-Century Britain* (London, 1977), p. 272.

53. Dickinson, *Politics of the People*, p. 272.

54. Happs, 'The Sheffield newspaper press and parliamentary reform, 1787–1831', pp. 42–3.

55. Happs, 'The Sheffield newspaper press and parliamentary reform, 1787–1831', pp. 42–3.

56. See chapter 3.

even in the annals of this favoured country, displays itself among all ranks of people'.[57] According to the *London Chronicle*:

> Since the Declaration of War ... a great number of Letters have been received from different Persons residing chiefly upon the coast opposite to France, wherein they have signified their Readiness of embodying themselves in order to resist any incursions which may be attempted to be made by the Enemy and have requested that Government will order them to be supplied with Arms and Accoutrements for their use during the continuance of hostility.[58]

English patriotic feeling was nowhere more evident that in the celebration of its navy, and in the figure of Horatio Nelson in particular. Just as Admiral Vernon became a popular hero in the 1740s (see chapter 6), so Nelson won much public acclaim in the 1790s, largely as a result of newspaper coverage. However, whilst Vernon was essentially an opposition figure, Nelson and British naval supremacy were celebrated for conservative and pro-government purposes and proved a boon to the administration's war effort (although Nelson himself was never an especially comfortable figure for the establishment). Newspaper reports of naval victories were greeted with great excitement and celebration, which was often explicitly anti-radical in tone. In 1794, the London *Sun* reported that celebrations surrounding Admiral Howe's victory against the French fleet off Brest had prompted the inhabitants of Uttoxeter to toast 'May the Axe of Government lop off the Heads of Sedition', whilst in Chester it was reported that 'not a street or an alley could be entered, but the heart-cheering tunes of God save the King, Rule Britannia, and other loyal songs met our ears'.[59]

According to Gerald Jordan and Nicholas Rogers, once Napoleon's territorial ambitions became clear and many radicals and reformers became disillusioned with the revolution, 'naval victories became less politically contentious and more unequivocally nationalist'.[60] Indeed, patriotism had never been solely the preserve of conservatives. Thus even those opposed to the war would congratulate British seaman on their bravery. The *Morning Chronicle* stated after the battle of Camperdown in 1797 that, 'However we may deplore the calamity, or condemn the impolicy

57. Emsley, *British Society and the French Wars*, p. 113.
58. Emsley, *British Society and the French Wars*, p. 38.
59. Gerald Jordan and Nicholas Rogers, 'Admirals as heroes: patriotism and liberty in Hanoverian England', *Journal of British Studies*, **28** (1989), pp. 211–12.
60. Jordan and Rogers, 'Admirals as heroes', p. 214.

of the war itself, it is with pride and pleasure that we witness the exploits of our defenders on our natural element, and that we see our Country saved against the incapacity of our Government by the courage of our Tars'.[61] Even the radical *Sheffield Iris*, which opposed the war on humanitarian grounds, declared itself in 1798 as reluctant to see Britain 'bowing the neck to that yoke, which humbled Holland and Switzerland and Italy'.[62] Despite the fact that Britons were conspicuously unwilling to join the armed forces,[63] papers such as the *Northampton Mercury* urged: 'surely no man, who has any regard for himself, his family, or his country can object to take his chance of being called upon if [an invasion] should arise.'[64] Like Admiral Vernon before him, Nelson was fêted for delivering the nation from a foreign foe. After his success at the Battle of the Nile in 1798, the *Sussex Weekly Advertiser* announced that 'there has been scarcely anything heard but the echoes of loyalty from one end of the country to the other'.[65] Nelson's symbolic importance remained after his death. In 1806 the *York Herald* urged that if Britain was invaded, its inhabitants should remember 'the noble and auspicious words of the Hero Nelson – "England expects every man to do his duty"'.[66]

Newspapers' promotion of patriotic sentiments were also evident in the treatment given to George III. As we saw in the last chapter, from the mid-1780s the King's popularity began to increase and the advent of war with France and the growth of loyalism and conservative sentiment only served to further this development. Linda Colley has argued that press reports and incitement played an important part in the wider endorsement of the monarchy's public appeal.[67] When the *Morning Herald* diverged from this loyalist trend in March 1789 and declared the King to be incapable of reigning because of ill health, it was publicly burnt outside the Carolina Coffee House near the Royal Exchange.[68] It was not just the monarch, but the whole royal family who attracted increasing

61. Jordan and Rogers, 'Admirals as heroes', p. 214.

62. Emsley, *British Society and the French Wars*, p. 69.

63. Linda Colley, *Britons: Forging the Nation 1707–1837* (New Haven, 1992), ch. 7.

64. Clive Emsley, 'Revolution, war and the nation state: the British and French experiences 1789–1801', in Mark Philp, ed., *The French Revolution and British Popular Politics* (Cambridge, 1991), p. 110.

65. Jordan and Rogers, 'Admirals as heroes', p. 215.

66. Emsley, *British Society and the French Wars*, p. 122.

67. Linda Colley, 'The apotheosis of George III: loyalty, royalty and the British nation 1760–1820', *Past and Present*, **102** (1984), p. 113.

68. Arthur Aspinall, *Politics and the Press, c. 1780–1850* (London, 1949), p. 271.

support during this period. When over 160 addresses were sent primarily to the Queen upon the King's recovery in 1789, *The Times* stated that 'no female ever more justly deserved it ... She is a pattern of domestic virtue, which cannot be too much admired.'[69] The role of the press in encouraging patriotism and royal support was particularly evident during the run-up to the jubilee in 1809. Newspapers in Chester, for example, 'played an indispensable part in jubilee organization by printing readers' suggestions and suitably emotive editorials, as well as mayoral notices about jubilee meetings, advertisements for royal souvenirs, and details of the procession route'.[70] In places such as Bristol, where the local authorities were not eager to organise jubilee celebrations, the local press was even more important in applying pressure. *Felix Farley's Bristol Journal* was indignant in its October issues: 'Every provincial paper, that we have perused, proclaims the universal attention which this day has excited. Why is this ancient and loyal, this opulent City, the last to announce its intention to join in the universal joy?'[71]

In such an atmosphere of popular patriotism and conservatism, coupled with the introduction of repressive legislation which culminated in a series of state treason trials and the suspension of habeas corpus, radicalism was increasingly forced underground. Radical organisations which flourished before the mid-1790s, such as the Manchester Corresponding Society, operated thereafter on a largely secretive basis. Stories of conspiracy began to circulate in Manchester, London, the Midlands and the West Riding of Yorkshire. The failed Irish rebellion of 1798 served to heighten further conservative fears of domestic insurrection, particularly when government spies uncovered a plot to organise simultaneous Irish and English risings. Benjamin Flowers, editor of the radical *Cambridge Intelligencer*, was one of the few to defend the Irish rising, claiming that it was caused by the brutality of the system of rule.[72]

Even more alarming for most English men and women were the revolutionary plots of Colonel Despard and his followers. During Despard's trial in 1803, newspapers served to increase fears of domestic insurrection. The *Morning Post* claimed that 'The poor ... believe him a martyr', and that Despard thought that a revolution could be caused simply 'by a small party of desperate men, who,

69. Colley, 'The apotheosis of George III', p. 125.
70. Colley, 'The apotheosis of George III', p. 116.
71. Colley, 'The apotheosis of George III', p. 116.
72. Murphy, *Cambridge Newspapers and Opinion*, p. 39.

having struck one great blow, such as the assassination of the King, and filled the city with consternation, would find thousands to support them'.[73] The *Leeds Mercury* attacked English 'Jacobins' and accused them of being motivated by 'bad designs' and of shrinking into 'lurking holes like a lawless banditti'. Once again, the *Cambridge Intelligencer* was one of the few papers to raise a dissenting voice when it accused the *Mercury*'s editor of deliberately smearing reformers and bringing comfort to 'that corrupt and profligate system which has desolated a great part of Europe, murdered millions of our fellow creatures, robbed the people of this country of their most valuable rights, and brought the kingdom to the verge of ruin'.[74] The *Manchester Gazette* provided another minority radical viewpoint in 1800 when it attacked the war for its futility:

> *Glory* ... never cultivated a yard of land, never added a grain to the poor man's loaf, nor put an ounce of warp into the poor man's loom; ... Can stabs with the bayonet, can limbs blown from the body by gunpowder, can brains scattered by cannonballs, can the agonies of ten thousand men, oppressing the bare earth with horror, staining the rivulets with blood, writhing, groaning, and dying, can the inclemencies of the sky, the damps of marshes, the agues, fevers, and consumption of unsheltered ditches, can the pestilence, fire, frost, and famine, increase the sum of human happiness?[75]

However, the *Cambridge Intelligencer* and the *Manchester Gazette* were in a minority. Far more typical was the London paper, the *St. James's Chronicle*, which in 1800 pledged itself 'to persevere in the support of order and good Government; to show a uniform detestation of the French usurpations; and to resist every attempt, open or secret, towards the overturning of our valuable Constitution at home'.[76] From the mid-1790s onwards, many radical newspapers folded, were forced out of business or changed their politics. The decision of papers such as the *Sheffield Iris*, *Chester Chronicle*, *Morning Post* and *Newcastle Chronicle* to abandon radicalism suggests a major sea-change in public opinion. Fears of domestic insurrection were coupled with the reaction to the changing French situation. The coup of Fructidor of 1797 marked the return of arbitrary government in France and made a major impact on James Montgomery, editor of the *Iris*, who wrote at the time of his

73. Thompson, *Making of the English Working Class*, p. 528.
74. Thompson, *Making of the English Working Class*, p. 519.
75. Smith, 'English radical newspapers', p. 51.
76. Schweizer and Black, 'The eighteenth century British press: problems and perspectives', p. xiv.

hatred of tyranny, particularly 'under a Republican disguise'.[77]
More alarming was France's aim of territorial expansion, which
only the *Courier* defended.[78]

By the late 1790s, many of those newspapers which had formerly
supported France now trembled at the thought of a French
invasion. In August 1798, the *Morning Post* admonished those
radicals who might have been so deceived by French professions
of liberty as to countenance an invasion. 'She comes with the
rights of man in her mouth', the paper warned, 'and the rod of
oppression in her hand.' The *Newcastle Chronicle* agreed, and argued
that Britons must resist 'even that heavenly boon, *Liberty*, if it be
attempted to be crammed down our throats by *foreign bayonets*'.
According to Smith, the invasion scare of 1798 proved a turning
point for the *Morning Post, Newcastle Chronicle* and *Chester Chronicle,*
all of which 'jettisoned liberalism for patriotism'. Even those papers
that continued to promote parliamentary reform became less
critical of both the war and the government. By 1803, with the
failure of the Peace of Amiens, the change was complete. Formerly
radical newspapers now portrayed the British, not the French, as a
free people valiantly fighting for survival, whilst Napoleon became
a popular hate figure. The *Chester Chronicle* described the war as a
contest between 'liberty or slavery ... a war for all that is dearest to
a free people, for all that men value most in society'. The *Courier*
was in agreement, and described the war as necessary 'to confound
the devices of the most restless, rapacious, and tyrannical government that ever insulted and oppressed the earth ... WE SHALL
SUPPORT THE WAR, DECISIVELY, ARDENTLY SUPPORT IT.'[79]
Even the liberal *Manchester Gazette* called for unity in the present
crisis and ceased to claim that the war was unnecessary and unjust.[80]

However, loyalism and patriotic fervour were not constant from
the 1790s until 1815, nor was anti-radical sentiment. Indeed,
J.E. Cookson has noted how resilient was a section of the non-
loyalist, 'liberal' newspaper press during the 1790s and the early
years of the nineteenth century. The *Cambridge Intelligencer* is the
most famous example, but the *Newcastle Chronicle, Bath Chronicle,*
Bury and Norwich Post, Worcester Herald and *Salopian Journal* also

77. Smith, 'English radical newspapers', pp. 96–7.
78. Smith, 'English radical newspapers', pp. 98–9.
79. Smith, 'English radical newspapers', pp. 99–100 and 105.
80. H.T. Dickinson, 'Popular conservatism and militant loyalism 1789–1815', in
H.T. Dickinson, ed., *Britain and the French Revolution, 1789–1815* (Basingstoke,
1989), p. 111.

remained broadly in the refomist camp. And from about 1800, the number of such papers was increasing.[81] After 1807, domestic radicalism was revived by the followers of Sir Francis Burdett and the provincial 'Hampden Club' movement. Many of those involved in this new wave of radicalism were prolific writers. Men such as William Cobbett and Leigh Hunt were eager to spread the reformist word through print, and journals such as the *Political Register* and the *Examiner* were the result. In the autumn of 1808 the radical *Independent Whig* rumoured that 'corruption and undue influence' were at work in military promotions.[82] In January of the following year Gwyllm Lloyd Wardle, MP for Okehampton and Colonel of Volunteers, brought charges before parliament that the Duke of York had helped his mistress's corrupt practice of selling commissions. The revelations – widely circulated by the newspapers – prompted an outcry in the country and calls for reform from both outside and within parliament, which radicals such as Burdett rallied behind. The *Staffordshire Advertiser* pronounced that 'There is not an Englishman but must blush to see how the best interests of the army have been sacrificed to an inglorious dalliance.'[83] As a result of the scandal, the Duke of York was forced to resign from his post as Commander-in-Chief.

In 1810 Burdett was arrested for criticising the government's decision to imprison another radical, John Gale. Burdett was held up as a popular hero and riots ensued, followed by a flood of petitions to parliament demanding reform. In London, the radical press was joined by usually more moderate newspapers such as the *Morning Chronicle* and the *Evening Star* in supporting Burdett's cause.[84] In Kent, the *Maidstone Journal* and the *Kentish Gazette* were both critical of Burdett and his associates, however, the *Kentish Chronicle* sprang to his defence:

> had not the bare faced priests of corruption, traduced and villified his character; and most shamefully stigmatised and attempted to blacken the purest fame in the nation; by ascribing motives to this worthy, popular and justly esteemed man, which only tend to lessen themselves in the eyes of the discriminating; proving the horrid state of corruption and venality to which the British press is reduced; whilst it

81. J.E. Cookson, *The Friends of Peace: Anti-war Liberalism in England, 1793–1815* (Cambridge, 1982), pp. 92 and 108.

82. Emsley, *British Society and the French Wars*, p. 142.

83. *Staffordshire Advertiser*, 18 February 1809.

84. J. Ann Hone, *For the Cause of Truth: Radicalism in London 1796–1821* (Oxford, 1982), p. 197.

exalts the patriotic and envied Baronet, in the estimation of every dispassionate, reflecting and independent Man in the Kingdom.[85]

Newspapers were increasingly vocal about the public's right to know about corruption in high places (and the press's right to root it out), and in this they appeared to attract popular support. In Cambridge, the newly launched *Cambridge Independent Press* criticised Castlereagh, President of the Board of Control, for his tendency to 'designate as Jacobinical' everything that questioned government actions, and promised to work for 'the exposure and correction of the many abuses that exist both in and out of Parliament, to the subversion of the best interests of the public'.[86]

The campaigning role of newspapers was also evident in the calls for peace which became increasingly loud after 1807. In 1812 a largely Dissenting and provincial group generated a peace movement in opposition to the hardships and moral revulsion caused by the war. A petition organised by the politician Henry Brougham raised 150,000 signatures in support of the 'Friends of Peace'. Like many other provincial editors, Edward Baines of the *Leeds Mercury* strongly backed the campaign. As early as 1807 he had described the war as 'the harvest of Ministers' because of the increase in patronage, but, the *Mercury* protested, 'though to Ministers it is a time of *plenty*, a war like the present is a time of famine to merchants, to manufacturers, and to tradesmen'. The paper celebrated the withdrawal of the Orders in Council in 1812, which had restricted trade with the continent, as 'the most beneficial Victory which has been achieved during the present war'.[87] Demands for economic and parliamentary reform were heard from *The Times* in 1811 and 1812. The paper was also critical of the Orders in Council, and particularly hostile to government corruption. In 1812 *The Times* proclaimed:

> it is irritating beyond expression for a patient people, parting, and willingly parting, almost with their life-blood, in support of the independence of their country, to be told by the highest authority, that what is so hardly wrung from them, under pretence of public service, has been converted into sources of private emoluments; yet, for God's sake, if these things are done, let them not escape comment, and especially in the proper place, the House of Commons.[88]

85. Humphries, 'Kentish politics and public opinion 1768–1832', pp. 240–1.
86. Murphy, *Cambridge Newspapers and Opinion*, p. 62.
87. Donald Read, *Press and People 1790–1850: Opinion in Three English Cities* (Aldershot, 1993), p. 108.
88. Emsley, *British Society and the French Wars*, p. 142.

When a wave of machine-breaking swept through the industrial areas of the East Midlands, West Riding of Yorkshire and parts of Lancashire between 1811 and 1812, many attributed the cause to economic hardship. Luddism, as it came to be known, was a protest against mechanisation, exploitation and hardship. Those involved destroyed machinery, threatened employers and organised in secret. Historians have been divided over whether or not the movement should be described simply as 'industrial', or rather political and even revolutionary.[89] Certainly at the time, old fears of conspiracy and plotted insurrection were revived and the government was alarmed enough to make machine-breaking a capital offence and to station large numbers of troops in Nottinghamshire and Yorkshire. The spread of Luddism was partly attributed to newspaper stories. A Bolton magistrate blamed its emergence in Yorkshire on the dangerous example set by Nottingham, which Yorkshire Luddites 'were unfortunately in the habit of reading [about] in the newspapers'.[90]

Whether this was true or not, the newspaper press gave a good deal of coverage to Luddite disturbances, although newspapers were notably divided in their opinions in places at the centre of Luddite activity such as Nottingham and Leeds. The *Leeds Mercury* ascribed Luddism to the economic hardships caused by the war. A letter to the *Mercury* in April 1812, for example, urged voluntary subscriptions to alleviate the sufferings of the poor, which, it predicted, 'will be productive in pointing to the poorer class, the interest and feeling their towns-people take in their distresses, and may ultimately be the means of completely subduing that desperate association, which aims at nothing less than the destruction of the nation'.[91] Its rival, the *Leeds Intelligencer,* attacked the *Mercury* for encouraging insurrection by taking such a sympathetic line. The *Intelligencer* spoke of the 'dark, subtle and invisible agency' which was at work in Luddism, 'seducing the ignorant and the inexperienced'.[92] Such divisions represented opposing sides in the localities. However, the overall level of sympathy shown for the

89. Thompson, *Making of the English Working Class*; Eric Hobsbawn, 'The machine breakers' in Eric Hobsbawn, ed., *Labouring Men: Studies in the History of Labour* (London, 1964); F.O. Darvall, *Popular Disturbances and Public Order in Regency England* (Oxford, 1969); M.I. Thomis, *The Luddites: Machine Breaking in Regency England* (Newton Abbot, 1970).

90. Thomis, *Luddites*, p. 69.

91. Thomis, *Luddites,* pp. 17 and 22; Donna Hughes, 'Luddite disturbances in West Yorkshire' (Keele University BA dissertation, 1998), p. 9.

92. Thomis, *Luddites,* p. 78.

poor by the provincial press in this period is symptomatic of a significant change of attitude compared with earlier years. This was clear not just in the coverage of Luddism, but also in that of other forms of popular protest. For example, in 1812 the *Carlisle Journal* was critical of the behaviour of soldiers during food riots and blamed unrest not on revolutionary conspiracies, but on low wages, high food prices and the artificial scarcity caused by Liverpool grain agents.[93] The newspaper press was increasingly representing a country tired of war, no longer quite so paranoid about domestic insurrection and desperate for a return to prosperity and peace.

Conclusion

The period 1787–1815 was a particularly turbulent one in England. The French Revolution, in particular, had a profound impact on political life: causing popular politics to polarise; encouraging both a growth, and a significant lapse, in radical ideas and activity; prompting the rise of a new form of militant loyalism; and creating a large anti-war lobby in protest at the hardships caused by Anglo-French hostilities. In addition, the abolition movement promoted extra-parliamentary campaigning on a huge scale, and made a vital contribution to the ending of British involvement in the slave trade. In all these developments, the press played an important role. For societies and organisations as disparate as the Manchester Corresponding Society and the London Society of Planters and Merchants, newspapers gave publicity and spread propaganda. Newspapers also kept readers closely informed of the all-important events in France and the battlefields of continental Europe, and provided a commentary on their implication for those in Britain, whilst disseminating various, and often conflicting, ideas about the potential for domestic reform. In this way the newspaper press allowed both the propagation of different ideologies and arguments and the expression of popular sentiment on a variety of important issues. It was thus at the heart of a series of public debates which served at different moments to unite, divide, comfort and alarm contemporaries. Moreover, the newspaper press itself was profoundly affected by the politics of this period. There emerged a noticeably more politicised and politically divided

93. Joanne Fidler, 'The Carlisle food riots of 1812' (Keele University BA dissertation, 1998).

press, especially in the provinces, as well as a more democratic and demotic form of print culture associated with both loyalist and radical camps. As we shall see in the next chapter, after 1815, this section of the press and particularly its radical elements, was to thrive once again with renewed vigour.

CHAPTER NINE

1815–1855

After the war with Napoleonic France ended in 1815, the political influence of the public continued to grow. At the same time increasing demands were made for changes in the way in which the country was run. In 1820, Peel wrote:

> Do not you think that there is a feeling becoming daily more general and more confirmed – that is, independent of the pressure of taxation or any immediate cause, in favour of some undefined change in the mode of governing the country? It seems to me a curious crisis – when public opinion never had such influence on public measure and yet never was so dissatisfied with the share which it possessed...[1]

There is no doubt that the harsh postwar years were ones of intense politicisation amongst both the lower and middle classes. Historians who argue that the early nineteenth century witnessed the birth of class consciousness in Britain pay great attention to this period, and to the 1830s in particular, when campaigns for reform, and against newspaper taxes, the exploitation of factory workers and the New Poor Law, coupled with trade union activity and Chartism, seemed to mark a significant growth in the political awareness and activity of an emerging working class. In addition, many of these campaigns, and the movements for parliamentary reform and against the Corn Law in particular, attracted middle-class political activists in great numbers, many of whom perceived their cause to be that of a modern, industrial and liberal class fighting against an outmoded aristocratic ruling elite.

The role of the newspaper press became increasingly important for all strands of popular politics during the postwar period. For

1. Derek Fraser, 'The agitation for parliamentary reform', in J.T. Ward, ed., *Popular Movements c. 1830–1850* (London, 1970), p. 35.

those without formal political power, newspapers provided a focus for political activity as well as publicising particular causes and winning over new recruits. As the newspaper press became more closely associated with public opinion in the popular mind it wielded a sizeable degree of power, particularly during times of political crisis. As we shall see, throughout the period 1815–55 the press exerted a constant pressure on successive governments, whilst occasionally tipping the balance in governmental decision-making. This does not mean, however, that newspapers were a homogeneous force and always pushed in the same direction. Newspapers expressed a variety of political stances and ensured that public political debate in England remained both diverse and dynamic. Although *The Times* became increasingly prominent, especially in terms of metropolitan opinion, provincial newspapers such as the *Manchester Guardian* and the *Leeds Mercury* were powerful in mobilising and expressing provincial sentiment.[2] In addition, the radical press enjoyed periods of considerable success which profoundly altered the political life of the working classes in particular, as well as that of the population as a whole.

The transition to peace in England was not made easily. Demobilisation, deflation and distress compounded to make the postwar period both economically harsh and politically turbulent. Radical politics gained a degree of mass support once more, backed by a new infrastructure of clubs and a thriving radical press. In such an atmosphere, calls for changes in economic policy, and particularly for 'cheap government', became increasingly prevalent. In addition, demands for parliamentary reform – as a means to institute economic transformation – were also on the rise. The main sources of these complaints were a powerful reformist provincial press and the more strident and radical 'working-class' papers. The radical press included William Cobbett's *Political Register*, Thomas Wooler's *Black Dwarf* and the *Weekly Political Register*, run first by William Sherwin and then by Richard Carlile. In 1816, Cobbett began to issue his *Political Register* as an unfolded two-penny sheet, thus avoiding the newspaper stamp, and increasing the sales of the *Register* from 1,000–2,000 when it was priced at a shilling, to 40,000–60,000.[3] In some ways, these publications were more like weekly essay papers than newspapers. However, Kevin

2. Edward Baines [Jr.], *The Life of Edward Baines* (London, 1851); Archibald Prentice, *Historical Sketches and Personal Recollections of Manchester* (London, 1851).

3. D.G. Wright, *Popular Radicalism: The Working-Class Experience, 1780–1850* (London, 1988), p. 65.

Gilmartin makes a case for them to be classed as newspapers since, he argues, they only emerged in a less 'news-focused' form because of legal struggles over news content, whilst they did sometimes contain material which was news. More importantly, he argues, they were widely perceived by contemporaries to be newspapers.[4]

The radical press campaigned vigorously for parliamentary reform and against the excesses of 'Old Corruption'. It criticised the 'parasitic' class composed of the aristocracy, priesthood, holders of state pensions, placemen and all others living off the taxes of working men. According to Cobbett: 'The real strength and all the resources of a country, ever have sprung and ever must spring, from the *labour* of its people ... the *cause* of your present misery ... is the *enormous amount of taxes*, which the government compel us to pay for the support of its army, its placemen, its pensioners etc....'[5] Cobbett also asserted that 'The *success of the cause of Reform*, and of course, the happiness and peace of the country, must now, in a great degree, depend upon the efforts of the press.'[6] Such was the evangelising force of these arguments that the readers of radical papers often became the leaders of radical opinion in their communities and key figures in radical political campaigns.[7] The provincial reformist press was also deeply involved in local politics as well as campaigning vigorously on national issues. However, unlike the radical press, the focus of provincial newspapers' appeals was the industrial middle class. Newspapers such as the *Leeds Mercury* were strongly critical of the government's expenditure on the war and the distress which had continued into peace time. The paper attacked the Corn Law of 1815 and supported the movement in manufacturing districts against the measure. The burdens on industry were frequently taken up by the *Mercury*, and were linked with parliamentary reform. In 1815, it claimed that 'There can be no equity in the landed interest forming nine-tenths at least, of our representatives; while the commercial and trading interest, which is quite equal in magnitude and importance, is sunk into insignificance. – The natural fruits of such a defective system of representation are our Corn and Wool Bills.'[8] The *Nottingham*

4. Kevin Gilmartin, *Print Politics: The Press and Radical Opposition in Early Nineteenth-Century England* (Cambridge, 1996), pp. 77–8.

5. Wright, *Popular Radicalism*, p. 66.

6. Gilmartin, *Print Politics*, p. 65.

7. Wright, *Popular Radicalism*, p. 66.

8. Donald Read, *Press and People, 1790–1850: Opinion in Three English Cities* (Aldershot, 1993), pp. 111–12.

Review asked its readership to 'Awake from your lethargy', and appealed to 'ye men of property in trading towns' to 'resist this deadly blow aimed at you by the landed interest before it is too late – petition! petition! petition!', and indeed 18,000 did sign the hostile Nottingham petition, along with 50,000 in Birmingham and 54,000 in Manchester.[9] In common with the radical press, the *Manchester Times* also criticised selfish aristocratic governments for the nation's distress:

> when laws are in operation to double the price of their food, to lower their wages by excluding the produce of their labour from foreign markets, and to carry off their hard-earned savings in taxes upon almost every necessary of life, it is not less inhumane to deny them, when it is required, a portion of that abundance which has been produced by their labour.[10]

The re-emergence of radical politics in the early years after the war was marked by men such as the 'Patriotic' radical, Henry 'Orator' Hunt, who sought to represent the cause of the overtaxed and unrepresented 'common' people. Hunt hijacked the Hampden Club petitioning campaign in support of direct taxation household suffrage and organised a series of mass meeting at Spa Fields between 1816 and 1817 in order to propound his version of inclusive and democratic radicalism. When the reform petitions were rejected by parliament in 1817, the country was once more faced with rumours of insurrection. These were partly the fantasy of government spies, such as the *agent provocateur*, Oliver the Spy, whom Edward Baines of the *Leeds Mercury* famously exposed in 1817.[11] But the ruling class's fears were also based on real evidence, and not least on the rising at Pentrich in 1817. Hunt continued to be hailed in the North as the people's champion however, and in 1819 another series of mass meetings was organised. The demonstration planned for August at St Peter's Field in Manchester was to be the biggest yet. Somewhat prophetically, the *Manchester Gazette* had already denounced mass meetings on the grounds that they gave the government 'an excuse for arbitrary measures'.[12] However, such warnings were ignored and the general invitation to the public to attend the meeting in Manchester was issued in the *Manchester*

9. Donald Read, *The English Provinces c. 1760–1960: A Study in Influence* (London, 1964), p. 79.

10. Read, *Press and People*, p. 157.

11. Read, *Press and People*, p. 113.

12. Malcolm I. Thomis and Peter Holt, *Threats of Revolution in Britain 1789–1848* (London, 1977), p. 65.

Observer and in London newspapers.[13] The atmosphere in Manchester clearly became heated. A group of Lancashire magistrates took it upon themselves to inform the Home Secretary, Viscount Sidmouth, in May that radical meetings and 'the unbounded liberty of the press' were the principal causes 'of the evil which we apprehend'.[14] The same magistrates published a warning against attending the meeting in the *Manchester Observer*.[15]

The meeting at St Peter's Fields did take place, however. It was well attended and remained peaceful until an attempt was made to arrest Hunt and his companions. The decision of the Manchester magistrates to disperse the crowd using troops resulted in at least eleven deaths. The Peterloo massacre, as it was dubbed by the press, aroused the anger of both the middle and lower classes, and proved a propaganda victory for the radicals, not least because, as was increasingly common,[16] the hustings had included reporters from several major papers, including John Tyas of *The Times*, John Smith of the *Liverpool Mercury* and Edward Baines of the *Leeds Mercury*.[17] *The Times* published an influential account of events which blamed the authorities for the 'deplorable transactions' which took place and exonerated the crowd:

> Whatever may have been the preliminary or accessory circumstances concerned with that assembly – Whatever may have been the sense of the merits of those who promoted and presided at it ... of the unfitness of the season at which 50,000 people, half employed and half starved, were congregated to a single spot, there to be puffed up by prodigious notions of their own strength, and inflamed by artful pictures of their grievances ... all such considerations, all such suspicions, sink to nothing before the dreadful fact, that nearly a hundred of the King's unarmed subjects have been sabred by a body of cavalry in the streets of a town of which most were inhabitants, and in the presence of those Magistrates whose sworn duty it is to protect and preserve the life of the meanest Englishman.[18]

The radical press was far more sensationalist, with the *Cap of Liberty* accusing the government of 'High Treason against the People',[19]

13. Donald Read, *Peterloo: The Massacre and its Background* (Manchester, 1958), p. 111.

14. Read, *Peterloo*, p. 115.

15. Read, *Peterloo*, p. 117.

16. James Vernon, *Politics and the People: A Study in English Political Culture c. 1815–1867* (Cambridge, 1993), pp. 149–50.

17. Read, *Peterloo*, p. 132.

18. *The Times*, 19 August 1819.

19. John Stevenson, *Popular Disturbances in England 1700–1832* (2nd edn., London, 1992), p. 285.

whilst the *Black Dwarf* headlined the deaths at Peterloo for three weeks.[20] Reacting to such radical propaganda, a Manchester magistrate appealed to the Home Office in September for help to get some good 'loyal' articles to publish locally from newspapers in other parts of the country.[21] Such articles did exist. In Kent, for example, the Tory press regretted the deaths at Peterloo, but placed the blame firmly with the radicals as 'the odious instigators of the day's calamity'.[22] Yet most newspapers were extremely critical of the government. The extensive newspaper coverage given to Peterloo, and the stance which most newspapers took, did much to shatter the moral authority of the old order.

Following Peterloo, a number of new papers appeared in London which had a more fiercely aggressive style. However, papers such as the *Medusa*, the *Democratic Recorder* and the *Cap of Liberty* did not last long.[23] The failed Cato Street conspiracy discovered early the following year, in which a small revolutionary group in London plotted to assassinate members of the Cabinet, prompted the government to impose the repressive legislation of the 'Six Acts' in 1820. This included the Blasphemous and Seditious Libels Act which deemed all cheap periodical publications to be newspapers, and hence liable for stamp duty. This measure, which effectively outlawed unstamped radical papers, contributed significantly to the failure of many of them to survive into the 1820s. However, such papers were also hit by the lull in radical activity which descended in the 1820s and lasted for almost a decade.

Although popular clamour failed to effect change in the 1810s, the disaffected voice of popular opinion found a new target in 1820 when George IV, who was strongly associated in the public mind with repression and profligacy, attempted to divorce his wife, Caroline, on his accession to the throne. John Stevenson has claimed that 'in terms of coverage in the newspapers, radical agitation and popular involvement it was the most impressive display of public opinion in the capital since the days of Wilkes'.[24] The *Sheffield Mercury* complained, not unjustifiably, that the episode

20. Stevenson, *Popular Disturbances*, p. 250.

21. Read, *Peterloo*, p. 141.

22. Kenneth J. Eaton, 'Newspapers and politics in Canterbury and Maidstone 1815–1850: opinion in two Kentish towns' (University of Kent MA thesis, 1972), p. 69.

23. J.R. Dinwiddy, *From Luddism to the First Reform Bill: Reform in England 1810–1832* (Oxford, 1986), p. 37.

24. John Stevenson, 'The Queen Caroline affair', in John Stevenson, ed., *London in the Age of Reform* (Oxford, 1977), p. 117.

offered 'an excellent handle to the factious to vent their spleen against the government'.[25] Addresses and resolutions in favour of the Queen poured in from across the country. As Hazlitt noted, the Caroline affair 'excited a thoroughly popular feeling. It struck its roots into the heart of the nation; it took possession of every house or cottage in the kingdom.'[26] Cartoons such as 'Public Opinion!!' represented the Queen outweighing the King on the scales of justice whilst John Bull applauds and promises: 'I'll see fair play'.[27] The newspaper press tended to shy away from the worst excesses of anti-establishment satire and pornography with which the gutter press represented the affair.[28] However, they did pick up on the melodramatic potential of events, and almost all newspapers portrayed Caroline as a wronged woman: an emblem of victimisation and purity who was in need of rescue and protection from an immoral and corrupt husband. *The Times*, for example, described Caroline as 'but a poor female with nothing but her character to support her through these odious charges'.[29]

The radical press presented the attack on Caroline as symbolic of an assault on English liberties, and, above all, as the work of 'Old Corruption'. The *Black Dwarf* proclaimed that

> Her Majesty has perceived, that while her safety depends upon the people, her INTERESTS are the same with the interests of the *people!* She has done yet more – she has *proclaimed* those truths – and denounced that *corrupt faction*, which has persecuted her, as it has persecuted the nation at large.[30]

The general clamour over the affair meant that radical papers such as *Cobbett's Political Register*, the *Champion*, *Black Dwarf*, *Statesmen* and *Examiner* were joined by those not usually associated so closely with the radicals' cause such as *The Times*, *Star*, *Globe*, *True Briton* and *Traveller*, all of which boosted their sales significantly as a result.[31] The *Morning Post*, which opposed Caroline, not only lost

25. M.E. Happs, 'The Sheffield newspaper press and parliamentary reform, 1787–1831' (Oxford BLitt thesis, 1973), p. 127.

26. Wright, *Popular Radicalism*, p. 76.

27. E.A. Smith, *A Queen on Trial: The Affair of Queen Caroline* (Stroud, 1993), p. 33.

28. Iain McCalman, *Radical Underworld: Prophets, Revolutionaries and Pornographers in London, 1795–1840* (Oxford, 1993), pp. 162–77.

29. G.A. Cranfield, *The Press and Society: From Caxton to Northcliffe* (London, 1978), p. 115.

30. Smith, *A Queen on Trial*, p. 129.

31. J. Ann Hone, *For the Cause of Truth: Radicalism in London 1796–1821* (Oxford, 1982), p. 312.

sales, but had its offices stormed by a mob.[32] The extensive news-paper coverage of Queen Caroline's trial for adultery attracted some criticism. In September, J. Hatsell wrote to Lord Colchester that

> For several months the people of England have thought, talked and dreamt of no other subject than the Queen. The Lords, by permitting the evidence taken by the shorthand-writers to be published every morning, have not only supplied matter sufficient to occupy the leisure house of the whole reading world, from breakfast to dinner, with subjects of conversation for the remainder of the day, but have exhibited to the world such a scene of profligacy and vice as were never detailed in any novel...

Indeed, Hatsell noted that the scandalous nature of the testimony meant that Lord Sidmouth and Lord Lilford had prevented their daughters from reading the papers.[33] When Caroline accepted a pension of £50,000 in January 1821 her support began to wane. However, her funeral procession the following August was diverted through the city by popular force and became the occasion for another radical demonstration.

By the end of the decade English politics became dominated by another issue: that of Catholic emancipation. The Catholic Emancipation Act many have owed little to public opinion in England, but it did owe a great deal to mass pressure in Ireland. The campaigns of the Catholic Association during the 1820s combined religious and nationalist sentiment into a powerful movement, and by 1828, Ireland was fast descending into anarchy with the collapse of law and order and widespread violence to people and property. Wellington and Peel were forced to backtrack on earlier promises to oppose emancipation, and passed an Act in 1829 that allowed Catholics full civil rights. The reaction in Britain was mixed, but amongst many the Act provoked real horror, with Protestant alarm evident amongst Dissenters as well as Anglicans. Orange lodges and Brunswick Clubs provided the focus for nationwide opposition to the measure and the press acted to whip up popular hostility against the government and Catholics. However, opposition was not well organised, nor did it threaten much unrest. Indeed, even anti-Catholic newspapers, such as the *Leeds Intelligencer* and *John Bull*, advised their readers against taking

32. Stephen Koss, *The Rise and Fall of the Political Press in Britain*, vol. I: *The Nineteenth Century* (London, 1981), p. 40.

33. Smith, *A Queen on Trial*, p. 108.

any extra-parliamentary action, apart from petitioning.[34] The country was clearly divided over the issue of Catholic emancipation. The *Birmingham Journal* and *Birmingham Argus* were vehemently opposed, as was the *Nottingham Journal, Manchester Chronicle* and *Manchester Herald.* However, in Nottingham, the *Journal's* stance was challenged by the *Nottingham Review,* and in Manchester, the *Manchester Guardian* supported the change. *The Times* was broadly in favour of the measure, as was another London paper, the *Morning Chronicle.*

There were other divisions apparent in Preston, Leeds and Cornwall.[35] In Kent the *Kent Herald* and the *Kentish Chronicle* were in favour of emancipation, whilst the *Kentish Gazette* warned its readers that any such measure 'may place our children, if not ourselves, at the mercy of the professors of that religion, which was planted in ignorance, and maintained in blood!' 'Shall the Freemen of Canterbury stand idly by', the paper asked, 'while measures are taken which are likely to recall the scenes of Queen Mary's day? On the wall of our City we may stand and look into the very field where our forefathers were butchered...'[36] In Cambridge, whilst the *Independent Press* argued that emancipation was a 'civil right', the *Cambridge Weekly Journal* associated Catholicism with 'political tyranny and mental darkness'.[37] It was clear that the country's newspaper press was reflecting and promoting serious differences of opinion. However, despite the furore which the passage of the Catholic Emancipation Act prompted, arguably the greatest impact which the measure had in England did not concern Catholics, but rather the fate of the Tory Party. The Act caused the break-up of the Tory alliance, in power for over twenty years, and provided the Whigs with an opportunity to govern and to institute a series of far-reaching reforms.

As we have seen, calls for parliamentary reform had been common for many years. In the postwar period such demands began to be voiced more loudly, as growing numbers of middle-class men and women joined liberal Dissenters in demanding direct representation for the expanding manufacturing and commercial

34. G.I.T. Machin, *The Catholic Question in English Politics 1820 to 1830* (Oxford, 1964), p. 139.

35. Machin, *The Catholic Question,* pp. 197–8.

36. Peter L. Humphries, 'Kentish politics and public opinion 1768–1832' (Oxford DPhil thesis, 1981), p. 284.

37. Michael Murphy, *Cambridge Newspapers and Opinion 1780–1850* (Cambridge, 1977), pp. 64 and 71.

towns, and radical politicians and working-class groups increasingly linked the country's economic ills to the narrowness of the franchise. Still, despite the worsening economic situation and outbreak of serious rioting, the Reform Act would probably not have been passed had it not been for the great weight of public opinion behind the measure. This was made clear to parliamentarians through the unprecedented scale of petitioning (3,000 reform petitions were sent to parliament), the organisational work of the Political Unions and the combined efforts of the press. Such was the perceived influence of public opinion that in 1830 the *Sheffield Iris* proclaimed that 'this is the age ... when public opinion is setting in with a full tide against the antiquated absurdity of allowing the great mercantile interests of the country, as they are identified with certain manufacturing towns, to be risqued [*sic*] in the precarious support of county or rotton borough members'.[38] According to Lord John Russell, this powerful voice 'out of doors' came from the manufacturing towns where 'There sprang up a people whom it was easy to inflame and excite by popular harangues, and by the press, by large public meetings, and by inflammatory newspapers'.[39] Joseph Hamburger has argued that radical politicians used the press to intimidate those at Westminster into enacting parliamentary reform for fear that otherwise they would provoke a revolution. James Mill's advice to fellow radicals was that the press should make the people 'appear to be ready and impatient to break out into action, without actually breaking out'.[40] It is true that the press did help to summon up the spectre of uncontrollable popular anger if the bill was dropped or diluted. In February 1830, for example, the editor of the *Maidstone Gazette* claimed to 'tremble for the consequences' if reform failed.[41] The *Kent Herald* asserted: 'if the *prayer* for reform is now denied it [national agitation] will grow rapidly to a *demand* and who will dare refuse it?'[42] Rather more alarmingly, the *Poor Man's Guardian* published extracts from Colonel Macerone's *Defensive Instructions for the People*, which was a manual on street-fighting.[43]

38. Happs, 'The Sheffield newspaper press and parliamentary reform, 1787–1831', p. 137.

39. Joseph Hamburger, *James Mill and the Art of Revolution* (New Haven, 1963), p. 4.

40. Hamburger, *James Mill*, p. 64.

41. John A. Phillips, *The Great Reform Bill in the Boroughs: English Electoral Behaviour 1818–1841* (Oxford, 1992), p. 20.

42. Humphries, 'Kentish politics and public opinion 1768–1832', p. 331.

43. E.P. Thompson, *Making of the English Working Class* (London, 1963), p. 898.

But how much such threatening expressions were the work of radical politicians is open to question. The Political Unions, for example, were often involved in local propaganda campaigns, and indeed the seventh duty of every member of the Council of the Birmingham Political Union was 'to consider the means of organising a system of operations whereby the Public Press may be influenced to act generally in support of the public interests'.[44] But newspapers were not dictated to by such bodies. Instead, they constituted one factor for newspaper editors to consider in the complex make-up of popular sentiment. What was certainly true was that newspapers were crucial in making politicians such as Grey believe that revolution was imminent, and thus in compelling him to commit himself to reform despite the force of parliamentary opposition. In March 1830, Grey was already blaming newspapers for 'destroying all respect for rank and station and for the institutions of the Government', and a year later William IV complained bitterly to Grey of the 'poisonous influence of a licentious and unobstructed Press'.[45]

The bulk of English newspapers were firmly in favour of reform. *The Times* was particularly staunch in its support. In March 1831, the paper proclaimed:

> We are now arrived at the grand crisis for which the country has been so long preparing itself – a reform, or a dissolution within a few days or hours! – a reform, or the immediate reappearance of those who resist the just demands of the nation before their constituents! But it is impossible that the reform should not be admitted; for, if rejected, it is obvious that all connexion whatever between the men from thenceforth assembling themselves in Westminster, and the people of England, is at an end! ... All England wants reform: who are they to oppose it?[46]

In addition to asserting that the English public were clamouring for change, *The Times* encouraged mass agitation. In December 1830 it announced: 'We trust there is not a county, town, or village in the United Kingdom which will not meet and petition for a reform ... ' It also urged the people to recognise 'the solemn duty of forming themselves into political societies throughout the whole realm'.[47] When the House of Lords rejected the bill in October 1831,

44. Fraser, 'The agitation for parliamentary reform', p. 41.
45. Fraser, 'The agitation for parliamentary reform', p. 40.
46. E.A. Smith, *Reform or Revolution? A Diary of Reform in England, 1830–32* (Stroud, 1992), p. 49.
47. Thompson, *Making of the English Working Class*, p. 890.

London newspapers, including *The Times*, were published with black borders as a sign of mourning.[48] Support for the bill was also marked in the provinces, where newspapers such as the *Leeds Mercury*, *Leicester Chronicle* and *Nottingham Review* had campaigned for parliamentary reform for years. More recent papers such as the *Manchester Guardian*, *Manchester Times* and *Leeds Patriot* quickly joined the cause, in addition to traditionally Tory newspapers such as *Birmingham Argus*, *Leicestershire Herald* and *Nottingham Journal*.[49] The *Argus* complained of Birmingham's lack of MPs, and asserted that 'The very serious losses to which the trade of Birmingham has been exposed ... might have been greatly diminished, if not entirely prevented, had we been so fortunate as to have possessed two FAITHFUL REPRESENTATIVES IN PARLIAMENT during the last thirty of forty years.'[50]

It was not uncommon for provincial newspaper editors to be actively involved in pro-reform politics themselves. In 1830, the *Leeds Mercury*, edited by Edward Baines, was at the centre of a campaign in Yorkshire to elect the reformer, Henry Brougham. The *Mercury*'s rival, the *Leeds Intelligencer*, announced Brougham's election with scorn: 'Let it be proclaimed a warning to the race, that the Whig Aristocracy of the great County of York have been compelled to surrender to the Bainesocracy of Leeds; that ancient Whiggery ... lacked the spirit to hold up its head in face of Mr. Baines of the *Leeds Mercury*, aided by a small train of Unitarian and Presbyterian Dissenters, and the stray sheep of the Radical Interest.'[51] Both Edward Baines and his son, Edward Baines, Jr., were heavily involved in campaigning for reform. They not only championed it in their paper but also spoke at numerous reform meetings in York and Leeds.[52] Similarly active was Archibald Prentice of the *Manchester Times*. When the Reform Act was finally passed in 1832, Prentice rejoiced that 'the people and the press are, thank God! triumphant'.[53]

Not all provincial newspapers supported reform though. The *Cambridge Chronicle* felt the bill was too rushed and too radical,[54] and the *Kentish Gazette* observed that 'the inhabitants of this great nation

48. Smith, *Reform or Revolution?*, p. 91.
49. Fraser, 'The agitation for parliamentary reform', p. 41.
50. Dinwiddy, *From Luddism to the First Reform Bill*, p. 13.
51. Read, *Press and People*, p. 120.
52. Read, *Press and People*, p. 121; *Life of Edward Baines*, ch. 11.
53. Read, *Press and People*, p. 154; Prentice, *Historical Sketches*.
54. Murphy, *Cambridge Newspapers*, pp. 76–7.

are rapidly dividing themselves into two classes – the friends of order and a conservative constitution on the one hand, – the lovers of change at all risks and hazards on the other'.[55] However, such a line was not always popular. Sales in the Tory *Manchester Courier* were halved in 1831 when the paper attacked the prospect of reform.[56] Even before the Bill was passed, critical voices were also heard from the radical camp. 'Orator' Hunt was joined by the *Poor Man's Guardian* in criticising the bill for being too moderate. It was, according to the *Guardian*, 'purely a question between the aristocracy and the *middle*-money-getting classes'.[57] Reformist papers such as the *Manchester Guardian* argued that the interests of employers and workmen were inseparable: 'As the mass of the middle classes never can have any interests adverse to the happiness and prosperity of those below them in society, the rights of the humblest order would be quite safe from a constituency in which that mass had a preponderance.'[58] As we shall see, it was not an argument that most working-class radicals found either convincing or comforting. During the next two decades, an increasingly wide gulf opened up between middle- and working-class reformers. Newspapers generally allied themselves to one or other of the camps and in doing so helped to emphasise further their differences.

This divide became obvious during the factory agitation of the 1830s. The factory movement campaigned for a ten-hour day for women and child workers. It brought together individuals with a range of interests, including Tory paternalists and working-class radicals, and amounted to an impressive mass movement in the textile districts of northern England. The initial impetus for the campaign was a letter entitled 'Slavery in Yorkshire', written by Richard Oastler and published in the *Leeds Mercury* in October 1830. Oastler complained that 'Thousands of our fellow-creatures ... are this very moment existing in a state of slavery *more horrid* than are the victims of that hellish system, '*colonial slavery*' ... [they] hasten, half-dressed, *but not half-fed*, to those magazines of British infantile slavery – *the worsted mills in the town and neighbourhood of Bradford*'.[59] Oastler's letter provoked a furious controversy in the Yorkshire newspapers. Although his campaign for a ten-hour day

55. Humphries, 'Kentish politics and public opinion 1768–1832', p. 332.
56. Read, *Press and People*, p. 193.
57. Hamburger, *James Mill*, p. 80.
58. Dinwiddy, *From Luddism to the First Reform Bill*, p. 65; Norman McCord, *The Anti-Corn Law League 1838–1846* (London, 1958), p. 378.
59. J.T. Ward, *The Factory Movement 1830–1855* (London, 1962), p. 34.

began in the *Mercury*, it quickly moved to the Tory *Intelligencer*, after Edward Baines tried to cut the letters. Baines supported a compromise eleven-hour day and defended the rights of employers. As a result he was soon seen as the enemy of factory reform. In April 1832, 200 factory operatives marched through Leeds carrying a copy of the *Mercury* on a pole, bound in crêpe. This was set on fire outside the paper's office, and in the evening an effigy of the elder Baines was also burnt.[60]

As the factory movement began to gain momentum, other papers, such as *The Times*, *Standard* and *Morning Herald*, also gave support by publishing articles in favour of reform, reporting meetings and speeches, and demanding action from parliament.[61] Outside the North of England, papers such as the *Cambridge Chronicle* compared factory work to West Indian slavery, and spoke of the 'White slaves of Rochdale'.[62] In addition, the movement produced its own organs, the *Voice of the West Riding* and the *British Labourer's Protector and Factory Child's Friend*. Yet many other papers opposed change, particularly those such as the *Leeds Mercury* and the *Manchester Guardian*, which were associated with northern manufacturers. The *Guardian* argued that restrictive legislation would reduce wages and that higher prices would lose foreign markets. In 1832 it proclaimed that 'To yield to the senseless and mischievous popular outcry for a reduction to ten hours would be an act of suicidal madness'.[63] The apparent hypocrisy in the manufacturers' stance was quickly pounced upon by the proponents of factory reform. The *Stockport Advertiser* criticised employers who were 'the veriest liberals in the political sense, yet they exercise a terrible tyranny in their own establishments',[64] whilst in Kent, the *Gazette* attacked the 'hypocritical millocrats'.[65] The popular pressure exerted in favour of factory reform in the early 1830s was not enough to ensure the passage of an 1832 Bill specifically aimed at limiting child labour. However, an Act passed the following year did restrict children's work to some extent. After this, many factory activists turned their attention to the New Poor Law.

60. Read, *Press and People*, p. 124.
61. Ward, *The Factory Movement*, p. 51.
62. Murphy, *Cambridge Newspapers*, p. 93.
63. Read, *Press and People*, p. 144.
64. Ward, *The Factory Movement*, p. 315.
65. Kenneth J. Eaton, 'Newspapers and politics in Canterbury and Maidstone 1815–1850: opinion in two Kentish towns' (University of Kent MA thesis, 1972), p. 141.

The campaign against the Poor Law Amendment Act, or the New Poor Law, of 1834, reached its height in the manufacturing districts of Lancashire and Yorkshire in 1837–8. In terms of organisation and personnel it was based largely on the preceding factory movement. The New Poor Law was introduced by the government in response to rising poor rates and a desire to eradicate what reformers presented as parochial maladministration and idleness. It was hugely unpopular amongst the poorer sections of society. Samuel Kydd, a young shoemaker in the 1830s, later wrote that 'The passing of the New Poor Law Amendment Act did more to sour the hearts of the labouring population, than did the privations consequent on all the actual poverty of the land.'[66] Large numbers of men and women feared mass incarceration in the new workhouses, or 'bastilles'. It was not just the poor who were hostile to the Act either. Members of the middle classes also argued against the New Poor Law on Christian and humanitarian grounds. Newspapers were instrumental in the campaign against the changes, particularly the introduction of workhouses. The press not only publicised the arguments and activities of groups opposed to the New Poor Law, but helped to spread horror stories of the ill-treatment that workhouse inmates received. Some, like the tale spread by Feargus O'Connor of the *Northern Star* that a starving workhouse boy had gnawed his finger down to the first joint, proved not to be true.[67] Yet this story and others like that of a Lincoln labourer who had committed suicide, a crippled child of two who had been separated from its mother at Hampnett and a labourer who had died of starvation at Donnington, were widely circulated by newspapers and proved extremely influential in turning public opinion against the New Poor Law.[68] The Tory paper, the *Leeds Intelligencer*, attacked the new law as 'a monstrosity in legislation calculated to disgust as well as astonish'.[69] Other Tory papers including the *Bolton Chronicle* were joined by radical newspapers such as the *Sheffield Iris*, *Manchester and Salford Advertiser*, *Northern Liberator* and the newly formed *Northern Star*. These papers published extensive reports of anti-Poor Law meetings, as well as editorials, articles and letters condemning the measure.[70]

66. Wright, *Popular Radicalism*, p. 107.
67. M.E. Rose, 'The Anti-Poor Law agitation', in J.T. Ward, ed., *Popular Movements c. 1830–1850* (London, 1970), p. 85.
68. Ward, *The Factory Movement*, p. 233.
69. Read, *Press and People*, p. 187.
70. Rose, 'The Anti-Poor Law agitation', p. 87.

Bronterre O'Brien in the *Northern Star* denounced the Act as aimed at placing 'the whole of the labouring population at the utter mercy and disposal of the monied or property owning classes'.[71] In London, John Bell of the *London Mercury* angrily denied 'the existence of any *class* of idlers, out of the ranks of the aristocracy, and of the middle orders'.[72] More influentially, John Walter, the MP for Berkshire and proprietor of *The Times*, opposed the bill in parliament, whilst his paper took up the cause and became one of the Act's 'most formidable and consistent critics'.[73] Newspapers such as the *Manchester Guardian*, which supported the New Poor Law, were in a minority.[74] The popular clamour against the new law, and the practical difficulties which were experienced in trying to operate it, were such that the system soon collapsed. However, the bitterness caused by the measure lived on and continued to affect working-class politics in particular. It contributed in no small part to the growth of Chartism: an issue to which newspapers such as the *Northern Liberator* and the *Northern Star* increasingly turned their attention.

As the campaigns against the factory system and the New Poor Law raged during the 1830s, radical politics and a radical newspaper press were once more experiencing a period of vitality and growth. As we have seen, the cheap, unstamped radical press was largely driven out of circulation during the 1820s, but the radical revival after 1830 brought it back to the forefront of popular politics. Journals of opinion, which typified the radical press of the 1810s, gave way to popular newspapers, which increasingly came into competition with the stamped press and eventually outsold it.[75] Papers such as *Cosmopolite*, *Figaro*, *Crisis*, *Poor Man's Guardian*, *Working Man's Friend*, *Destructive* and *Gauntlet* were based largely in London. They were sometimes superseded by a new type of unstamped broadsheet, such as the *Twopenny Dispatch*, *Weekly Police Gazette* and *People's Hue and Cry*. By 1836, the unstamped press had grown to include the *New Weekly True Sun*, *Weekly Herald* and *Police Register*. These papers, like their counterparts earlier in the century, still attacked Old Corruption and taxation, but they also introduced new socialist critiques of the existing political economy,

71. Rose, 'The Anti-Poor Law agitation', p. 81.
72. Dorothy Thompson, *The Chartists* (Hounslow, 1984), p. 31.
73. Rose, 'The Anti-Poor Law agitation', p. 79.
74. Read, *Press and People*, p. 145.
75. Patricia Hollis, *The Pauper Press: A Study in Working-Class Radicalism of the 1830s* (Oxford, 1970), p. 105.

such as Spenceanism (which opposed all private property) and Owenism (which planned the reorganisation of society along utopian lines). Although the journalists of the unstamped press did not agree on many matters, certain tenets, such as the right of working men to vote, the belief that the working classes were productive whilst the rest of society were parasites on their labour, the argument that government was organised in the interests of the upper classes and the need for a secret ballot during elections, were generally agreed on.[76] In 1834, the *Poor Man's Guardian* stated:

> Now, since all wealth is the produce of industry, and as the privileged fraction produce nothing themselves, it is plain that they must live on the labours of the rest. ... The 'property' people having all the law-making to themselves, make and maintain fraudulent institutions, by which they contrive (under false pretences) to transfer the wealth of the producers to themselves. ... These and the like are the pretences under which the useful classes are plundered for the benefit of the useless.[77]

In addition to disseminating ideas about the way in which society was, and should be, run, the unstamped press also furthered working-class radical politics by relaying local information, advertising meetings and championing the cause of groups such as the National Union of the Working Classes.[78] According to D.G. Wright, it was the unstamped press which nurtured the more widespread radicalism which had emerged during the reform crisis by maintaining essential contact and a sense of participation in a common movement.[79] Certainly there were strong links between the unstamped press and working-class political organisations, whilst writing, publishing and distributing unstamped papers formed a vast working-class movement in its own right.

It has already been noted that the 'class'-based political divisions which followed 1832 made the 'reform alliance' of working-class and middle-class radicals extremely shaky. The campaign for the repeal of newspaper stamp duty which developed during the 1830s revealed the different sides struggling for the same ends in different ways and for very different reasons. As we saw in chapter 1, many

76. Hollis, *The Pauper Press*, chs. 6 and 7; Joel H. Wiener, *The War of the Unstamped: The Movement to Repeal the British Newspaper Tax, 1830–1836* (Ithaca, NY, 1969), ch. 8.
77. Hollis, *The Pauper Press*, pp. 222–3.
78. Wiener, *War of the Unstamped*, pp. 245–9.
79. Wright, *Popular Radicalism*, p. 96.

middle-class proponents of repeal believed that a cheap press would instruct and elevate the masses. James Mill felt that this would, in turn, counteract the effect of the more radical, and unsavoury, sections of the press:

> the illicit cheap publications, in which the doctrines of the right of the labouring people, who say they are the only producers, to all that is produced, is very generally preached. The alarming nature of this you will understand when I inform you that these publications are super-seding the Sunday newspapers, and every other channel through which the people might get better information. I am sure it is not good policy to give the power of teaching the people exclusively to persons violating the law, and of such desperate circumstances and character that neither the legal nor the moral sanction has sufficient hold upon them. The only effectual remedy is to remove the tax which gives them this deplorable power.[80]

Working-class radicals, on the other hand, argued that political education was a means to some form of political and social revolution. They acted in open defiance of the law and waged a 'war of the unstamped', publishing and selling a variety of cheap radical papers which challenged the establishment and alarmed the government. With their attacks on the competitive economic system, the ruling elite and the established Church, papers such as the *Poor Man's Guardian* and the *Voice of West Riding* provoked considerable hostility from amongst the ruling elite and the conservative middle classes. This is hardly surprising when radical writers such as Bronterre O'Brien proclaimed in the *Destructive* that:

> Some simpletons talk of knowledge as rendering the working classes more obedient and dutiful – better servants, better subjects, and so on, which means making them more subservient slaves, and more conducive to the wealth and gratification of idlers of all descriptions. But such knowledge is trash; the only knowledge which is of any service to the working people is that which makes them more dissatisfied, and makes them worse slaves.[81]

Not surprisingly, the stamped press was also hostile to the unstamped papers, which, they felt, were stealing their readers and reducing their profits. They too joined in the call for a reduction in tax in order to compete more easily.[82] In 1835

80. Hollis, *The Pauper Press*, p. 14.
81. Wright, *Popular Radicalism*, p. 97.
82. Hollis, *The Pauper Press*, pp. 79–80.

petitions were presented to parliament demanding the repeal
of stamp duty, and a series of meetings was held which sent
deputations to the Chancellor. Under growing pressure both from
out-of-doors – and not least from the newspaper press – and
from an influential lobby group within parliament, and faced with
the knowledge that attempts to enforce the law were largely
unsuccessful, the government reduced the stamp tax on newspapers to one penny in 1836. Some radicals still campaigned for
the total repeal of newspaper taxation (finally achieved in 1855),
but the issue largely died out during the following decade as
Chartism increasingly dominated working-class and radical politics.

Chartism grew out of a belief that the people had been
manipulated and misled by middle-class reformers in order to
provide the 'muscle' to ensure the Reform Bill's success in 1832,
and had subsequently been abandoned once the measure was
passed. More than that, the 'betrayal' had been compounded by
the middle class's support of a government which subsequently
imposed the New Poor Law, repressed trade unions and the Swing
rioters, resisted the Ten Hours Bill and attacked the unstamped
press. Chartists believed that redress for these grievances lay in
obtaining political power and that economic inequality sprang
from political inequality, and not vice versa. It addressed the
politically excluded and promised them protection and deliverance
from the 'class' legislation of the aristocratic government by
ensuring them direct representation.

The Charter was drawn up in 1837 and was quickly followed by a
national petitioning campaign. The six points of the People's
Charter demanded universal manhood suffrage, secret ballots,
annual parliaments, constituencies of equal size, the payment of
MPs and the abolition of property qualifications for members of the
Commons. Chartism drew its strength from across the country,
particularly from industrial communities. With no common
economic base and a high degree of localism in its organisation, it
was not a particularly unified movement and lacked inner coherence and an organisational identity. However, individuals such as
Feargus O'Connor did much to draw the different areas and groups
together in national protest using the mass platform, as Chartism
built upon the methods of Hunt and the postwar radicals. In
addition, a formal structure of organisation, most importantly the
National Charter Association, helped provide the movement with a
sense of unity. Yet arguably the most important single unifying
element in Chartism was the Chartist press, not least because, as

Gareth Stedman Jones has shown, the sophisticated ideology of Chartism was dependent upon print for its dissemination.[83]

Over fifty Chartist newspapers and journals appeared during the movement's life.[84] These drew largely on the tradition – and often the personnel – of the unstamped press.[85] Every Chartist group or leader had their own periodicals or newspapers, such as Lovett's *Charter* (1839–40) or the London *Democrat*, which put forward the views of Harney. In the North-East there was the *Northern Liberator* (1837–40), and in the West Country, the *Western Vindicator*.[86] Many were short-lived, or expressed regional or sectional Chartist opinion, but the *Northern Star* quickly established itself as the comprehensive and definitive voice of the movement. This was a role which earlier radical papers had proved unable to fulfil and helped unite Chartism by publicising local and regional initiatives and according them national significance.[87] As the *Northern Star* itself explained:

> If the people were unanimous upon any measure, but it suited not the press to convey that unanimity, the identity of opinion would be useless. The great value of the Press to its party [the People's party], then, is that it serves as a herald to proclaim to all the united opinion of all, and under its banners the forces are mustered without the expenditure of much time or money.[88]

According to James Epstein, 'The *Star* was the most important agency for the integration and transformation of disparate local radical agitation and organisation into the national Chartist movement'.[89] The early Chartist historian, Reginald Gammage, agreed. 'Never was a journal started more opportunely,' he wrote. 'It caught and reflected the spirit of the times.'[90] The paper was founded in Leeds in 1837 as a Factory and Anti-Poor Law journal, but after it was bought by Feargus O'Connor it became a national vehicle for his brand of Chartism. However, O'Connor's paper was never

83. Gareth Stedman Jones, 'Rethinking Chartism', in Gareth Stedman Jones, ed., *Languages of Class: Studies in English Working-Class History, 1832–1982* (Cambridge, 1983).

84. David Jones, *Chartism and the Chartists* (London, 1975), p. 99.

85. Thompson, *The Chartists*, pp. 37–9.

86. Edward Royle, *Chartism* (2nd edn., Harlow, 1986), p. 74.

87. John Belcham, *Popular Radicalism in Nineteenth-Century Britain* (Basingstoke, 1996), p. 76.

88. J.A. Epstein, 'Feargus O'Connor and the *Northern Star*', *International Review of Social History*, **xxi** (1976), p. 91.

89. Epstein, 'Feargus O'Connor and the *Northern Star*', p. 51.

90. Jones, *Chartism and the Chartists*, p. 100.

exclusive in terms of politics, and unlike earlier radical papers whose editors had ignored the voices of rivals, the *Star* allowed different views within Chartism to be expressed. It reported, for example, on Robert Owen's tours and trade union activity as well as Christian radicalism and co-operation.[91] Indeed, Engels noted that the *Star* was 'the only sheet which reports all the movements of the proletariat'.[92] O'Connor was not always popular amongst the Chartist leadership, but Holyoake's one tribute to him was that 'In the *Northern Star* he let every rival speak, and had the grand strength of indifference to what anyone said against him in his own columns'.[93] The paper thus became *the* paper of Chartism, and unlike earlier radical weeklies, gave good coverage to more general news in addition to material relating strictly to the Chartist movement. The *Star* was in every sense a 'newspaper' and not just a campaign sheet, and therein lay much of its strength. The *Northern Star* was tremendously successful, achieving sales of 50,000 at the height of Chartist activity in 1839 (although these dropped substantially in the 1840s). Although the paper was stamped and relatively expensive, we have already seen in chapter 3 how widespread its readership was. Circulation was so great that 'the Post Office authorities were in some cases obliged to hire carts or wagons for its transmission, as it occasionally overflowed the restricted accommodation of the mail coaches'.[94] The distribution of the paper also became a political campaign in its own right, as paid agents became local Chartist organisers, and vice versa.[95] Many of these individuals were veterans of the 'war of the unstamped'.[96]

The excitement, expectation, unity and mass involvement that Chartism managed to secure in its early years was not repeated. The movement's political leadership soon split into opposing factions: some of which proposed peaceful, constitutional progress, others of which favoured the use of physical force and prompted the failed risings in Newport and Bradford. The movement subsequently became even more diverse, with the emergence of such trends as 'Teetotal' and 'Knowledge' Chartism and the development of Complete Suffrage Unions constituted a general shift towards 'respectability' A severe economic depression in 1842 helped to

---

91. Thompson, *The Chartists*, p. 48.
92. Epstein, 'Feargus O'Connor and the *Northern Star*', pp. 85–6.
93. Royle, *Chartism*, p. 77.
94. Epstein, 'Feargus O'Connor and the *Northern Star*', p. 70.
95. Wright, *Popular Radicalism*, p. 143.
96. Epstein, 'Feargus O'Connor and the *Northern Star*', p. 77.

revive the movement's political radicalism. This was pre-empted by a meeting of delegates in Manchester to found the National Charter Association, which was in turn largely prompted by O'Connor's letters to the *Northern Star* from gaol.[97] In 1848, Chartism experienced its final push as Chartist leaders attempted to exploit the excitement caused by revolutions throughout Europe. Yet despite attempts to present an acceptable image, public opinion appeared firmly opposed to Chartist activity and linked it with unrest in Ireland. On the morning of a planned mass demonstration on Kennington Common, *The Times* warned that 'The present movement is a ramification of the Irish conspiracy. The Repealers wish to make as great a hell of this island as they have made of their own'.[98] Although the Kennington meeting passed off peaceably enough, further radical activity elsewhere in the country was met with repressive government action.

Indeed, Chartism had always received a generally hostile reception in the country at large and outside of the ranks of its own publications. The *Leeds Mercury* was, like many other provincial newspapers, strongly opposed to the Chartist cause. In 1838 the paper claimed that 'The true objects to which the attention of the Working Classes should be directed, and the only means by which they can ever attain either political influence or personal happiness, are these – Education, Religion, Virtue, Industry, Sobriety, Frugality. These are *Six Points* of a thousand times more importance than the Six of "the People's Charter". These would make them *deserve* the suffrage.'[99] According to the Tory *Leeds Intelligencer*, the Six Points, if achieved, would produce 'a regular Democratic tyranny'.[100] The *Manchester Guardian* was also critical, and argued that annual parliaments would only increase 'the expense, the trouble, and the turmoil of electioneering', that the payment of MPs would bring 'the lucre of private gain' into politics, and that universal suffrage would give the vote 'to every drunkard and blackguard in the kingdom'. Moreover the paper proclaimed that the Chartist leaders hoped 'to bribe the poor to aid their designs, by holding out hopes of wholesale plunder and confiscation'.[101] In Suffolk, both the *Bury and Norwich Post* and the

97. James Epstein, *The Lion of Freedom: Feargus O'Connor and the Chartist Movement, 1832–1842* (London, 1982), pp. 220–35.

98. Belcham, *Popular Radicalism in Nineteenth-Century Britain*, p. 91.

99. Read, *Press and People*, p. 132.

100. Read, *Press and People*, p. 189.

101. Donald Read, 'Chartism in Manchester', in Asa Briggs, ed., *Chartist Studies* (London, 1967), pp. 38–9.

Ipswich Journal proved hostile. In 1838 the *Journal* announced that the Chartists planned to effect a form of levelling:

> When men like these talk of 'rights of equality by nature' and blurt out their venom at those who have amassed property ... and call them knaves and plunderers of the working classes; their object is too apparent to be concealed by the transparent veil of 'patriotism' which they invariably raise to hide their real motives.[102]

In Kent, the *Maidstone Journal* proclaimed in 1839 that 'Chartism is now revealing itself in its proper colours – pillage and spoliation are evidently its immediate objects, anarchy and revolution are its ultimate aim'.[103] Such a hostile press contributed in no small part to the widespread attacks made on Chartists and their cause.

Whilst the working-class campaign for the Charter met with a largely poor reception from the provincial newspaper press, the same fate did not befall another great popular campaign of the 1840s for the repeal of the Corn Law. As we have seen, complaints against the Corn Law had been made since it was originally introduced in 1815. By the late 1830s it provided a focus for middle-class freetraders and radicals of all classes concerned with the condition of the poor. To campaigners the Corn Law constituted both a symbol of aristocratic misrule and a major impediment to free trade. The radical *Nottingham Review* claimed that 'an unparalleled mass of wretchedness, distress, privation and consequent disease among the poor labouring classes of the community' had been caused by it,[104] whilst the *Kent Herald* proclaimed the Corn Law to be 'the abominable fruits of an aristocratic system of government'.[105] At the end of 1838 the *Leeds Mercury* called upon both men and masters in the North 'to meet in all your towns and villages, and petition parliament for an *Abolition of the Bread Tax*'.[106] 'The iron is hot', the paper proclaimed, 'strike it with a Yorkshire hammer, and let us see if we cannot shape it into the beautiful form of Freedom.'[107] As had been the case with parliamentary reform, many provincial newspaper editors were

102. Hugh Fearn, 'Chartism in Suffolk', in Briggs, ed., *Chartist Studies*, p. 159.

103. Eaton, 'Newspapers and politics in Canterbury and Maidstone 1815–1850', pp. 157–8.

104. W.H. Chaloner, 'The agitation against the Corn Laws', in Ward, ed., *Popular Movements*, p. 137.

105. Eaton, 'Newspapers and politics in Canterbury and Maidstone 1815–1850', p. 151.

106. Read, *Press and People*, p. 134.

107. Read, *Press and People*, p. 135.

actively involved in organised opposition to the Corn Law in the shape of the Anti-Corn Law League. Archibald Prentice of the *Manchester Times* was one of the founders of the Manchester Anti-Corn Law Association in 1838 and later a member of the Anti-Corn Law League.[108] The editor of the *Sheffield Independent*, Thomas Ward, was also active in his local Anti-Corn Law association, and his paper, like the *Manchester Times*, consistently opposed the Corn Law.[109]

Not only did the movement to repeal the Corn Law attract support from newspapers, but the Anti-Corn Law League – the campaign's governing body – actively sought to promote its cause in the press. Soon after the League was founded in 1839, the movement's own paper, the *Anti-Corn Law Circular*, was established, which in 1841 changed its title to the more emotive *Anti-Bread Tax Circular* and later to the *League*. Members of the League also launched the *Economist* in 1843 as a journal devoted to the ideas of free trade, although not an avowed organ of the League. The League then purchased bulk copies of the journal and distributed them to its members.[110] The League also organised other forms of propaganda, and in 1839 it arranged to pay the owner of the London *Sun* £500 a year to publish the League's material. The organisation also agreed in 1842 to buy copies of eight of the capital's weekly papers in bulk in preparation for a major fund-raising drive, and in exchange for the newspapers concerned including an editorial recommending the League to its readers. These papers were then distributed free of charge in shops, inns, clubs, trains and ships.[111] The Anti-Corn Law League also distributed tracts, handbills and other propaganda devices as it grew into a national organisation of considerable size and political clout.

The anti-Corn Law campaigners were not without their enemies. Many radicals, as well as conservatives, accused them of narrow class interest. The *Morning Chronicle* called the Leaguers 'narrow-minded bigots'.[112] The *Leeds Intelligencer* attacked the Anti-Corn Law League as a selfish organisation of employers, seeking cheap labour rather than the well-being of their employees.[113] In the agricultural county

---

108. Read, *Press and People*, p. 163.
109. Read, *Press and People*, p. 171.
110. McCord, *The Anti-Corn Law League*, pp. 182–4.
111. McCord, *The Anti-Corn Law League*, pp. 181–2.
112. McCord, *The Anti-Corn Law League*, p. 84.
113. Read, *Press and People*, p. 190.

of Kent, the *Kentish Gazette* also denounced the Leaguers: 'The outcry against the agricultural interest has emanated from the manufacturers of the North – the most tyrannical and unjust of whom towards their own dependants are the principal members of the Anti-Corn Law League', whilst the *Kentish Observer* described Leaguers as men who had 'accumulated enormous fortunes in the course of a very few years, by the most heartless sacrifice of life and health on the part of those they employ, that ever disgraced a Christian country'.[114] In Cambridge, where the local economy was also based on land, the *Cambridge Chronicle* reminded its readers of the disastrous effects which a repeal would bring.[115]

Although the League was not directly responsible for the repeal of the Corn Laws in 1846, it had kept the question of repeal at the forefront of public attention for some years and had certainly influenced opinion both inside parliament and out-of-doors. Debates concerning the Corn Law often revealed the gulf between many working-class and middle-class reformers. Thus the London *Charter* newspaper in 1839 tried to persuade working men in Sheffield against 'leaving the people' to support the Anti-Corn Law League, which was described as 'a party comprised of avaricious, grasping, money-mongers, great capitalists, and rich manufacturers'.[116] Yet by the late 1840s, there were some signs that a rapprochement was possible. The *Northern Star* was fulsome in its praise of Peel's conversion to repeal in 1846; three years later, a significant editorial appeared in the paper which said of the National Parliamentary and Financial Reform Association – a group of middle-class reformers and moderate Chartists founded that year to campaign for the 'Little Charter' of household suffrage, the ballot, triennial Parliaments and a more equal distribution of seats – that

> The middle and working classes have joined hands, without reserve of dissimulation. The one party says they cannot go further at present – the other, that they will accompany them as far as they go, but they do not mean to stop there. The ancient and honoured motto is not even in abeyance. We still exclaim, 'The Charter and no Surrender!' but, taught by dear-bought past experience, we have varied the mode of operation by which it is to be attained.[117]

114. Eaton, 'Newspapers and politics in Canterbury and Maidstone 1815–1850', pp. 164 and 179.
115. Murphy, *Cambridge Newspapers*, p. 105.
116. Edward Royle and James Walvin, *English Radicals and Reformers 1760–1848* (Brighton, 1982), p. 177.
117. Royle and Walvin, *English Radicals and Reformers*, p. 180.

Newspapers were helping to set the stage for more unified activity in the future.

In addition to their intense discussion of domestic politics, the press continued to feed the public appetite for news about foreign affairs in the post-Napoleonic period. Improvements in communications – particularly the introduction of the telegraph – meant that by the 1850s, news from France could reach London in a matter of minutes. When Julius Reuter established his telegraph agency in the capital in 1851, the public could read about events on the continent often the day after they happened.[118] The sense of immediacy in foreign news coverage which such improvements produced, coupled with a series of dramatic events in Europe – not least the revolutions of 1848 – helped promote a growing public demand for sensation, news and outrage which publications such as the *Illustrated London News* (founded in 1842 and with a circulation of over 200,000 copies a week by 1856[119]) were aimed at satisfying. It was the more sensational elements of the newspaper press that persuaded large sections of the English public that they were threatened with a French invasion in 1848,[120] whilst an even larger section of the press whipped up a huge scandal surrounding the Crimean War (1854–6). Initially, both newspapers and the public appear to have supported hostilities against Russia, and anti-Russian sentiments were evident in books, pamphlets and the periodical press from as early as 1815.[121] But the war soon became deeply unpopular as its conduct was subjected to unprecedented levels of publicity and public discussion. Here newspapers played a crucial role, and the pioneer war dispatches of William Howard Russell in *The Times* were particularly important in revealing levels of incompetence amongst British officers and the poor state of the troops. Most newspapers laid the disasters of the campaign firmly at the door of the existing system of aristocratic government, and arguments were made for an alternative model based on 'middle-class' values of efficiency and meritocracy.[122] On 23 December

118. Donald Read, *The Power of the News: The History of Reuters 1849–1989* (Oxford, 1992), pp. 5–7.

119. Dennis Griffiths, ed., *The Encyclopedia of the British Press 1422–1992* (London, 1992), p. 330.

120. David Large, 'London in the year of revolutions, 1848', in *London in the Age of Reform*, p. 149.

121. Asa Briggs, *Victorian People: Some Reassessments of People, Institutions, Ideas and Events 1851–1867* (London, 1954), ch. 3; Peter Hopkirk, *The Great Game: On Secret Service in High Asia* (London, 1990).

122. Olive Anderson, *A Liberal State at War: English Politics and Economics During the Crimean War* (New York, 1967), ch. 2.

The Times declared that 'the noblest army England ever sent from these shores has been sacrificed to the grossest mismanagement. Incompetence, lethargy, aristocratic hauteur, official indifference, favour, routine, perverseness and stupidity reign...'[123] The famous Charge of the Light Brigade was a case in point, when the lack of tactical grasp and poor communication which beset the whole Anglo-French campaign was graphically and tragically displayed as Lord Cardigan's Light Brigade was ordered to charge against the main artillery of the Russian Army at Balaclava.

Although high political machinations were clearly important, public distaste concerning the Crimean War was certainly a contributory factor in the fall of the Aberdeen administration in 1855.[124] In February of that year the patriotic radical MP J.A. Roebuck carried a resolution in the Commons calling for an enquiry into the conduct of the war, and with the help of other anti-war radicals helped to bring down Aberdeen's unhappy coalition government. It was widely believed that the press had helped to promote the ministerial crisis. Indeed, the Foreign Secretary, the Earl of Clarendon, claimed in January 1855 that by exciting the public 'almost to madness', *The Times* had caused the government to fall.[125] Such claims were certainly dramatic, but they were not new. As we have seen in chapter 6, similar statements had been made more than a century earlier. However, what had changed was the social diversity and sheer size of the political nation which the newspaper press was thought to represent in such protests, as well as the degree of political clout which public opinion was thought to wield. By the end of our period, the newspaper press in England was largely free from government interference and was able – with some justification – to proclaim itself the fourth estate of the British constitution.

Conclusion

The postwar period was an extremely turbulent one in Britain. Economic hardship and increasing extra-parliamentary activity acted to make the political climate particularly heated and fuelled demands for radical changes in the way in which the country

---

123. J.B. Connacher, *The Aberdeen Coalition, 1852–1855: A Study in Mid-Nineteenth-Century Party Politics* (Cambridge, 1968), p. 518.

124. Connacher, *The Aberdeen Coalition*.

125. Anderson, *A Liberal State at War*, p. 75.

was run. In such a situation, newspapers became increasingly prominent as they encouraged and focused popular political campaigns, at the same time as becoming more strongly linked with public opinion. As such, the newspaper press was capable of wielding a sizeable degree of political power, and of influencing the decisions of government. This was particularly true of *The Times*, which by the 1840s was the most prominent English newspaper, although provincial newspapers were also extremely influential during the 1830s and 1840s, as was a radical press which was prominent both during these years and the immediate postwar period.

Between 1815 and 1855 English newspapers were involved in a huge variety of political campaigns and sustained a series of heated public debates. Movements for political reform and against government repression and 'Old Corruption' all motivated sections of the press at particular times. Certain issues – such as the Peterloo massacre, Queen Caroline's trial, Catholic emancipation, the demand for parliamentary reform in the early 1830s, factory reform, the New Poor Law, the Corn Law and the Crimean War – succeeded in provoking great waves of public indignation. Such outbursts of popular resentment were something which newspapers and newspaper editors were actively engaged not just in reflecting, but in promoting and perpetuating as well. However, for radical politics during this period, the impact of the press was arguably of even greater importance. Newspapers did not just publicise and galvanise support for the radical cause. It was also in the pages of the press that much of radical political ideology was worked out and disseminated. Print thus formed the backbone of radical politics, and in so doing, confirmed all the fears of earlier conservative commentators that newspapers would challenge the very existence of the old order.

Conclusion

Between the lapsing of the Printing Act in 1695 and the removal of
stamp duty in 1855, English newspapers were transformed from the
reading matter of a handful of the political and social elite to
the main source of information on current debates and contemporary affairs for the majority of the population. By the end of our
period, the scale of the newspaper press – both in terms of overall
circulation and the number of titles produced – was at a level which
would have been inconceivable (and unsupportable) in the early
eighteenth century. In addition, the character of most newspapers
in the mid-nineteenth century was self-confident, opinionated,
probing and critical in ways which would also have appeared alien
to earlier newspaper readers. Many late nineteenth-century claims
for the importance of newspapers would have seemed equally
astonishing. Not least that made in 1871 by James Grant, the
former editor of the *Morning Advertiser,* that the press had 'one of
the most glorious missions in which human agencies ever were
employed', namely, 'to enlighten, to civilise, and to morally transform the world'.[1] The degree to which Grant's prophesy came true,
is, of course, open to debate. What is less contentious is the
increasingly prominent role which newspapers played in English
political life.

Most importantly, newspapers helped to articulate, focus and
formulate the growing force of public opinion. For the German
sociologist Jürgen Habermas, this process can be understood by
seeing the newspaper press as part of a new public literary sphere
which emerged in late eighteenth-century England. This provided
the basis for a political public sphere, linked to the growth of a self-
conscious bourgeoisie and the emergence of a 'reasoning public'
which could be critical of administration and sought to influence
public power. The formation of this new public was dependent

---

1. James Grant, *The Newspaper Press: Its Origins, Progress and Present Position*
(London, 1871).

upon new networks of communications, not just because factors like a press and a reading public ensured the exchange of information and ideas, but in the larger sense of a new institutional context for political action.[2] Although historians of other European countries – France in particular – have applied the same model of social transformation to their own national contexts, it is clear that there were important differences between countries. As we have seen, such differences were a source of some surprise to foreign visitors, who were struck by the novelty of the English press and clearly unused to the degree of freedom which it enjoyed. Like many domestic contemporaries (and Whig historians), foreign commentators tended to celebrate the liberty with which the newspaper press operated in England, and claimed that the influence it exerted over politics and public opinion was a blessing which both prevented politicians from abusing their power and gave the people a voice. In an address to the Liverpool Chatham Society in 1858, W.S. Robinson went even further, and proclaimed that 'The present glory – the present social, moral, political and educational superiority of England in the great family of nations, is, in a vast measure, owing to her free, untrammelled, outspoken, and patriotic newspaper press.'[3]

Although we have also seen that such views were far from universally held between 1695 and 1855 – and others felt equally strongly that newspapers had a more sinister character and were capable of misleading the public and creating unrest and dissent – by the end of our period such negative assessments of the press were seldom heard. Aled Jones has noted a modification of the political language used in the debate on journalism from the mid-nineteenth century, so that even amongst conservative commentators, terms such as 'sedition' and 'licentiousness' all but disappeared in favour of a more tolerant attitude, which accepted the power and permanence of the newspaper press and reflected a more optimistic approach to its impact on public opinion. Thus Sir Algernon Borthwick, proprietor of the conservative *Morning Post*, argued in 1884 that local newspapers were capable of persuading working men 'not, perhaps, that the Conservative cause is the

---

2. Jürgen Habermas, *The Structural Transformation of the Public Sphere*, trans. Thomas Burger (Cambridge, Mass., 1989); Geoff Eley, 'Re-thinking the political: social history and political culture in eighteenth- and nineteenth-century Britain', *Archiv für Sozialgeschichte*, **21** (1981).

3. Aled Jones, *Powers of the Press: Newspapers, Power and the Public in Nineteenth-Century England* (Aldershot, 1996), p. 180.

absolutely right one, but that much of what they have heard from their Radical friends and associates is untrue'.[4] As the world of clubland and the lobby system ensured that journalists and politicians became increasingly intimate towards the end of the nineteenth century, politicians' acceptance, and indeed promotion, of the political and constitutional role which the newspaper press had assumed, only increased. It was now impossible to imagine the political world operating without newspapers. Thus W.T. Stead wrote in 1886 that although he was a 'comparatively young journalist', he had 'seen Cabinets upset, Ministers driven into retirement, laws repealed, great social reforms initiated, Bills transformed, estimates remodelled, programmes modified, Acts passed, generals nominated, governors appointed, armies sent hither and thither, war proclaimed and war averted', all as a result of 'the agency of newspapers'.[5]

4. Jones, *Powers of the Press*, pp. 165–74, quote from p. 174.
5. Stephen Koss, *The Rise and Fall of the Political Press in Britain*, vol. 1: *The Nineteenth Century* (London, 1981), p. 14.

Select Bibliography

CHAPTER ONE: NEWSPAPERS AND PUBLIC OPINION

BARKER, HANNAH, *Newspapers, Politics, and Public Opinion in Late Eighteenth-Century England* (Oxford, 1998).

BREWER, JOHN, *Party Ideology and Popular Politics at the Accession of George III* (Cambridge, 1976).

GUNN, J.A.W., *Beyond Liberty and Property: The Process of Self-recognition in Eighteenth-century Political Thought* (Kingston, Ont., 1983).

HELLMUTH, ECKHART, 'The palladium of all other English liberties: reflections on the liberty of the press in England during the 1760s and 1770s', in ECKHART HELLMUTH, ed., *The Transformation of Political Culture: England and Germany in the Late Eighteenth Century* (Oxford, 1990), p. 493.

JONES, ALED, *Powers of the Press: Newspapers, Power and the Public in Nineteenth-Century England* (Aldershot, 1996).

CHAPTER TWO: THE GROWTH OF NEWSPAPERS

BARKER, HANNAH, *Newspapers, Politics, and Public Opinion in Late Eighteenth-Century England* (Oxford, 1998).

BLACK, JEREMY, *The English Press in the Eighteenth Century* (Beckenham, 1987).

CRANFIELD, G.A., *The Development of the Provincial Newspaper* (Oxford, 1962).

SNYDER, HENRY L., 'The circulation of newspapers in the reign of Queen Anne', *Library*, 5th ser., **xxiii** (1969).

SUTHERLAND, JAMES R., 'The circulation of newspapers and literary periodicals, 1700–30', *Library*, 4th ser., **15** (1934).

WADSWORTH, A.P., 'Newspaper circulations, 1800–1954', *Transactions of the Manchester Statistical Society* (1955).

CHAPTER THREE: NEWSPAPER READERS

ASPINALL, ARTHUR, 'The circulation of newspapers in the early nineteenth century', *Review of English Studies*, **xxii**, 85 (1946).

BARKER, HANNAH, *Press, Politics, and Public Opinion in Late Eighteenth-Century England* (Oxford, 1998).

BRIGGS, ASA, 'Press and public in early nineteenth-century Birmingham', *Dugdale Society Occasional Papers*, **8** (1949).

CRESSY, D., *Literacy and the Social Order* (London, 1975).

HARRIS, BOB, *Politics and the Rise of the Press: Britain and France 1620–1800* (London, 1996).

SCHOFIELD, ROGER, 'Dimensions of illiteracy in England 1750–1850', in H.J. GRAFF, ed., *Literacy and Social Development in the West* (Cambridge, 1981).

SMALL, HELEN, TADMOR, NAOMI and RAVEN, JAMES, eds., *The Practice and Representation of Reading in England* (Oxford, 1992).

VINCENT, DAVID, *Literacy and Popular Culture: England 1750–1914* (Cambridge, 1989).

CHAPTER FOUR: POLITICIANS AND THE PRESS

ASPINALL, ARTHUR, *Politics and the Press c. 1780–1850* (London, 1949).

BARKER, HANNAH, *Press, Politics, and Public Opinion in Late Eighteenth-Century England* (Oxford, 1998).

BREWER, JOHN, *Party Ideology and Popular Politics at the Accession of George III* (Cambridge, 1976).

DOWNIE, J.A., *Robert Harley and the Press: Propaganda and Public Opinion in the Age of Swift and Defoe* (Cambridge, 1979).

HARRIS, BOB, *Politics and the Rise of the Press: Britain and France 1620–1800* (London, 1996).

HOLLIS, PATRICIA, *The Pauper Press: A Study in Working-class Radicalism of the 1830s* (Oxford, 1970).

KOSS, STEPHEN, *The Rise and Fall of the Political Press in Britain*, vol. I, *The Nineteenth Century* (London, 1981).

READ, DONALD, *Press and People 1790–1850: Opinion in Three English Cities* (Aldershot, 1993).

SIEBERT, FREDERICK SEATON, *Freedom of the Press in England 1476–1776: The Rise and Fall of Government Control* (Urbana, Ill., 1965).

CHAPTER FIVE: NEWSPAPER MANAGEMENT AND EDITORIAL STRATEGIES

ASQUITH, IVON, 'The structure, ownership and control of the press, 1780–1855', in GEORGE BOYCE, JAMES CURRAN and PAULINE WINGATE, eds., *Newspaper History From the Seventeenth Century to the Present Day* (London, 1978).

BARKER, HANNAH, *Press, Politics, and Public Opinion in Late Eighteenth-Century England* (Oxford, 1998).

CHRISTIE, I.R., 'British newspapers in the later Georgian Age', in I.R. CHRISTIE, *Myth and Reality in Late-Eighteenth-Century British Politics and Other Papers* (London, 1970).

CRANFIELD, G.A., *The Development of the Provincial Newspaper* (Oxford, 1962).

HARRIS, M., *London Newspapers in the Age of Walpole: A Study in the Origins of the Modern English Press* (London, 1987).

READ, DONALD, *Press and People 1790–1850: Opinion in Three English Cities* (Aldershot, 1993).

CHAPTER SIX: 1695–1759

HARRIS, BOB, *A Patriot Press: National Politics and the London Press in the 1740s* (Oxford, 1993).

HARRIS, BOB, 'England's provincial newspapers and the Jacobite rebellion of 1745–1746', *History*, **80** (1995).

LANGFORD, PAUL, *The Excise Crisis: Society and Politics in the Age of Walpole* (Oxford, 1975).

PERRY, THOMAS W., *Public Opinion, Propaganda, and Politics in Eighteenth-Century England: A Study of the Jew Bill of 1753* (Cambridge, Mass., 1962).

PETERS, MARIE, *Pitt and Popularity: The Patriotic Minister and Public Opinion during the Seven Years War* (Oxford, 1980).

SPECK, WILLIAM, 'Politics and the press', in MICHAEL HARRIS and ALAN LEE, eds., *The Press and English Society From the Seventeenth to Nineteenth Centuries* (London, 1986).

CHAPTER SEVEN: 1760–1786

BARKER, HANNAH, *Newspapers, Politics, and Public Opinion in Late Eighteenth-Century Britain* (Oxford, 1998).

BREWER, JOHN, *Party Ideology and Popular Politics at the Accession of George III* (Cambridge, 1976).

BRADLEY, JAMES E., *Popular Politics and the American Revolution in England: Petitions, the Crown and Public Opinion* (Macon, Ga. 1986).

CANNON, JOHN, *The Fox–North Coalition* (Cambridge, 1969).

LUTNICK, SOLOMON, *The American Revolution and the British Press 1775–1783* (Columbia, Mo., 1967).

MONEY, JOHN, *Experience and Identity: Birmingham and the West Midlands 1760–1800* (Manchester, 1977).

WILSON, KATHLEEN, *The Sense of the People: Politics, Culture and Imperialism in England, 1715–1785* (Cambridge, 1995).

CHAPTER EIGHT: 1787–1814

ASPINALL, ARTHUR, *Politics and the Press, c. 1780–1850* (London, 1949).

COLLEY, LINDA, 'The apotheosis of George III: loyalty, royalty and the British nation 1760–1820', *Past and Present*, **102** (1984).

COOKSON, J.E., *The Friends of Peace: Anti-war Liberalism in England, 1793–1815* (Cambridge, 1982).

DICKINSON, H.T., *The Politics of the People in Eighteenth-century Britain*, (Basingstoke, 1995).

DRESCHER, SEYMOUR, 'Whose abolition? Popular pressure and the ending of the British slave trade', *Past and Present*, **143** (1994).

EMSLEY, CLIVE, *British Society and the French Wars 1793–1815* (London, 1979).

OLDFIELD, J.R., *Popular Politics and British Anti-Slavery: The Mobilisation of Public Opinion Against the Slave Trade 1787–1807* (Manchester, 1995).

PHILP, MARK, *The French Revolution and British Popular Politics* (Cambridge, 1991).

READ, DONALD, *Press and People 1790–1850: Opinion in Three English Cities* (Aldershot, 1993).

WALVIN, JAMES, 'The public campaign in England against slavery, 1787–1834', in DAVID ELTIS and JAMES WALVIN, eds., *The Abolition of the Atlantic Slave Trade: Origins and Effects in Europe, Africa, and the Americas* (Madison, Wisc. 1981).

CHAPTER NINE: 1815–1855

ANDERSON, OLIVE, *A Liberal State at War: English Politics and Economics during the Crimean War* (New York, 1967).

ASPINALL, ARTHUR, *Politics and the Press, c. 1780–1850* (London, 1949).

EPSTEIN, J.A., 'Feargus O'Connor and the *Northern Star*', *International Review of Social History*, **xxi** (1976).

GILMARTIN, KEVIN, *Print Politics: The Press and Radical Opposition in Early Nineteenth-Century England* (Cambridge, 1996).

HOLLIS, PATRICIA, *The Pauper Press: A Study in Working-Class Radicalism of the 1830s* (Oxford, 1970).

KOSS, STEPHEN, *The Rise and Fall of the Political Press in Britain*, vol. I: *The Nineteenth Century* (London, 1981).

McCORD, NORMAN, *The Anti-Corn Law League 1838–1846* (London, 1958).

MACHIN, G.I.T., *The Catholic Question in English Politics 1820 to 1830* (Oxford, 1964).

READ, DONALD, *Press and People, 1790–1850: Opinion in Three English Cities* (Aldershot, 1993).

WARD, J.T., ed., *Popular Movements c. 1830–1850* (London, 1970).

WRIGHT, D.G., *Popular Radicalism: The Working-Class Experience, 1780–1850* (London, 1988).

Index